PROFESSIONAL ISSUES IN INFORMATION TECHNOLOGY

Second edition

Frank Bott

Published by BCS Learning and Development Ltd, a wholly owned subsidiary of BCS, The Chartered Institute for IT, First Floor, Block D, North Star House, North Star Avenue, Swindon, SN2 1FA, UK.
www.bcs.org

Paperback ISBN: 978-1-78017-180-7
PDF ISBN: 978-1-78017-181-4
ePUB ISBN: 978-1-78017-182-1
Kindle ISBN: 978-1-78017-183-8

British Cataloguing in Publication Data.
A CIP catalogue record for this book is available at the British Library.

Typeset by Lapiz Digital Services, Chennai, India.
Printed at CPI Antony Rowe Ltd, Chippenham, UK.

CONTENTS

LIST OF FIGURES AND TABLES

AUTHOR

Frank Bott studied mathematics at Trinity College, Cambridge, where he was awarded the Yeats Prize. After several years working in the University's Computer Laboratory he joined SPL International and managed large projects in shipbuilding, the electronics industry and the NHS. He was for two years a visiting professor at the University of Missouri. For ten years he was Head of the Aberystwyth University Computer Science Department, where he still lectures part-time. He has been an active member of BCS since 1963 and is a long-standing member of its Professional Examinations Board, as well as of a number of other committees.

Frank has published extensively in the field of software engineering and professional issues in IT. He also writes on classical music and is joint author of a biography of the Welsh-American composer Joseph Parry.

ACKNOWLEDGMENTS

Special thanks are due to Professor Mike Tedd, my friend and colleague for more years than either he or I would wish to admit to. He it was who, in 1986, first encouraged me to put together a lecture course on professional issues in software engineering; he read the complete draft of the first edition of this book and his wise advice and suggestions proved invaluable. This second edition has benefited from the advice of colleagues from BCS, both the mid-Wales branch and the Professional Examinations Board, for which I am most grateful. Over the years Dr Fred Long has drawn my attention to many reports of incidents relevant to the topics covered here and the fruits of the ensuing discussions can be found throughout the text. The faults that remain are, of course, entirely my responsibility.

Finally, I would like to thank my wife for her patience, forbearance, love and support, not only during the period that this book was being written, but throughout our years together.

ABBREVIATIONS

ACAS	Advisory, Conciliation and Arbitration Service
ACM	Association for Computing Machinery
BCS	BCS, The Chartered Institute for IT
CEng	Chartered Engineer
CEPIS	Council of European Professional Informatics Societies
CITP	Chartered IT Professional
CMA	Computer Misuse Act 1990
CPD	continuing professional development
DCF	discounted cash flow
DPA	Data Protection Act 1998
ECDL	European Computer Driving Licence®
EEA	European Economic Area
EHRC	Equality and Human Rights Commission
EU	European Union
EUCIP	European Certification of IT Professional
FoI	Freedom of Information Act 2000
GATT	General Agreement on Tariffs and Trade
ICANN	Internet Corporation for Assigned Names and Numbers
ICRA	Internet Content Rating Association
IEE	Institution of Electrical Engineers
IEEE	Institute of Electrical and Electronic Engineers
IEEE-CS	IEEE Computer Society
IET	Institution of Engineering and Technology
IRR	internal rate of return
ISEB	Information Systems Examination Board
ISM	Industry Structure Model
ISP	internet service provider
IT	information technology
IWF	Internet Watch Foundation
LLP	limited liability partnership

MBO	management by objectives
MP	Member of Parliament
NPV	net present value
PIDA	Public Interest Disclosure Act 1998
PJA	Police and Justice Act 2006
PLC (or plc)	public limited company
QA	quality assurance
RAM	random access memory
RCVS	Royal College of Veterinary Surgeons
RIBA	Royal Institute of British Architects
RIPA	Regulation of Investigatory Powers Act 2000
SFIA	Skills Framework for the Information Age
TUPE	Transfer of Undertakings (Protection of Employment) Regulations
UKCES	UK Commission for Employment and Skills
UML	Unified Modelling Language
URL	uniform resource locator
W3C	World Wide Web Consortium
WIPO	World Intellectual Property Organization

USEFUL WEBSITES

The following are the URLs of the websites referred to in the text. In most cases I have given the URLs of the home pages, since these are much less likely to change than those of individual pages. All the URLs were checked and found to be correct in August 2013.

UK government and official bodies

www.parliament.uk
This website covers both the House of Commons and the House of Lords. It includes materials placed before Parliament, records of all debates, details of all members and much else.

www.legislation.gov.uk
All UK legislation from 1988 to the present can be found on this website, as well as most primary legislation from before that date.

www.gov.uk
This general government website includes a great deal of information relating to the law, to running a business, to the rights of disabled people and many other topics.

www.equalityhumanrights.com
The website of the Equality and Human Rights Commission contains much valuable guidance for organisations that have to comply with anti-discrimination legislation.

www.ico.org.uk
The website of the Information Commissioner's Office contains useful information relating to data protection and freedom of information, including reports of cases that have been taken to court.

www.acas.org.uk
The website of the Arbitration, Conciliation and Advisory Service (ACAS).

www.ukces.org.uk
The website of the UK Commission for Employment and Skills.

www.innovateuk.org
The Technology Strategy Board's website.

US government sites

www.house.gov
The website for the US House of Representative.

www.senate.gov
The website for the US Senate.

Trade associations

www.corporate-responsibility.org/wp-content/uploads/2009/09/directors_guidance_final.pdf
The Corporate Responsibility (CORE) Coalition has produced a guide to directors' responsibilities.

www.sfia-online.org
The website of the SFIA Foundation.

www.iwf.org.uk
The website of the Internet Watch Foundation.

http://opensource.org
The Open Source Initiative's website.

www.fsf.org
The Free Software Foundation's website.

www.gnu.org
The website of the Gnu Project.

www.ukbusinessangelsassociation.org.uk
The website of the UK Business Angels Association.

www.eban.org
The website of the European Business Angels Network.

www.wbaa.biz
The World Business Angels Association's website.

Professional bodies and international organisations

www.bcs.org
The website of BCS, The Chartered Institute for IT.

www.theiet.org
The website of the Institute of Engineering and Technology.

www.computer.org/portal/web/guest/home
The Institute of Electrical and Electronic Engineering – Computer Society's website.

www.acm.org
The Association for Computing Machinery's website.

www.ifip.org
The website of the International Federation for Information Processing (IFIP).

www.cepis.org
The website of the Council of European Professional Informatics Societies (CEPIS).

www.wipo2.int
The website of the World Intellectual Property Organization.

Company reports

www.cgi.com/en/investors/annual-reports

The section of the CGI website that provides annual reports.

www.microsoft.com/investor/reports/ar12/index.html
The section of the Microsoft website that provides annual reports.

www.investors.sage.com/reports_presentations/reports
The section of the Sage website that provides corporate reports.

Legal case reports

www.humphreys.co.uk/articles/software_1.htm
A report on Cantor Fitzgerald versus Tradition (UK).

www.5rb.com/docs/Navitaire-v-Easyjet%20Airline%20Co%2030%20Jul%202004.pdf
A report on Navitaire Inc versus easyJet and Bulletproof Technologies Inc.

http://en.wikipedia.org/wiki/Oracle_Corporation_v._SAP_AG
A report on Oracle Corporation versus SAP AG.

www.scotchspam.org.uk/transcom.html
A report on Gordon Dick versus Transcom Internet Services Ltd.

www.pcworld.com/article/148780/spam.html
An article about Robert Soloway.

www.bailii.org/ew/cases/EWHC/Admin/2009/2021.html

www.publications.parliament.uk/pa/ld200708/ldjudgmt/jd080730/mckinn-1.htm
Two reports about Gary McKinnon.

Other legal material

www.bitlaw.com/software-patent/index.html
A clear statement of the position regarding software patents in the USA.

www.bitlaw.com/software-patent/bilski-and-software-patents.html
This gives an excellent description of the confused situation regarding software patents in the USA as it stood at the beginning of 2012.

www.lawcom.gov.uk/files/defamation2.pdf
The Law Commission report entitled *Defamation and the Internet*.

http://webjcli.ncl.ac.uk/1996/issue3/akdeniz3.html.
http://usir.salford.ac.uk/15815/7/MacEwan_Crim_LR.pdf
The two papers referred to in Chapter 15 that discuss the operation of the Computer Misuse Act.

Other sites

www0.cs.ucl.ac.uk/staff/A.Finkelstein/las/lascase0.9.pdf
This website provides information about the London Ambulance System disaster, including a copy of the official report.

http://sunnyday.mit.edu/therac-25.html
An updated version of the original Leveson and Turner paper on the Therac 25 Disaster.

www.midstaffspublicinquiry.com/report
Report of the Mid-Staffordshire NHS Foundation Trust Public Enquiry (the Francis report).

http://philarcher.org/icra/ICRAfail.pdf
Report on the failure of the ICRA initiative.

www-hcid.soi.city.ac.uk/research/DRC_Report.pdf
The Disability Rights Commission's report on disabled access to the internet.

PREFACE

When employers of newly qualified information systems professionals are asked what it is they would most like them to know, the answer is very rarely technical. Much more commonly, the answer is an understanding of the business environment. For this reason, BCS, The Chartered Institute for IT insists that accredited courses contain a significant element of 'professional issues' and, in its own examinations, BCS requires candidates to take a compulsory paper entitled *Professional Issues in Information Systems Engineering*. This book has been written as a guide for students taking that paper and it covers the whole syllabus. It is hoped, however, that the book will also prove useful to others, both students on other courses and those who are already embarked on a career in the information systems industry.

It is important for candidates to realise that mere knowledge of the syllabus is not enough, by itself, to pass the paper. Candidates are expected to be able to apply that knowledge to simple scenarios. Failure to do this is one of the commonest reasons for failing the paper. The book includes many such scenarios, some real and some fictitious.

Many of the candidates for the Institute's examinations are from overseas. BCS is a British institute and it has to give priority to the situation of the IT professional in the United Kingdom. For this reason the syllabus refers to Acts of the UK Parliament and to the laws of England and Wales (and Scotland where Scottish law differs significantly). However, it is expected that overseas candidates will be concerned with the position in their own countries and, where relevant, this book tries to illustrate how this varies from country to country. (Nowhere is this more evident than when discussing the legal status of professional engineers.) UK candidates should also find it beneficial to learn about the position in other countries.

Despite the existence of some very large and well-known multinational companies, much of the IT industry consists of small enterprises with less than six employees. Many young entrants to the profession aim to set up such a business of their own. One of the purposes of the Professional Issues module in the Institute's Diploma examination is therefore to give practical guidance in a range of legal, financial and organisational areas relevant to small IT businesses. This is reflected in many aspects of the book.

A word of warning is needed here. This book tries to explain the central principles and issues in the areas covered, so that you will be aware of areas you need to think about and areas where you will need professional advice. The book should give you enough knowledge to talk intelligently to professionals in the fields that it covers. But what the book covers is inevitably introductory and much is omitted. Just as you would not regard an accountant who had read a book on computing and learned to use a spreadsheet and a word processor as competent to design the software for the space shuttle, so you must not regard yourself as a competent lawyer, accountant or other professional on the strength of having studied this book.

The book can be regarded as falling into four main parts. Chapters 1 to 4 are concerned with the general context in which professionals work – the law and how it is created, the professions and the nature and structure of commercial organisations.

Chapters 5 to 8 are concerned very specifically with financial matters – the financing of start-up companies, the nature of financial statements, costing, budgeting and cash flow and the evaluation of investment proposals. Chapters 9 and 10 cover the human aspects of running a company, including human resources and anti-discrimination legislation.

More specific legal issues are covered in the final chapters, including software contracts and licences, intellectual property rights and legislation that affects the way in which computers and the internet are used or misused. Many of these topics are matters of day-to-day concern for most computer users.

There are *Further Reading* sections at the end of each chapter. These are intended to:

- enable those who are teaching courses for the examination to deepen and broaden their knowledge so that they can respond to questions and initiate discussion in their classes;
- help students who feel they need to read more in order to get a better understanding of the material;
- provide guidance to readers who need or want to go more deeply into particular topics to satisfy their own professional needs.

The first edition of this book was written in 2004. In the nine years since then there have been many changes in the law and important new legislation, such as the Equality Act 2010 and the Companies Act 2006, has been enacted. The way the internet is used has also developed in many important ways and is the subject of some political controversy. All these developments are reflected in the revisions that have been made.

Since the first edition was published, the structure of the IT industry has changed considerably. Although there are still many very small independent companies – under six employees, say – takeovers and mergers have dramatically reduced the number of small to medium-sized independent companies in the sector. Many of the companies referred to in the first edition no longer exist. A new section on takeovers and mergers has been added, along with additional material on outsourcing, and references to specific companies have been comprehensively revised to reflect the current state of the industry.

Frank Bott
Aberystwyth
August 2013

1   LAW AND GOVERNMENT

After studying this chapter, you should:

- *understand the nature of the law and the difference between criminal law and civil law;*
- *understand what is meant by the terms legislature, judiciary and executive and appreciate the variety of ways in which these concepts are implemented in different countries;*
- *understand the ways in which law comes into existence.*

1.1 WHAT IS THE LAW?

There are many ways of defining the law. For the purpose of this book we shall take a very straightforward definition. We shall define law as 'a set of rules that can be enforced in a court'. These rules are different in different countries. The best known examples of such differences are probably in the rules governing things like divorce or the sale of alcohol. From the point of view of the IT professional, however, differences in the rules governing data protection, the rights of access to information and the misuse of computers are much more significant.

As well as having different laws, different countries have different legal systems, that is, different systems of courts, different rules for court procedure, different procedures for appealing against a court decision and so on. The word **jurisdiction** is used to mean the area covered by a single legal system and set of laws.

Even within a single country, the law and the legal system may be different in different areas. This is most obviously the case in large countries with a federal system of government, where the country is divided into a number of states each of which can make its own laws in certain areas. Obvious examples are India and the United States.

In the UK, for historical reasons, Scotland, Northern Ireland and the Isle of Man each have different legal systems and different laws. However, as far as the topics covered in this book are concerned, their laws are, in almost all cases, the same as those of England and Wales. When we refer to British law or UK law, we shall be referring to laws that apply across the UK. Sometimes we shall refer to the law of England and Wales, indicating that there are differences elsewhere in the UK.

1.2 CRIMINAL LAW AND CIVIL LAW

The popular image of the law sees it as the set of mechanisms that tries to punish wrongdoers by fines or imprisonment. This aspect of the law is known as the criminal law. It can be considered to represent society's view of the minimum standard of acceptable behaviour. It defines what constitutes a crime, lays down the mechanisms for deciding whether a person accused of a crime is guilty or innocent and specifies the range of punishments applicable to different categories of crime.

In general, the police are responsible for discovering who has carried out a specific criminal offence and for collecting evidence that will convince a court that the person in question really did commit the offence. The state, in the form of the Crown Prosecution Service in England and Wales, will then start proceedings by prosecuting the person concerned (who is known as the **accused** or the **defendant**) in a criminal court. The court will decide whether or not the case against the person has been proved and, if it finds the case proved, will sentence the offender to a suitable punishment.

We shall not be very concerned with the criminal law in this book. We shall be much more occupied with the **civil law**. The purpose of the civil law is to provide rules for settling disputes between people.

Notice that we have referred to disputes between people. Does this mean that the civil law doesn't apply if one or both sides in a dispute are companies, or organisations of some other kind? It doesn't mean this, of course, but, in order to overcome the difficulty, we need the idea of a **legal person**. A legal person is an organisation that has gone through a process called **incorporation** that gives it the same legal status, so far as the civil law is concerned, as a **natural person**, that is, a human being. There are several different ways in which an organisation can be incorporated. In Britain, an organisation can be incorporated by an Act of Parliament, by registering as a company or by the grant of a royal charter. We shall discuss this process in Chapters 2 and 3.

Court action under the civil law is known as litigation. It must be initiated by one of the **parties to the dispute**, that is, by the person, legal or natural, who feels they have been wronged. The person who initiates the court action is known as the **claimant**, although in the United States and some other countries the older term **plaintiff** is still preferred.

Two important differences between British civil law and criminal law relate to the **standard** of proof and the **burden** of proof.

For a person to be found guilty of a criminal offence, the prosecution must demonstrate that he or she is guilty beyond all reasonable doubt. For a claimant to win his case under civil law, he only has to show that his claim is correct on the balance of probabilities. In other words, the standard of proof required in criminal cases is higher than that required in civil cases.

In a criminal case, the burden of proof lies on the prosecution. This means that it is up to the prosecution to prove its case. Defendants do not need to prove their innocence. They are assumed to be innocent until they are proven guilty. In a civil case, on the other hand, both parties present their arguments and must convince the court of their correctness.

1.3 WHERE DOES THE LAW COME FROM?

The two main sources of law in England and Wales are the **common law** and **statute law**. The common law is essentially traditional law that is not written down but which depends on the judgement of judges over the centuries. When deciding the rights and wrongs of a case, a court will look at the way in which similar cases have been decided in the past; such cases are known as **precedents**.

The common law tradition is shared by many other countries. Almost all the countries of the Commonwealth share the tradition; so, most importantly, does the United States of America. This means that a judgement made by a judge in the United States can be used as a precedent in, for example, a court in Singapore, or vice versa.

The tradition of common law is not found in the countries of continental Europe, such as France and Germany. Their law is based entirely on written codes, one for the criminal law and one for the civil law. Those parts of the world that were once colonised by such countries have generally kept such a system of written codes. Confusingly, this system of written codes is often also referred to as civil law. However, in this book, we shall always use the term civil law in the sense described in the previous section, that is, the law used for settling disputes between people.

Statute law is law laid down by Acts of Parliament. It is often referred to as **legislation**. Two hundred years ago, most cases that came to trial would have been tried under the common law. There was comparatively little statute law. Over the past two hundred years the position has changed a lot. On the one hand, technical developments and social changes make new laws urgently necessary. Laws to regulate child labour and laws to prevent the misuse of computers are just two examples of Parliament creating new laws for such reasons. On the other hand, in some areas the millions of common law judgements from the past make it increasingly difficult for courts to apply the common law and Parliament has passed legislation to bring together the common law in these areas into a single statute. A good example of this is the Theft Act 1968, which consolidated the common law provisions regarding crimes involving stealing.

1.4 THE LEGISLATIVE PROCESS IN THE UK

Like many other democratic countries, the UK has what is known as a **two-chamber** or **bicameral legislature**. This means that the law-making body (the legislature) is made up of two chambers or groups of people.

The British legislature is known as **Parliament**. One of the chambers is called the House of Commons; its members are elected and everyone over the age of 18 has a vote. The country is currently divided into 659 constituencies, each of which elects one member of parliament, who is the person who gets the most votes in the election. This is known as the 'first past the post' system.

The other chamber in the UK Parliament is known as the House of Lords; most of its members are appointed but a significant number are chosen from amongst the hereditary peers, although this situation may not last very much longer. (Reform of the House of Lords has been an active political issue in Britain for over a hundred years but, although most people agree that reform is needed, it has proved possible to get agreement only on some very limited reforms.)

The British government is made up of members from both the House of Commons and the House of Lords. Members of the House of Lords are never more than a small proportion and the Prime Minister, the Chancellor of the Exchequer, the Foreign Secretary and the Home Secretary are now always members of the House of Commons.

Most new legislation is initiated by the government although it is possible for individual members of parliament to initiate legislation in certain circumstances. It is introduced in the form of a **bill**; this is a set of proposals that parliament is invited to discuss, possibly modify and then approve. The bill is usually introduced first in the House of Commons. It will be discussed and possibly amended there, a process that includes a number of stages. If it is approved by the House of Commons, it is passed to the House of Lords. If the House of Lords approves the bill, it becomes an Act of Parliament. It is then passed to the Queen for her formal approval (the **royal assent**), after which it becomes law. (The Queen cannot refuse to give her approval when parliament has approved a bill.) Acts of Parliament are usually referred to by their title, followed by the year in which they received the royal assent, e.g. Computer Misuse Act 1990.

If the House of Lords rejects a bill or modifies it, the bill is returned to the House of Commons for further consideration. The House of Commons has the power to override any changes that may have been made by the House of Lords or even to insist that a bill rejected by the House of Lords should, nevertheless, be passed and proceed to receive the royal assent. The justification for this is that the House of Commons is democratically elected and so represents the will of the people in a way that the members of the House of Lords, not being elected, cannot do.

In many cases, the government may want to canvass opinion before asking Parliament to approve legislation. It may publish a **green paper**, which typically explains why the government wants to create new laws in a certain area and discusses a number of possible approaches. The green paper will be discussed by Parliament and comments on it will be invited from the public and from bodies that have an interest in the area. Thus BCS, along with many other bodies, was specifically asked for its views when the question of legislation to address the problem of computer misuse was raised.

Once the government has decided on its general approach, it may publish a **white paper**, which describes the proposed legislation and will be used as the basis for discussing and possibly modifying the details of what is proposed. At the end of this process the government will take into account these discussions and produce a bill.

Acts of Parliament constitute what is known as **primary** legislation. The complexity of modern society makes it impossible for all laws to be examined in detail by parliament. To overcome this difficulty, an Act of Parliament will often make provision for **secondary** legislation to be introduced. This means that detailed regulations can be introduced without full discussion in parliament. Instead, the proposed regulations are placed in the library of the House of Commons so that members of either house can look at them. If no objections are raised within a fixed time period, the regulations become law. An example of secondary legislation in the computer field are the regulations that were produced to apply the Copyright, Designs and Patents Act 1988 to protect the design of semi-conductor chips.

The UK is a member of the European Union (EU). This is a grouping of 28 European countries which are working towards a high level of economic and social integration involving the harmonisation of many of their laws. The EU has its own parliament, elected by individual voters in all the member countries. The EU is run by a Commission that has the power to issue directives that require member countries to modify their own legislation, if necessary, to meet a common standard. These directives must be discussed by the European Parliament and approved by the member states before they come into effect. Several of these directives relate to topics, such as data protection and the protection of software, that are particularly important for IT professionals and we shall be referring to many of them later in the book.

In addition to the British national parliament, there are separate elected assemblies in Wales and Northern Ireland and a Scottish parliament. These have certain limited powers but they do not affect the topics covered in this book.

1.5 THE LEGISLATIVE PROCESS IN OTHER COUNTRIES

Although this book is concerned primarily with the UK, the influence and power of the United States in the world of information technology is so great that IT professionals need to know something of how government in the USA works.

In the US, the legislature is known as Congress. It consists of two houses, the Senate and the House of Representatives. Both houses are elected but on very different terms. Members of the House of Representatives (representatives) are elected for a period of two years. Each congressman represents a district and each district contains (roughly) the same number of people. The Senate contains two members (senators) for each state; senators are elected for seven years.

Legislation must be approved by both the Senate and the House of Representatives before it can become law; neither chamber can override the other. Furthermore, the President must also give his assent before an Act of Congress becomes law. Unlike the Queen, who cannot withhold her assent to legislation passed by Parliament, the President is allowed to veto legislation passed by Congress and this regularly happens. As in other countries with a written constitution, there is also a Supreme Court, which can strike out legislation approved by Congress and the President, on the grounds that it is unconstitutional. As we shall see in Chapter 14, this has happened with legislation concerned with pornography on the internet. This is in contrast to the situation in the UK, where the doctrine of the **sovereignty of Parliament** means that the courts cannot override primary legislation made by Parliament, although they can override secondary legislation.

The members of the government of the US are not members of Congress. The President is, in practice though not in theory, directly elected by the people. The members of the government are individuals chosen by the President and their appointment must be approved by Congress. The founders of the United States believed that it was very important to separate three functions, that of:

- the legislature, that is, Congress, which makes laws;

- the judiciary, that is, the judges and other legal officials, which applies and enforces these laws in particular cases; and

- the executive, that is, the President and the other members of the government, which carries on the actual business of government.

The separation of these functions is recognised in many other countries. Historically, they have not been separated in the UK but recent reforms, embodied in the Constitutional Reform Act 2005, have moved the UK much further in this direction by establishing a Supreme Court.

The legislative situation in the US is made more complicated by the fact that the country is a federation of 50 states. Each state has its own legislature, most of them modelled on the federal legislature, and its own government. On some topics each state can make its own laws but in other areas the law is made at federal level. For example, as we shall see in the next chapter, each state has its own laws regarding who can call themselves an engineer. The issue of states' rights, that is, the extent to which federal law can override laws made by individual states, has been a live political issue throughout the existence of the US and remains so today. Most recently, this has led the Federal Supreme Court to declare unconstitutional laws passed by individual states to regulate use of the internet. This issue of states' rights also arises in other countries with a federal constitution, such as India or Australia.

Smaller countries such as Singapore, Sri Lanka and Mauritius often have a **unicameral** legislature, that is, a parliament that consists of a single chamber. Where there is a historical connection with Britain, much of the legislation may be based on British legislation, as a way of avoiding the expense of law-making on a large scale.

1.6 THE LAW ACROSS BORDERS

What are the geographical limits of the jurisdiction of a country's courts? The immediate reaction is likely to be that a country's courts can only deal with crimes committed within the country's boundaries. This is not in fact true. Most countries would claim that their courts have the power, for example, to deal with a spy who passed on secrets to an enemy country, even though the passing on of the secrets took place on foreign soil. And many countries, including the UK, have legislation intended to combat sex tourism, that is, legislation that enables criminal charges to be brought in their courts against their citizens who have engaged in sexual activity with underage partners in foreign countries.

The development of the web and other innovations in the field of telecommunications has, however, created further problems. The very notion of the place where a crime is committed has ceased to be well defined. If a hacker sitting in an apartment in New York hacks into a European air traffic control computer located in the Netherlands so as to cause a mid-air collision over Denmark, where was the crime committed and which country's laws and legal procedures should be used in prosecuting the crime? What happens about an action that is criminal in some of the countries it affects but not in others – publishing obscene material over the internet is a case in point?

Closely related to these questions is the issue of extradition. Under what circumstances can a person be extradited, that is, sent from one country to another in order to face trial for an alleged offence?

Some recent cases have turned these questions into very live issues and we shall have more to say about them in later chapters. However, they are immensely complex questions and anything like a complete answer is well beyond the scope of this book.

Jurisdiction in civil cases that cross borders is in some ways a much simpler matter in that it is up to the claimant to decide in which country to initiate action. That decision will depend very much on the circumstances of the case but may well also be influenced by the reputation of a country's courts and how favourable its laws will be to the claimant's case.

FURTHER READING

Twenty years ago, it was difficult to get information about the legislative process in countries other than the one in which you were living. It meant going to specialist libraries or to the embassies of the countries concerned. The development of the web has changed all this and it is now very easy to obtain this material from websites.

The following pages explain how the legislative process works in the UK and in the US.

United Kingdom
www.parliament.uk

United States of America
www.house.gov/content/learn
www.senate.gov
http://bensguide.gpo.gov/9-12/lawmaking/index.html

Copies of acts of Parliament and acts of Congress for the past 30 years or so are available on the web.

In the US, most of the individual states have similar sites describing the legislative process in the state and, in many cases, most of the statutes of the state are available on the web.

Most other countries have similar sites, although the quality is variable.

2 THE COMPUTING PROFESSION

After studying this chapter, you should:

- *understand what is meant by the terms profession and professional, and be aware of the main professional bodies in the field of information technology;*
- *be familiar with BCS Code of Conduct and understand the obligations that it imposes on members;*
- *understand the concepts of reservation of title and reservation of function in the context of professional responsibility for public safety.*

2.1 THE CONCEPT OF A PROFESSION

Words like **profession** and **professional** are used in many different ways. Professional footballers are footballers who make their living from the game. Professional employees are employees of a certain status, who are expected, within limits, to put the interests of the organisation they work for above their own convenience. To describe someone as a real professional implies that they can be relied on to carry out their work competently and conscientiously regardless of the circumstances. A professional piece of work means a piece of work that meets established standards of quality. However, the terms can also have negative overtones – professional fouls are fouls committed deliberately by professional footballers who calculate that, on the balance of probabilities, the outcome will be in their favour.

There is no single definition of a profession. The meaning of the word depends on who is using it and what the context is. However, if we look at a range of occupations that would commonly be described as professions – lawyers, doctors, dentists, accountants, veterinary surgeons, architects and so on – we see that there are a number of characteristics that most of them have in common:

- Substantial education and training are required in order to practise the profession.
- The members of the profession themselves decide the nature of this training and, more generally, control entry to the profession.
- The profession is organised into one or more professional bodies.
- Members of the profession are expected to conduct their professional activities in accordance with codes of conduct laid down by the professional bodies and enforced by them.

Many, but by no means all, professions also enjoy a sort of monopoly: either the use of a certain title, such as architect, or the carrying out of certain functions, dentistry for example, or both, may be restricted by Act of Parliament to members of certain professional bodies. We shall discuss this in more detail later in this chapter.

A professional body usually starts by a group of people coming together because of a shared interest in a particular type of activity. There are many professional bodies in Britain and they cover a very wide range of professions, including the law, medicine, many different branches of science and engineering, accountancy, architecture, surveying and many others. BCS, The Chartered Institute for IT (BCS) was set up in 1957 as the British Computer Society by a group of people working in the new and expanding field of computers, who wanted the opportunity to exchange ideas. It currently has about 70,000 members. The Institution of Engineering and Technology (IET) is the other main body in the UK that includes information technologists among its members. It was formed in 2006 by a merger of the Institution of Electrical Engineers, which was set up in 1871 by people with an interest in the developing field of electrical engineering, and the Institution of Incorporated Engineers. It covers electrical engineering, electronic engineering and a number of other fields in addition to IT, and has a membership of around 150,000.

Although the role of professional bodies in the USA is somewhat different from their role in the UK, there are two professional computing bodies based in the USA whose importance is worldwide and immense. The Institute of Electrical and Electronic Engineers (IEEE) is a professional engineering society based in the USA but with members and activities spread worldwide. It was under the aegis of the IEEE that the first professional society in the field of computing was founded in 1946. This was the IEEE Computer Society (IEEE-CS); today it has over 100,000 members. It was closely followed by the **Association for Computing Machinery**, universally known as the ACM. This was founded in 1947 and now has over 75,000 members. Like the IEEE-CS, it is primarily an American organisation, but it has members and activities in many countries.

2.2 ROYAL CHARTERS

In the UK, any organisation that believes its main objectives are in the public interest can enter into discussions with the Privy Council with a view to being awarded a *royal charter*. A royal charter is a formal document, written in rather quaint language and signed by the monarch, which establishes the organisation and lays down its purpose and rules of operation. As they grow into mature organisations, most professional bodies seek and obtain a royal charter.

BCS was awarded its royal charter in 1984. The Institution of Electrical Engineers was awarded its first charter in 1921 and the IET received its charter in 2008, shortly after the merger.

The charter of BCS sets out very clearly the purposes of the institution:

> to promote the study and practice of Computing and to advance knowledge and education therein for the benefit of the public.

There follows a lengthy list of things that the institution is authorised to do in order to fulfil these purposes. The most important of these can be summarised as follows:

- establishing a code of conduct to regulate the way members of the body behave in their professional lives and a disciplinary procedure to discipline members who breach this code;
- promoting education in the field of computing;
- setting standards of education and experience that must be met by people wishing to become members of the body;
- establishing mechanisms for disseminating knowledge of good practice and new developments to its members, typically through publications and conferences but also through the use of the internet;
- to promote and support standards and codes of practice;
- to advise government and regulatory bodies about matters within its area of expertise.

In the following sections we shall look at the way that BCS addresses some of these functions.

2.3 PROFESSIONAL CONDUCT

The BCS charter specifically requires BCS to 'establish and maintain a sound ethical foundation for the use of computers...'. All professional bodies are under a similar obligation; this, indeed, is one of the most important characteristics of a professional body. It is normally done by laying down a code of conduct to which their members are required to adhere. A **code of conduct** sets out the standards of behaviour that members of the body are expected to follow in their professional life. Sometimes the code is called a code of ethics. It looks outwards, in the sense that it is concerned with the relationship between members and society as a whole. Although all codes of conduct have much in common, they also have significant differences, if only because the nature of the activities of different professions places different temptations in the path of their practitioners.

Codes of conduct should not be confused with codes of **practice**, which are concerned with the way in which the professional activities should be carried out.

BCS's Code of Conduct is currently divided into the following sections (please consult the BCS website for the latest version at www.bcs.org/codeofconduct):

1. The Public Interest
2. Professional Competence and Integrity
3. Duty to the Relevant Authority
4. Duty to the Profession.

2.3.1 The public interest

This section requires members to be aware of and comply with aspects of the law and regulations that govern acting in the public interest. For example, members need to safeguard public health, protect the environment, have due regard for privacy and human rights and avoid discrimination.

Some of these elements can cause problems for members working for clients or companies in countries whose governments practice or encourage systematic discrimination on, for example, grounds of race, religion or sexual orientation. Information systems developed in such countries often have such discrimination embedded in their design – this was certainly the case, for example, in some government information systems developed in South Africa during the era of apartheid. The effect of this clause is to forbid members of BCS from working on such systems.

The section is also concerned with the rights of third parties as well as copyright and intellectual property (which will be discussed in detail in Chapter 11).

Finally, the section invites members to take any opportunity to address the so-called digital divide, that is, the inequality that exists, for whatever reason, among different groups with respect to their ability to benefit from information and communication technologies. It includes, on the one hand, the lack of appropriate skills amongst many elderly people, which means they cannot take advantage of technologies that could very much improve the quality of their lives. On the other hand, it includes the gap between the way that middle-class children in Britain can use these technologies and the lack of facilities for children in rural Africa to do the same.

2.3.2 Professional competence and integrity

This section addresses what has been, and to some extent continues to be, a serious problem for the IT industry. Only too often, individuals and companies claim to be able to undertake work that they are not competent to carry out, and this leads to system failures. One of the most serious system failures, that of the London Ambulance Service's Computer Aided Despatch System, in 1994 (see Further Reading section), was caused, at least in part, by a small software company claiming expertise that it did not have. It was not deliberate deception: the company in question had so little expertise that it failed to recognise that the system required expertise that it did not have.

Under this section members are also required to keep their professional skills up to date and be familiar with the legislation that is relevant to their professional activities. Thus, web developers building an ecommerce site for a retail company are required to be conversant with legislation such as the Consumer Protection (Distance Selling) Regulations 2000 (see Chapter 14). A software engineer working on a railway signalling system would not be expected to be familiar with those regulations but should be familiar with the regulations laid down by the Rail Safety and Standards Board.

2.3.3 Duty to the relevant authority

This section starts by saying that members should carry out their professional duties with 'due care and diligence', that is, with the proper care and attention. This is what society has the right to demand of any professional.

The term 'relevant authority' means the person or organisation that has authority over what you are doing. If you are employed by an organisation, this is likely to be your employer; if you are an independent consultant, it will be your client; and if you are a student, it will be your school, college or university. In some cases, there may be several relevant authorities; for example, if you are a part-time student who is also employed part time, then the relevant authority as far as your work as a student is concerned will be your school or college but the relevant authority in your employment will be your employer.

According to this section, behaving professionally towards relevant authorities means, in particular, avoiding the following:

- *Conflicts of interest*: These are situations in which there are incentives that might encourage you to do things or take decisions that are not in the best interests of your relevant authority. If, for example, you have been asked by your employer to recommend a payroll package for your company and it happens that your sister works in the sales section of a company that supplies such a package, you might well be tempted to recommend that package, whether or not it is the most suitable for your company's needs. In such circumstances, you should explain the situation to your employer and suggest that it might be better to ask someone else to recommend a suitable package.

- *Disclosing confidential information without permission*: Confidential information may include technical information about a company's products, its financial position, sales leads and so on. (The law relating to confidential information is covered in more detail in Chapter 11).

- *Misrepresentation*: This is a failing that occurs only too often in the software industry. In their eagerness to make a sale, sales staff in particular, but also technical staff, will claim that software that they are selling will do things that, in fact, it will not, or they will claim their company is competent to do things that it cannot. Although most people will try to avoid making claims that they know are wrong, in many cases they will be prepared to claim things of which they are uncertain, if the claims seem plausible. The Code forbids such behaviour.

2.3.4 Duty to the profession

Like other professionals, information systems professionals have not always had a good press. System developments have been plagued by delays, budget overruns and complete failures, and these have been well publicised. Too often, the systems themselves do not meet the needs of their users. And information systems professionals have, on occasions, been perceived as behaving in an unprofessional manner. The purpose of this section of the Code is to impress on members what is expected of them in order to uphold the reputation and good standing of BCS in particular, and the profession in general.

2.3.5 Status of professional codes of conduct

Like most professional bodies, BCS has procedures that allow it to take disciplinary action against members who infringe the Code, with expulsion as the ultimate sanction. Where membership of the professional body confers a licence to practise, as in the case of the Law Society for example, this is a very serious punishment, since expulsion deprives expelled members of the right to earn their living in their chosen profession. Even in the case of BCS, expulsion or other sanctions, although not directly affecting a member's ability to earn a living, can certainly affect their professional standing. A member who has been subject to disciplinary action can thus take the matter to the civil courts, which will expect the disciplinary proceedings to have been conducted in accordance with the rules of natural justice. This places limits on the extent to which codes of conduct can be enforced.

Most codes of conduct contain some very precise rules and some rather vague or aspirational ones. Clause (e) in the *Duty to the Profession* section of the BCS Code of Conduct is an example of a very precise rule. It states:

> [You shall] notify BCS if convicted of a criminal offence or upon becoming bankrupt or disqualified as a Company Director and in each case give details of the relevant jurisdiction.

This is quite clear. There is little doubt about what it means and, in any specific case, it should be clear whether a member has complied with this rule. There is no difficulty in taking action against a member who has broken this rule.

The first clause of the *Public Interest* section, on the other hand, is much vaguer:

> [You shall] have due regard for public health, privacy, security and wellbeing of others and the environment.

Although no one can quarrel with this precept, there may not be general agreement as to whether a particular development is or is not consistent with improvement in public health, safety and the environment. Some people would regard any work carried out for the nuclear industry as being detrimental to public health, safety and the environment. Others will argue that the use of nuclear power stations to generate electricity is beneficial to the environment because it avoids carbon dioxide emissions. It would thus be unreasonable for the Institute to take disciplinary action against members working in the nuclear industry, even though many other members might feel passionately that such work was dangerous to health, safety and the environment.

2.4 EDUCATION

BCS promotes education in a number of ways:

- it runs its own system of professional examinations and grants approval to suitable organisations that provide courses to prepare students for them;

- it accredits degree programmes offered by universities and other institutions of higher education;
- it designs and franchises short courses leading to qualifications in specific areas.

2.4.1 Higher education

BCS offers examinations to students in higher education. These consist of three stages, the **Certificate**, the **Diploma** and the **Professional Graduate Diploma**. As well as the normal written examinations, projects are assessed at Diploma and Professional Graduate Diploma levels. The Professional Graduate Diploma with the project is considered to be the equivalent of an honours degree.

A few other computer societies operate examination schemes. The Australian Computer Society has, for a number of years, operated its own system of examinations, somewhat comparable with the BCS Certificate and Diploma examinations but without the project. The IEEE-CS has recently introduced a scheme that allows someone with 9,000 hours of appropriate professional experience to take an examination set by the Society and, if successful, to be registered with the IEEE as a Certified Software Development Professional.

2.4.2 Accreditation and exemption

The term accreditation is used with a confusing variety of related meanings. In the present context, it refers to the process by which a professional body recognises specific academic awards made by specific institutions of higher education as satisfying, wholly or partly, the academic requirements for professional membership. Awards that are recognised in this way are referred to as accredited awards and the courses that lead to them are referred to as accredited courses. It is in this sense that the term is used by a range of professional bodies in such fields as medicine, law, engineering and science.

In deciding whether to accredit an award, BCS takes into consideration:

- the academic content of the programme, to see whether it meets the Institute's requirements, which are based on the computing benchmark statement produced by the UK Quality Assurance Agency for Higher Education;
- the quality of the learning and teaching facilities provided for students, including laboratory facilities and staff qualifications;
- the quality control and assurance procedures of the institution offering the award.

The process involves a written submission and a visit by a BCS panel during which there will be meetings with both staff and students.

2.4.3 Professional certifications

BCS offers a substantial range of qualifications, known as certifications, which are achievable through short courses. The courses are intended as training courses for staff working in the industry. Typically, they last around 40 hours.

Courses are available in a wide range of topics including, for example, business analysis, sustainable IT, IT governance and information security, project management and support, and software testing.

At the level of the computer user rather than the systems developer, BCS manages and promotes the European Computer Driving Licence (ECDL) in the UK on behalf of the ECDL Foundation. This is a European-wide qualification, which enables people to demonstrate their competence in computer skills. It is designed specifically for those who wish to gain a basic qualification in computing to help them with their current job, develop their IT skills, and enhance their career prospects.

2.5 THE ADVANCEMENT OF KNOWLEDGE

The royal charter of BCS states very specifically that one of its objects is to advance knowledge of computing, and many other professional bodies include this among their objects. In practice, however, much of the research that contributes to the advancement of knowledge takes place in universities and in research establishments both public and private. As a result, professional bodies tend to be more concerned with the dissemination of knowledge through their publications, conferences that they organise or sponsor and various other activities.

One of the first actions of BCS when it was formed was to establish *The Computer Journal*. The first issue was published in 1958 and it has been published regularly ever since. The journal carries articles that present the results of research carried out in industry, in research establishments and in universities all over the world. The IET publishes a number of journals covering various topics in IT, including *IET Software*, which concentrates on new developments in software engineering, and *IET Networks*.

Most of the articles in *The Computer Journal* and the IET journals are targeted at specialists. For the information systems professional who is not engaged in research and development, the three most useful publications are probably *Computer* (the flagship publication of the IEEE-CS), *IEEE Software* and the *Communications of the ACM*. These contain authoritative articles on new developments and current issues written at a level that practising professionals can understand.

BCS also supports a considerable number of specialist groups. These groups bring together people with interests in specific areas. They cover a wide range of specialist areas, from artificial intelligence to software testing, from human computer interaction to law. They are particularly effective in spreading knowledge of good practice because they bring together practitioners from different organisations, all working in the same field, who learn from each other. Many specialist groups have gone on to develop an extensive range of resources, from books and reports to special software, to disseminate knowledge about their specialist topic.

2.6 CONTINUING PROFESSIONAL DEVELOPMENT

For many years, little attention was given to how professionals kept their knowledge up to date after qualifying. Thus, it was possible for a doctor, a dentist or a solicitor to practise for 40 years without any formal requirement to update their knowledge. Of course, most professionals were aware of the need to do this and would take whatever opportunities are available. Nevertheless, these opportunities might not be readily available and the pressures of day-to-day work might make it difficult for busy professionals to take advantage of them.

The increasing rate at which new knowledge was becoming available and existing knowledge was being used in new ways led, in the 1970s, to increasing concern that professionals should keep their qualifications up to date and this process became known as **continuing professional development** (CPD). It can be defined as the systematic maintenance and improvement of professional knowledge and skills throughout an individual's professional working life.

2.6.1 CPD services to individual members

In common with other professional bodies, BCS supports CPD both by providing a formal structure through which it can be recorded and assessed, and by providing some of the means by which it can be achieved. For example, all members of BCS receive a copy of its monthly publication, *ITNOW*, which helps to keep them aware of new developments and current topics of interest to the profession. Additionally, the Institute provides its members with many opportunities for CPD through its branches and specialist groups. These provide an opportunity for members to meet together to share experiences, talk about common problems and listen to talks about new developments both technical and professional.

Although CPD serves to encourage professionals to keep their expertise up to date, there is a real danger that the knowledge and experience that qualified a member for a professional grade within the Institute may atrophy if they are not used. Accordingly, BCS offers a service to allow members to revalidate their skills every five years so that they can demonstrate to employers that these skills have been maintained.

2.6.2 Career development and CPD services to the industry

For many years, managing IT staff presented problems to their employers. The chronic shortage of qualified and experienced staff together with the rapid pace of change made the problems particularly acute for large user organisations. Such organisations were faced with the problem of where to place IT specialists in their staffing structures. Because of their scarcity, such staff could command high salaries but, elsewhere in the organisation, such salaries would be associated with substantial managerial responsibility. IT staff were anomalies who provoked both envy and disdain among their colleagues.

BCS started to tackle this problem in the mid-1980s with the development of the Industry Structure Model (ISM) – now SFIAplus, an enhanced model based on the Skills Framework for the Information Age (SFIA). The SFIA is a common reference model for the identification of IT skills, which has been developed by the SFIA Foundation, a not-for-profit organisation set up and owned by BCS, the IET, the Institute for the Management of Information Systems and e-skills UK, an industry body.

Such a model means that a large employer has a systematic way of structuring IT roles and is therefore in a much better position to address the problems referred to above.

2.7 REPRESENTING THE PROFESSION

Professional bodies are widely regarded as the source of the most authoritative advice on their disciplines. It is normal, therefore, for them to be consulted by the government about changes in the law as it affects the discipline or is affected by it. This consultation may extend over a period of several years, as happened, for example, when BCS was consulted over the EU Directive on Data Protection and the 1998 Data Protection Act. As well as such official consultation, professional bodies are also regularly invited to talk to groups of members of parliament who are interested in their disciplines.

Professional engineering bodies are also routinely asked by standardisation bodies, such as the American National Standards Institute or the British Standards Institute, to nominate members of committees developing standards in the field. Indeed, the IEEE itself runs the standards-making process in the field of local area networks through its Project 802.

Individual BCS members are also able to influence and shape policy by playing an active part in discussions and contributing to consultations from government and other bodies on a wide range of professional, economic and societal issues through joining the BCS 'policy hub'.

2.8 MEMBERSHIP GRADES

BCS has three major membership categories: standard grades, professional grades and chartered professional status. Membership in the professional grades requires degree level qualifications in IT or substantial experience. For chartered professional status, both degree level qualifications and substantial experience are required.

The criteria for membership in the professional and chartered professional grades are flexible but, for that very reason, they are complicated. The BCS website should always be consulted for precise and up-to-date information.

Membership at any level requires a commitment to compliance with the Institute's Code of Conduct. There are two professional grades: Member and Fellow, and members are entitled to use the letters MBCS after their name. Fellow is the most senior professional grade. It is open to applicants who can demonstrate a minimum of five years' IT practitioner experience and hold a senior IT position or who have an established reputation of eminence or authority in the field of IT. Fellows may use the letters FBCS after their names.

To achieve Chartered IT Professional (CITP) status you will be a professional Member or Fellow and will have spent at least three of the last five years working in an IT role carrying significant responsibility, full accountability and presenting a challenging range of complex work activities. Chartered IT Professionals are entitled to use the letters CITP after their names, along with their membership post-nominal (MBCS or FBCS).

In addition to awarding CITP status, the Institute is licensed by the Engineering Council to award Chartered Engineer (CEng) status and Incorporated Engineer (IEng) status, and by the Science Council to award Chartered Scientist (CSci) status.

2.9 RESERVATION OF TITLE AND FUNCTION

As mentioned at the beginning of this chapter, in certain cases, where it is considered to be in the public interest, the members of a profession may be granted some sort of legal monopoly. There are two different ways in which this can be done. First, the use of the name of the profession may be restricted to those people who are appropriately qualified. A restriction of this sort is called **reservation of title**. In the UK, for example, the Architects Act 1997 makes it a criminal offence to call yourself an architect unless you are registered with the Architects Registration Board.

Secondly, the law may state that certain activities are restricted to people with appropriate qualifications or to members of particular specified professional bodies. This is called **reservation of function**. For example, in England and Wales, only members of the Institute of Chartered Accountants in England and Wales and the Association of Certified Accountants are allowed to audit the accounts of public companies. Auditing accounts is an example of reservation of function where there is no corresponding reservation of title. Anyone can call himself or herself an accountant, provided this is not done for fraudulent purposes.

An example where both reservation of title and reservation of function apply is veterinary surgery. Under the Veterinary Surgeons Act 1966, you are not allowed to call yourself a veterinary surgeon unless you are registered with the Royal College of Veterinary Surgeons (RCVS); in order to be registered you must have the proper qualifications. And, subject to certain limitations, it is a criminal offence to carry out surgical procedures on animals unless you are registered with the RCVS.

In the US, title and function are usually reserved not to members of professional bodies but to people whose names are on a register maintained by a state government. In the UK, a somewhat similar provision has been in operation for many years for doctors and dentists. Recent developments have shown a tendency for the UK to move further in the same direction. For example, until the passage of the Architects Act 1997, it was an offence to 'practise or carry on business under any name, style or title containing the word "architect"', unless you were a member of the Royal Institute of British Architects (RIBA). The 1997 Act established the Architects Registration Board, registration with which now replaces membership of the RIBA as the requirement for calling yourself an architect. The reason for this change is that professional bodies are often seen as white-collar trade unions, which use their monopoly power to limit competition and maintain high charges for their services, while doing little to enforce the codes of conduct that they publish.

Whatever the mechanism adopted, there are strong arguments for protecting the public by ensuring that only suitably qualified people are allowed to practise professions in which unqualified people can do serious damage, be it physical or economic. It was a series of civil engineering disasters that led to the introduction of a licensing scheme for engineers in the USA in the 1920s and 1930s. A number of disasters can be traced directly to lack of professional competence on the part of the software engineers who developed the systems. Therac 25 (see the Further Reading section) in the US and the London Ambulance System in the UK are only two of many examples that show how the professional incompetence of software developers can lead to avoidable deaths. In both these examples, the developers lacked any professional qualifications in software engineering and were ignorant of such elementary topics as the risks of concurrent access to shared memory and the dangers of dynamic memory allocation, as well as many more advanced topics. Although the immediate cause of the failure of these systems was programming error arising from ignorance of elementary topics, these errors occurred in a context that showed a much broader lack of professionalism. It is not surprising, therefore, that there have been calls for the compulsory registration of software engineers and for legislation to ensure that software engineering activities are carried out under the supervision of registered software engineers.

Some members of the profession have advocated a legal requirement that all software must be written by registered software engineers, or at least under their supervision. Such a regulation would be impossible to enforce. The number of people qualified to be registered as software engineers is vastly fewer than the number of people developing software. If such a regulation were introduced, the amount of new software that could be developed would be enormously reduced or, more likely, software development would go underground. Furthermore, there would be considerable opposition to the regulation. Many software developers would see it as an attempt to establish a monopoly by a small number of people with specific qualifications, with the intention of pushing up their own earnings. The public would share this view and see the move as unnecessary, because most software is not critical.

It would be more realistic and more defensible to require that the design and implementation of all 'critical' systems should be under the control of a registered software engineer; in the UK, this would probably mean a chartered engineer or a CITP whose experience and qualifications are in software engineering. By a critical system we mean a system whose failure to operate correctly could result in physical injury or loss of life, or catastrophic economic damage. Society is justified in demanding that such systems are designed and implemented by properly qualified and experienced engineers.

One difficulty is that the boundary between critical and non-critical systems is not always well defined. Although it is clear that an air traffic control system should be considered critical, because a failure can result directly in loss of life, should we consider a medical records system to be critical, because the loss of information concerning, say, a patient's allergy to penicillin could in some circumstances lead to the death of the patient? A second difficulty is that many software engineers have not studied the rather specialised techniques needed for working on critical systems. Nor, for the jobs they are doing, is it necessary that they should.

In the UK context, compulsory reservation of function for software engineers, even for critical systems work, is unlikely to be realistic except as part of a move towards reservation of function for engineers more generally. The UK has shown no inclination to follow the US in making registration of engineers compulsory and there is little likelihood of this happening. If anything, it is indirect pressures from the Health and Safety Executive or from insurers providing professional indemnity insurance that is likely to increase the emphasis on registration as CEng or CITP.

In the US, the certification and registration of software engineers remains a contentious issue, although there has been some progress towards integrating software engineering into the more general schemes for registration of engineers. However, since such registration is carried out at the level of the individual state, progress is extremely slow.

A large number of vendor or product specific qualifications are now available and serve further to confuse the situation. Although such qualifications are useful for demonstrating that individuals have specific expertise, they are of little relevance when it comes to ensuring that critical systems are built by people who know what they are doing.

FURTHER READING

The websites of the main professional bodies referred to in this chapter are as follows:

- BCS, The Chartered Institute for IT
  www.bcs.org

- Institution of Engineering and Technology
  www.theiet.org

- IEEE – Computer Society
  www.computer.org/portal/web/guest/home

- Association for Computing Machinery
  www.acm.org

All four websites include the organisation's code of conduct/ethics, as well as much information about the organisations and the way they function. The websites of BCS and the IET also include the full text of their royal charters.

Websites of the two international bodies connected to BCS:

- International Federation for Information Processing
  www.ifip.or.at
- Council of European Professional Informatics Societies
  www.cepis.org

Website of the SFIA foundation:
  www.sfia-online.org

The authoritative description of the London Ambulance Service disaster was published as follows:
  Thames Regional Health Authority. (1993) *Report of the Inquiry into The London Ambulance Service*. Communications Directorate, South West Thames Regional Health Authority.
This report and some related material are also available on the web:
  www0.cs.ucl.ac.uk/staff/A.Finkelstein/las/lascase0.9.pdf

The Therac 25 disaster is described in a number of books and articles, such as the following readily available source:
  Leveson, N. and Turner, C. S. (1993) 'An Investigation of the Therac-25 Accidents'. *IEEE Computer*, 25, No. 7, 18–41.
An updated version of the paper is also available on the web:
  http://sunnyday.mit.edu/therac-25.html

3   WHAT IS AN ORGANISATION?

After studying this chapter, you should know and understand:

- *the different ways in which an organisation can be become a legal entity;*
- *the situations for which the different types of legal entity are appropriate;*
- *what a limited company is and why it is the preferred legal form for a commercial organisation;*
- *what is meant by the terms* takeover, merger, management buyout *and* outsourcing;
- *the most important ways in which the law regulates limited companies.*

3.1 THE ROLE OF ORGANISATIONS

An organisation is a group of people working together in a formal way. Our life in a modern society is dominated by our interactions with organisations. We go to school and to college; schools and colleges are organisations. We or our friends and relatives go to hospital; a hospital is an organisation. We have a bank account; a bank is an organisation. We take the examinations of BCS; it is an organisation. And we work for a company or a government department, both of which are organisations. We may even set up a business of our own and thus create an organisation ourselves. However, as we mentioned in Chapter 1, organisations need to have a legal existence. In this chapter we shall describe the different ways in which an organisation can acquire a legal existence, concentrating on the idea of a limited company because this is the most important type of commercial organisation.

A very broad distinction can be made between commercial organisations, which are in business to make money, and public organisations or other non-profit-making bodies. This distinction is reflected in the different procedures used to set up the organisations and the different ways in which they are governed. Most of this chapter will be concerned with commercial organisations but in the last section we shall look briefly at non-commercial organisations.

3.2 COMMERCIAL ORGANISATIONS

The law offers several different ways of setting up and operating a commercial organisation. Depending on the circumstances, the business may be operated as a sole trader, a partnership, a cooperative or a limited company.

A **sole trader** is an individual who runs his or her own business. There are no legal formalities attached to becoming a sole trader; you become a sole trader simply by starting to run a business. If the income of your business is large enough you will need to register with HM Revenue & Customs (HMRC) for VAT (value-added tax) purposes, and you may need to negotiate with HMRC about your income tax status but neither of these is necessary simply in order to become a sole trader.

A sole trader is personally liable for all the debts of the business so that all the trader's assets, including the family home, are at risk if the business fails. For this reason, anyone who is in business in anything other than a very small way should not operate as a sole trader. It is usually better to form a limited company, as discussed later in this chapter.

If a group of people carry on a business with a view to making profits, and the business is not a limited company, then the law will treat them as being in a **partnership**. This will happen whether the people in question intend it to or not. The legal framework governing partnerships was established in the Partnership Act 1890 and has since been changed only in minor ways. The Act has important consequences for people going into business together.

The most important consequence of the Partnership Act is that the liability of the partners is unlimited and that the partners are **jointly and severally** responsible for the partnership's liabilities.

What does this mean in practice? Suppose that you and a friend are working together to write software for local company. Your friend is doing most of the work and you have agreed that he will get most of the money. Unfortunately, his software doesn't work and the company decides to claim damages for the harm it has suffered because of the defective software. You own a house and a car and have money in the bank; your friend doesn't. The company can sue you for the entire amount of the damages, despite the fact that it was your friend's software that didn't work.

A second problem with partnerships is the difficulty of making changes in the ownership. If one of the partners wishes to leave the partnership, perhaps to retire, how much money are they entitled to receive in return for relinquishing their share of the partnership? And how do the remaining partners raise this money? In the extreme case that one of the partners dies, how much is due to his or her estate?

Partnerships are mainly used in professions such as the law, medicine or architecture. The bodies that govern these professions have often insisted that their members practise in partnerships because the draconian rules regarding liability are seen to be a way of discouraging recklessness and ensuring the probity of the professionals concerned.

A more recent innovation is the **limited liability partnership** (LLP), which was introduced in the Limited Liability Partnership Act 2000. Unlike an ordinary partnership, an LLP is a corporate body, that is, it is a legal person and has a continuing existence independent of its members. The members of an LLP have a joint or collective responsibility to the extent that this is agreed when setting up the partnership but they have no responsibility for each other's actions. The LLP structure is commonly used by such professionals as accountants, solicitors and patent attorneys but is being increasingly used by groups of professionals such as management consultants and even web designers.

Another way in which an organisation can acquire a legal existence is as a **cooperative**. They are important in fields such as agriculture and enjoy a special legal status. They are, however, unusual in the information systems industry and we shall say no more about them.

By far the commonest form of commercial organisation, however, is the limited company. It is also the most suitable form of organisation for most businesses. Most of the remainder of this chapter will be dedicated to describing this type of organisation.

3.3 LIMITED COMPANIES

There are three principles that are fundamental to the concept of a limited liability company:

- The company has corporate legal identity, that is, it is a legal person, completely separate from the people who work in it or the people who own it.

- The ownership of the company is divided into a number (usually large) of shares. These shares can be bought and sold individually. The people who own these shares are known as the members of the company or shareholders. If the company is profitable, it may decide to distribute some or all of the profit to shareholders, in proportion to the number of shares that each of them holds. Profit distributed to shareholders in this way is known as a dividend.

- In the event that the company incurs debts or other legal liabilities, the owners of the company have no obligation to pay these. The most that shareholders stand to lose is the money they paid for their shares.

The UK recognises two main types of **limited company**, the public limited company (plc) and the private limited company. The essential difference is that a plc can, if it so wishes, offer its shares for sale to the public but a private limited company cannot. The name of a private limited company will end with the word Limited or Ltd, for example Augusta Technology Ltd, while the name of a public limited company will end with plc, for example, Lloyds Bank plc.

In return for the privileges, particularly limited liability, that the status of being a limited company confers, a limited liability company has certain obligations. It must provide details about itself to Companies House. This is a government agency that handles the formation and dissolution of UK companies, receives and stores information about companies that is required by law, and makes such information available to the general public. Companies must produce annual accounts (see Chapter 6) and an annual report; these must be submitted to Companies House and will be publicly available. Some of the reporting requirements are eased for small companies, while there are more stringent requirements for companies whose shares are quoted on a stock exchange.

Until the middle of the 19th century, the only way to create a limited company was through an Act of Parliament or the issue of a royal charter, both very slow and expensive routes. The modern idea of the limited company was developed through a number of acts of the UK parliament in the middle of the 19th century and was rapidly taken up in other countries. It has played a very important part in subsequent economic development, which would probably have taken place much more slowly if the convenient mechanism offered by the limited company had not been available.

It can be safely said that the three principles stated at the start of this section hold in any country that recognises the concept of a limited company. Within this framework, however, the details vary widely from country to country (as does the terminology – in particular, the term corporation is commonly used in the US to denote a large limited company). Several countries (New Zealand, Canada, Australia, for example) have enacted legislation in recent years that simplifies the law relating to companies.

The UK government carried out a review of company law that was trailed as being a complete overhaul that would greatly simplify the law. It resulted in the Companies Act 2006. This act proved to be **consolidating** act, that is, an act that brought together into a single place all the provisions relating to company law, which were previously distributed through many pieces of legislation. This undoubtedly made it easier to understand the existing law and some useful new provisions were introduced. Nevertheless, pressure from those who had a vested interest in the status quo meant that many opportunities for simplification were missed. The Act contains 1,300 sections, making it one of the longest and most complicated pieces of UK legislation.

3.4 SETTING UP A COMPANY

A limited company is created by a group of people each agreeing to subscribe a certain amount of money to set up an organisation to pursue some stated goal and to register the organisation as a limited company in accordance with the law. In the UK the process of setting up a limited company is straightforward and it can be done online, quickly and cheaply. It is not necessary to employ a lawyer or an accountant, although this may be advisable if you have little experience of dealing with formal documents.

The commonest way of setting up a company is to buy an 'off-the-shelf' company. There are a number of company formation agents that set up companies with a standard constitution; they hold a stock of such companies, which never actually trade, and they sell them to customers wanting a company through which to run their business. Once the customers have bought the company, they can make changes to its constitution, including its name, at their leisure.

The alternative is to create a company specifically to meet the requirements of the business. The process of registering the business is quick and cheap; the Registrar of Companies offers a same day service for less than £100. In practice, however, there are decisions to be made and forms to be completed, with the result that the process is likely to be slower and more expensive than buying a shelf company.

There are only a few countries in which companies can be set up as cheaply and as conveniently as in the UK or the USA. At the other extreme, in some countries it can take up to six months to register a new company and the cost can run into several thousands of pounds.

3.5 THE CONSTITUTION OF A LIMITED COMPANY

When a new company is incorporated, it is necessary to produce a memorandum of association signed by the founding shareholders. This simply states their wish to form a company under the Companies Act 2006 and the agreement of each of them to take at least one share. (Up until 2009, the memorandum of association was a longer and more complicated document.) The document must be filed with Companies House, the central repository of information about companies registered in the UK.

In order to become incorporated, in addition to the memorandum of association the company requires **articles of association**. These are much more complicated and technical. They relate to such matters as the number of directors, how directors are appointed and removed, what their powers are, what happens when new shares are to be issued, what process is required in order to modify the articles, and so on. In order to simplify the setting up of companies, the Companies Act 1948 included a specimen set of articles of association, which have been regularly updated; these were known as *Table A*. Following the Companies Act of 2006, these were replaced by a set that are now known as **model article**. Most new companies adopt these model articles as the basis of their articles of association and specify only the way in which their articles differ from the model ones.

Once a company has been registered, the memorandum of agreement and the articles of association are deposited at Companies House and are public documents, in the sense that anyone may visit Companies House and inspect them. It often happens in private companies that the shareholders wish to conclude a further agreement among themselves. Such an agreement is called a **shareholders' agreement**. It might, for example, say that, if a shareholder wishes to dispose of shares, the recipient of the shares must be a person acceptable to the remaining shareholders. Unlike the memorandum and the articles, a shareholders' agreement is not a public document.

3.6 DIRECTORS

In small companies, it may well be that the shareholders run the company directly but this is not feasible if there are more than a handful of shareholders; in any case, some shareholders may not wish to be involved directly in the day-to-day operations of the business. The law requires that the shareholders appoint directors to take responsibility for running the company on their behalf.

In small companies, the shareholders may actually be directors or at least be in regular contact with them. In large public companies, however, the shareholders have very little opportunity to influence the directors. To compensate for this, the law makes directors subject to certain obligations.

First, the Companies Act 2006 lays down that the overall duty of a director is to promote the success of the company for the benefit of its members as a whole, having regard to the following factors:

- the likely consequences of any decision in the long term;
- the interests of the company's employees;
- the need to foster the company's business relationships with suppliers, customers and others;
- the impact of the company's operations on the community and the environment;
- the desirability of the company maintaining a reputation for high standards of business conduct;
- the need to act fairly as between members of a company.

More specifically:

- Directors must act in good faith and for the benefit of the company. Suppose, for example, that you are a director of a small company that writes software and that someone approaches you to have some software written. If you decided that you could do this yourself in your spare time rather than having it written by the company, you would not be considered to have acted in good faith for the benefit of the company, and you could be required to pay the company compensation for the loss of the contract.

- Directors must exercise the skill and care in carrying out their duties that might be expected from someone of their qualifications and experience. This means, for example, that a director with long experience of purchasing computers who signed a contract to buy a computer system that was not suitable for the use the company intended to make of it might be ordered by a court to pay back to the company the cost of the computer. Furthermore, directors must take the same care as an ordinary person might be expected to take on his or her own behalf.

- A director who has an interest in a contract made with the company (e.g. owning an office cleaning company that the company is thinking of employing) must disclose this interest to the board of directors. The model articles stipulate that the director must not be allowed to vote or be counted in the quorum when the matter is discussed but, in the case of a small company, this may well be varied.

The obligations described above can be described as domestic, that is, they are obligations owed to the company. In addition, there are certain external or legal obligations that the directors must fulfil:

- Directors are required to keep themselves aware of the company's financial position and not allow it to continue to incur debts when they know or should

> have known that the company will be unable to repay them. If they fail to do this, a court can make them personally liable for the company's debts.
>
> - The directors are responsible for drawing up the company's annual report, including its accounts, and for filing this report with Companies House. We shall explore this in more detail in Chapter 6.
>
> - The directors are responsible for ensuring that the company complies with all relevant provisions of the law. Although the company itself, having a legal existence, can be prosecuted for criminal breaches of the law, in some cases directors can be made personally responsible. Thus the Health and Safety at Work Act 1974 provides that in appropriate circumstances a director or other senior manager can be criminally liable if a company is found to be in serious breach of the Act.

Many companies have both executive directors and non-executive directors. Executive directors are normally also employees of the company, with specific responsibility for certain areas of its activities. Non-executive directors are directors who act in advisory capacity only. Typically, they attend monthly board meetings to offer the benefit of their advice and serve on committees concerned with sensitive issues such as the pay of the executive directors and other senior managers; they are usually paid a fee for their services but are not regarded as employees. It is important to realise that, legally, the duties and responsibilities of non-executive directors are precisely the same as those of the executive directors.

Every public company must have a company secretary; private companies can choose not to have a secretary. The company secretary is legally responsible for keeping the various records that the company has to maintain and for submitting various statutory returns to Companies House in Cardiff. He or she will normally also take responsibility for a variety of related matters. The company secretary is often also a director. Small companies often appoint an outsider, typically a solicitor or accountant, as company secretary, because such people are likely to have the necessary professional expertise.

3.7 TAKEOVERS, MERGERS AND OUTSOURCING

Limited companies, whether private or public, are, on the whole, short-lived. They disappear, not because they fail – although, of course, some do – or are wound up for other reasons, but because they are taken over by other companies.

3.7.1 Takeovers

How and why do such takeovers take place? The commonest scenario in the IT industry is of a private company, A, being taken over by a larger company, B, probably but not necessarily a public one. The mechanism of such a takeover is that B acquires all the shares of A, paying for them either in cash or in its own shares or in a mixture of both. It is likely that the shareholders of A will also be its directors and that much of the value of the company derives from the skills of these people and their contacts. Accordingly, there may well be an agreement that they will work for B for, say, the next three years.

Why might the owners of A want to sell the company? First, although as the owners of a successful small company they will be quite wealthy on paper, they are probably only able to pay themselves a comparatively modest salary and they certainly don't feel wealthy. Furthermore, their wealth on paper is critically dependent on the continued success of the company and probably vulnerable to a change in market conditions. By selling the company, they are able to convert their paper wealth into real money and, at the same time, protect themselves against fluctuations in the value of the company. A second reason for wanting to sell the company may be the need for further capital investment.

One reason why B may wish to buy A is that A has intellectual property or high level skills that complement those of B. In one such case, A was a small company that had developed software for automatically carrying out failure mode analysis on the electrical system of a car, that is, it would predict the result of all the different possible ways in which the electrical system could fail. Such an analysis, formerly done by hand, is a requirement before a new model of car can be put on the market. Although A's technical development had been successful, it did not have the resources to market its software successfully. B was a large US-based multi-national company that produces electronic design automation tools. A's software complemented B's software perfectly and B already had excellent access to all its potential customers. B bought A, and A's software became one of B's products and continued to be maintained and developed by staff who had developed it originally.

A very different type of takeover occurred in 1991, when the British software house SD-Scicon, which specialised in defence and other hi-tech systems, was taken over by the American company Electronic Data Systems (EDS). EDS was in the business of providing IT services to large organisations, particularly in the field of health services. It showed no interest in SD-Scicon's traditional markets and rapidly shed the considerable number of highly skilled professional staff who worked for the company. It used the acquisition of SD-Scicon as a means of getting a foothold in the much more profitable market for IT services in the UK but SD-Scicon effectively lost its identity and completely disappeared.

In contrast, when EDS itself was acquired by Hewlett-Packard for $13.9 billion in 2008 it was able to retain its identity, staff and structures, although it now trades as HP Enterprise Services. In this instance, Hewlett-Packard wanted to enter the large and profitable area of IT services and it chose to do so by acquiring a company that was a major player in the field. To have broken up EDS would have defeated the purpose of the takeover.

In cases such as these last two examples, where the company being acquired is a public company, the stock exchanges on which the companies' shares are quoted impose strict regulations in an attempt to prevent improper exploitation of the situation.

REASONS FOR TAKEOVERS

From the point of view of the owners and managers of the acquiring company, the fundamental reasons for taking over another company are to make more money and to get bigger. In more detail these amount to:

- expanding the customer base. This occurs particularly when the company taken over offers services similar to those of the buying company but in a different geographical area;
- expanding its range of offerings. This occurs when the company taken over offers products or services that are complementary to those of the buying company, for example, when a company offering a human resources package acquires a company that offers a payroll package;
- acquiring new staff. There has been a shortage of high quality IT staff for most of the past 40 years and this has prevented many companies expanding as they would have wished. Taking over another company can be a quick way of acquiring additional staff;
- economies of scale. The larger company's human resources (HR) department, for example, may be able to take on HR responsibilities for the company being taken over, without itself requiring any extra staff. It is frequently claimed that such savings will result from a takeover but the reality is that the savings are usually small and often negligible;
- vertical integration;
- eliminating a competitor.

These benefits do not come without risks. The acquisition in 2007 of the Dutch bank ABN AMRO by a consortium including the Royal Bank of Scotland is a recent example of an acquisition that, far from yielding the expected benefits, resulted in disaster for the purchaser. There are many similar, if less well-publicised, examples in the IT industry.

3.7.2 Mergers

In a takeover, one company gains control of another by acquiring a majority, if not all, of its shares. Although the terms takeover and merger are commonly used synonymously, strictly speaking there is a difference. In a merger, the two companies come together on equal terms. A common mechanism is that a new company is set up, which acquires all the shares of the merging companies in exchange for its own shares; the merging companies themselves cease to exist.

Mergers in this strict sense are comparatively uncommon. A good example, however, was the merger of the two telephone operating companies Bell Atlantic and GTE to form Verizon Communications Inc. This merger, completed in June 2000, was one of the largest mergers in American industrial history. There is a risk that mergers on this scale can have a serious effect on competition and work against the public interest. For this reason, they may be subject to examination under monopolies legislation (anti-trust legislation in the USA). It took two years to obtain complete approval of the merger of Bell Atlantic and GTE.

3.7.3 Management buyouts

It may happen that some of the senior employees of a company decide to purchase the company from its existing owners. This is known as a management buyout. It will usually require a lot of capital to do this and the purchasers will need to borrow this. However, the lenders are likely to demand that the purchasers shoulder a significant part of the risk by raising a substantial amount of capital, for example, by mortgaging their homes. At first sight a management buyout looks praiseworthy – the people who are running the company become its owners. In practice, there are many potential conflicts of interest. The management may run the company down over a period before bidding to buy it, thus reducing its apparent value and the sum they have to pay to buy it. Once they have bought it, they rapidly build the company up again before selling it at a considerable profit.

3.7.4 Outsourcing

Outsourcing is contracting out activities or processes from one business to another. Fifty years ago, large companies would employ their own cleaners, their own gardeners to look after their grounds, their own maintenance staff and painters to look after their premises, their own catering staff to run the staff canteen, and so on. Nowadays all, or most of, these activities will be outsourced, that is, contracted out to other, specialist companies. More surprisingly, perhaps, so will the processing of the company's payroll and the maintenance of staff records. Theatres and airlines outsource the sale of tickets. And some organisations outsource the whole of their IT operations.

Historically, outsourcing in the UK was associated particularly with IT and the civil service and was introduced by the Conservative government under Margaret Thatcher that came to power in 1979. The Conservative party was committed to the politically popular goal of reducing substantially the number of civil servants. By outsourcing the provision of government IT services, the number of civil servants could be cut dramatically. At the same time, there were good reasons for thinking that this might lead to an improvement in the quality of those services – the civil service had difficulty in recruiting and retaining high quality IT staff, while specialist outsourcing companies, not being subject to the same staffing restraints as the civil service, had fewer problems.

As a result of this policy, which has been accepted by all succeeding governments, of whatever complexion, almost all government operational IT is now outsourced. The policy has been by no means universally successful and there have been many examples of serious problems. However, it must be borne in mind that the size and scope of government IT systems is much greater than that of systems in use in private industry. If outsourcing companies have often failed to appreciate this, so also have politicians and civil servants.

ARGUMENTS FOR OUTSOURCING

Outsourcing is now widely practised by private industry as well as by the public sector. The arguments put forward in favour of outsourcing IT provision can be summed up as follows:

- It frees management to concentrate on the core business of the company.
- It makes the costs of IT more visible and therefore easier to control.
- Specialist companies are able to produce and operate more effective systems because:
  - they have much wider experience of system development than do user companies;
  - they can justify employing highly specialised staff;
  - working in a specialised IT company provides a better career path for IT staff than working for a user organisation.
- Overall, it saves money.

There is an element of truth in all these points but there is also a danger that the company that outsources too much of its IT provision may lose control and understanding of its own operations.

Outsourcing is often associated with **off-shoring**, that is, moving activity to other countries. Thus, companies in Britain may outsource software development to companies in India. The reason for doing this is straightforwardly one of cost. Well qualified and experienced software engineers in India earn much less than they do in the UK and there are plenty of them available.

Employment issues connected with outsourcing are considered in Chapter 9 and outsourcing contracts are discussed in Chapter 12.

3.8 NON-COMMERCIAL BODIES

3.8.1 Statutory bodies

Roughly speaking, about 80 per cent of jobs in the UK are in the private sector and provided, on the whole, by limited companies. The remaining 20 per cent are in the public sector – local government, the National Health Service, education, the police, the armed services and so on. It is in the nature of the public sector that it deals with data on a much larger scale than most private sector organisations – very few private companies have as many as a million customers but the Department for Work and Pensions holds records for everyone in the UK over the age of 16 – about 50 million people. Because of the large numbers involved, such public sector bodies make great demands on IT services; they employ many IT staff directly and many more work for private sector companies that provide IT services to the public sector. Large public sector IT projects also have very poor record of success, precisely because of their size.

Many public sector organisations come into existence by statute, that is, by Act of Parliament. Such organisations are often referred to as statutory bodies. Frequently the organisations themselves are created by secondary legislation. In the terms of object-oriented programming, the Act of Parliament defines a class of organisations, specifying their structure, their duties and their powers. Secondary legislation is then used to create objects belonging to that class, that is, specific instances of it. Thus, in the field of local government, the Local Government Act 1992 created the class of unitary authorities together with a body, the Local Government Commission, which would make recommendations for the creation of specific unitary authorities; these authorities would then be created by secondary legislation. The unitary authorities themselves are empowered to create and run schools and certain other public services.

The overall objective of the directors of a limited company is fairly straightforward even if achieving them is difficult: they have to run the company in order to make as much money for the shareholders as they reasonably can, while having due regard to the interests of the employees and certain other defined considerations. If the shareholders are unhappy they can either sell their shares or, if enough of them are unhappy, they can vote to replace the directors. If the directors fail to run the company profitably it will ultimately be forced to close or it will be taken over.

The position in the public sector is very different. The overall objective of a public body is to provide some sort of public service such as keeping the roads in an area in good condition, providing education for children or administering state pensions. There are no shareholders but everyone has an interest in seeing that the body does its job satisfactorily. But profitability is not a measure of success and the option of closure if the body does not perform satisfactorily is not usually acceptable. There thus needs to be some mechanism for making the management of the body accountable to the general public.

Many different mechanisms have been adopted to achieve accountability in the public sector. At the level of national and local government, accountability is achieved through the ballot box. Members of Parliament and local councillors are elected for limited terms and they take responsibility for the activities of national and local government respectively. However, their role is fundamentally different from that of directors of a company. Company directors – or, more precisely, executive directors – are expected to run a part of the company and are usually selected on the basis of their ability to do this. Members of Parliament and local councillors are elected to represent the public and to contribute to council policy making, rather than to the carrying out of policy. The national government and local councils employ professionals – civil servants, engineers, IT staff, social workers, teachers and so on – to carry out their policy. There is often a tension between politicians, who are motivated by policy issues, and the professionals, who are motivated by practical considerations. Too often, professionals feel that the politicians are stick-in-the-muds who are opposed to all change, while the professionals feel that the councillors have their heads in the clouds and don't understand the practicalities. A particular problem that frequently arises is that politicians decide that a change to, say, the social security system is required. They fail to realise how long it will take to make and test the necessary changes to the IT systems and insist that the changes are implemented too quickly. The result is that the system fails and causes serious problems for some members of the public. The IT professionals – or, increasingly often, the company to which the development is outsourced – are blamed for the failure. In most such cases, the blame should be shared: on the one hand, those responsible for setting over-ambitious goals and timescales and insisting on them, against professional advice, must take their share of the blame but, on the other hand, outsourcing companies are too eager to sign lucrative contracts whose timely fulfilment depends on a lot of very optimistic assumptions.

3.8.2 Other non-profit-making bodies

As well as statutory bodies, there are very many organisations whose activities are generally seen to be in the public interest and which are not intended to be profit-making. Such organisations include professional bodies, such as BCS or the Institute of Physics, political parties, charities such as Oxfam or Christian Aid and so on. Such organisations usually take the legal form of a **company limited by guarantee**. In this case, rather than subscribing for shares, the members agree that, in the event that the body has to be wound up, each will pay a small fixed amount (typically £1) to cover liabilities. A company limited by guarantee is not allowed to distribute its profits to its members. It can apply for charitable status and for the grant of a royal charter.

Like most of the larger professional bodies, BCS is a company incorporated by royal charter and a registered charity. The royal charter states that 'the government and control of the Institute and its affairs shall be vested in the Trustee Board'. This means that the Trustee Board performs the functions of the board of directors of company and of the trustees of a charity. The Trustee Board consists of the President, Deputy President and the immediate past President, all of whom serve for one year, plus the four Vice-Presidents and five other members. All the members of the Trustee Board are elected by the Council, which consists of the members of the Trustee Board, together with 27 members elected directly by the membership of BCS and the chief executive, who is the only member who is a paid employee of BCS.

An organisation the size of BCS is much too large to be run solely by its members and so, like most professional bodies, it is run by a combination of full-time employees and volunteers from amongst its members. The structure described in the previous paragraph seems, on the face of it, to ensure control of the Institute rests firmly with its members. In practice, however, the short tenure of the senior elected officers and the limited amount of time that members, who have full-time professional commitments elsewhere, can devote to BCS business, mean inevitably that the senior full-time employees have a great deal of influence over BCS policy and the way it is carried out.

FURTHER READING

The UK government has a website that describes in simple language the duties of a director of a private limited company:
www.gov.uk/running-a-limited-company

The Corporate Responsibility (CORE) Coalition has produced a much more sophisticated guide to directors' responsibilities, which can be found at:
http://corporate-responsibility.org/wp-content/uploads/2009/09/directors_guidance_final.pdf

The Companies House website provides detailed information about registering a company, filing a company's annual return, changing a company's details and so on:
www.companieshouse.gov.uk

4 STRUCTURE AND MANAGEMENT OF ORGANISATIONS

After studying this chapter, in the context of organisations with which you are familiar, you should:

- *be able to recognise how they are structured;*
- *be able to suggest alternative possible structures and identify their advantages and disadvantages;*
- *be aware of the effect that decisions about organisational structure may have on individual employees.*

4.1 ORGANISATIONAL MODELS

As we said at the start of Chapter 3, an organisation is a group of people working together in a formal way. What this means is that the work that has to be done is shared between these people and that there are rules about who does what. How the work is shared and how tasks and people are grouped together – the structure of the organisation – will vary very much from organisation to organisation. It is surprising, however, that organisational structures have much more in common than might be expected. In this chapter, we shall describe the most common ways of structuring organisations.

4.1.1 The bureaucratic model

Organisational theory, the study of how organisations are structured and how they work, goes back to end of the 19th century. The founders of the theory were sociologists like Max Weber and Mary Parker Follett, and practical business people like Henri Fayol and Lyndall Urwick. They developed what is known as the bureaucratic model. In a modified form, this model still describes the organisational structures to be found in most large, and many smaller, organisations. (Note that **bureaucratic** here is simply descriptive; the pejorative sense developed later.)

The ideal bureaucratic organisation was thought to have the following characteristics:

1. All tasks are split up into specialised jobs, in which jobholders become expert; management can thereby hold them responsible for the effective performance of their duties.

2. The performance of each task is governed by precise rules. This means that there should be no variation in the way tasks are carried out and therefore no problems with the coordination of different tasks.

3. Each individual (and hence each unit) in the organisation is accountable to one and only one manager.

4. In order to ensure that personalities and personal relationships do not interfere with the organisation's performance, employees are required to relate both to other employees and to clients in an impersonal and formal manner.

5. Recruitment is based on qualifications and employees are protected against arbitrary dismissal. Promotion is based on seniority and achievement. Life-time employment is envisaged.

These ideas have proved surprisingly long-lasting. Remnants even of the fourth were certainly still to be found in banks and local authorities in the 1980s. In the 1970s it was still the case in some companies that if two employees became engaged to be married, one of them would be required to resign.

It is an inevitable consequence of these rules that the organisation will be hierarchical and that its structure can be represented as a tree.

Despite the obvious weaknesses of the approach (at least in this form), it brings many benefits and many companies were run successfully along these lines for many years. Modernised and liberalised versions are still to be found working successfully, particularly in production line industries. Much grief has ensued when companies whose main business is appropriately organised in this way have applied these ideas to software production, for instance by separating the tasks of writing code, compiling it and correcting compilation errors, and testing it, and assigning them to different groups of specialists.

4.1.2 The organic model

The best known alternative model is the **organic** model, particularly associated with Rensis Lickert. He expresses the basic assumption of the model in the following (rather verbose) terms:

> An organisation will be effective to the extent that its structure is such as to ensure a maximum probability that in all interactions and in relationships within the organisation, each member, in the light of his background, values, desires, and expectations, will view the experience as supportive and one which builds a sense of personal worth and importance.
> (*The Human Organisation*. McGraw-Hill, New York, 1967, p.47)

This view underlies the organisational structure of most small professional companies – software houses, advertising agencies, even solicitors' and GPs' practices; it is also common in academic institutions, both schools and universities. The view is not necessarily consciously articulated – nor is this view and the adoption of the structures it suggests sufficient to achieve effectiveness!

Proponents of the bureaucratic model claim that it is universally applicable. Proponents of the organic model make similar claims. It says little for common sense that those who hold the obvious view that each has its appropriate place should be christened adherents of the contingency school of organisational design.

4.1.3 Matrix management

It is an essential feature of the bureaucratic model that every individual and every unit in the organisation is responsible to only one manager. This is not realistic in the context of project-based, high technology companies. A specialist in high speed communications working for a systems integrator may well find him- or herself working on two or three projects simultaneously, as well as having a more general responsibility for maintaining the company's expertise in the area. In the past 30 years or so the idea of matrix management has become fashionable, as a way of addressing such situations. It accepts that individuals may be responsible to more than one manager and requires rules that will enable possible conflicts to be resolved. In a software company, for example, database specialists may belong to a database group and report to its manager, while at the same time reporting to the project manager of the project they are working on.

Some organisations and some management consultants have tried to formulate the matrix management model much more formally. The results are not encouraging.

4.2 STRUCTURING PRINCIPLES

The bureaucratic model tells us something about the way individuals and groups in an organisation relate to each other. It tells us nothing, however, about how to group together the tasks and activities that have to be carried out. In practice, there are many different ways of doing this and we shall describe some of them in the following sections. It should not be thought that these models are mutually exclusive. In all but the smallest companies, different parts of the organisation are likely to reflect different ways of producing a structure. Furthermore, the structures produced by the different criteria may be combined in a matrix structure.

4.2.1 Structure by function

In almost every organisation, we can identify certain groups of activities that have to be carried out and that fit naturally together.

First of all, there are the activities that are the primary purpose of the organisation. These activities are known as **operations**. The primary purpose of a school is to teach students. The primary purpose of a hospital is to cure sick people. The primary purpose of a software company is to provide software for its customers. In each case, these activities constitute the operations of the organisation concerned. The term **core business** is often used to mean the primary purpose of an organisation.

Secondly, almost all organisations have to pay their bills and pay their employees. They will need to ensure that the buildings they use are cleaned regularly. If they charge for their services, they may need to send out bills and ensure that these are paid. They will probably need to hire new employees from time to time. These activities are generally known as **administration**. Although operations in different types of organisation will be very different, administration varies much less.

Thirdly, many organisations will need to publicise their services or their products and try to persuade people to use them or buy them. In the business world these activities are usually known as **sales and marketing**. Strictly speaking, marketing means the activities involved in making potential customers aware of the products the business can offer; it also includes planning new products on the basis of what the company might provide and what customers would like. Selling or sales is the activity of persuading individual customers to buy from the company.

It is often thought that sales and marketing are activities restricted to commercial organisations. This is not the case. Health services try to persuade people to go for check-ups and to participate in screening programmes. Publicising these services is a marketing activity; sending out specific invitations to individuals is a sales activity. In Britain, as part of the policy of giving parents a choice of schools for their children, schools are encouraged to compete for pupils. This means schools must produce publicity material, a marketing activity, and must try to persuade parents visiting the school to send their children to it, a sales activity.

Finally, many organisations need to be continually developing new products or services, or developing new ways to deliver them. These activities are known as research and development.

A structure based on functions, with an administrative division, an operations division, a sales and marketing division and possibly a research and development division, is the commonest type of structure to be found in medium-sized companies. It is illustrated in Figure 4.1.

Figure 4.1 A function-based structure

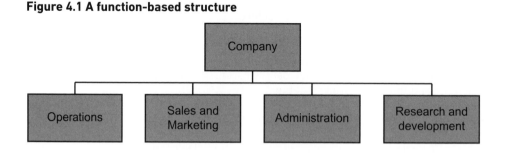

4.2.2 Structure by geography

In many cases it makes sense to group activities together on a geographical basis. Multinational companies, that is, companies that operate in a number of different countries, are usually forced to have some geographical elements in their structure. In most cases, in order to operate effectively in a country, they will need a permanent presence there, and this requires that they have a legal personality, usually in the form of a subsidiary company registered in the country but owned by the parent. The subsidiaries are subject to the laws of the countries in which they are registered, in particular, the laws regarding employment, accounting and taxation. These laws differ markedly from country to country so each subsidiary will need its own administrative capability. Linguistic and cultural factors will usually mean that sales and marketing have to be locally based; certainly this is the case if the company's customers are consumers.

An example of a company that is structured on a geographical basis at the top level is CGI. It is the fifth largest IT services company in the world and is based in Montreal. It operates in 40 countries across the world and its operations are structured into six geographically-based divisions.

Within a single country, geographical factors have become less important as a result of the development of modern communications and, as a result, geographical structures have been replaced by structures based on other factors. British banks, for example, used to operate through local branches that provided all but the very largest customers with all the banking services they required. The local branches themselves were under the control of regional management, based on geographical regions. Now that customers can do much of their banking online over the internet, the role of the local branch and the extent of its manager's authority are steadily declining. Instead, the banks have moved towards a product line organisation, in which different banking services (current accounts, loans, investment advice and so on) are provided by different divisions of the bank, independent of the local branches.

4.2.3 Product line structure

A product line structure is a structure that is based around the different types of product that an organisation produces. This type of structure is very common in the engineering industry, for example, where a motor vehicle manufacturer may be structured into three divisions: cars and light vans, heavy goods vehicles, and replacement parts.

Companies that produce and market a substantial piece of software for corporate customers – a multi-user accounting package, for example – often organise themselves into three main operational divisions: development and maintenance of the software, consultancy and training. This should be regarded as a product line structure since the three types of activity, providing software, giving advice to companies in how to use it, and provide training for customer staff, can be considered to be different services that the company provides and they are typically provided by different teams of people.

MIXED STRUCTURES

Large multinational companies often show a mixture of functional, geographical and product line structures. Microsoft, for example, operates its business in five 'segments' based on a product line structure:

Windows Division develops and markets PC operating systems, related software and online services, and PC hardware products.

Server and Tools develops and markets server software, software developer tools and services for information technology professionals and developers.

Online Services Division develops and markets information and content designed to help people simplify tasks and make more informed decisions online, and help advertisers connect with audiences. Its products include Bing, MSN, adCenter and advertiser tools.

Microsoft Business Division handles Microsoft Office, SharePoint, Exchange, and related products.

Entertainment and Devices Division develops and markets products and services designed to entertain and connect people. These include the Xbox and Skype.

Long-term research and development is organised as a separate, corporate activity, spread geographically across ten countries but structured internally on a project basis rather than by location. Support services such as finance, human resources and legal services are provided at a corporate level, structured by function.

4.2.4 Structure by market sector

Structure by market sector means structure based on the different market sectors to which its customers or prospective customers belong.

This approach is very popular within the IT industry. From the sales and marketing point of view it has the great advantage that each division can fairly readily identify its potential customers and its staff, both sales and technical, are likely to be familiar with customers' problems and to speak a language that the customer will understand.

There are two dangers with this approach. First, there is the risk one division may be unaware of technological expertise that exists in another division. This may lead to inefficient use of resources, through unnecessarily hiring additional specialists or employing consultants, or, worse, to failing to learn from mistakes that have been made by other parts of the company.

The second danger with a structure based on market sector is that, by continuing to concentrate on its traditional areas even when these markets are becoming saturated, the company will miss new opportunities and will stagnate.

4.2.5 Structure by technology

A technology-based structure was once a favourite model for software companies. Thus, a company might have divisions specialising in artificial intelligence, communications, web-based systems, databases and real-time systems. There are several problems with this type of structure:

- It usually requires several different technologies to meet a customer's needs.
- There are many applications that cannot be said to require specific technologies.
- There are many competent software engineers whose expertise runs across a number of technologies.
- It is difficult, if not impossible, for sales and marketing staff to predict which potential clients will need which technology.

The last of these is particularly serious and companies that are primarily structured by technology have serious problems finding their clients. In marketing jargon, they are not sufficiently 'customer-focused' – they concentrate on selling the technologies that they have, rather than finding out what the customer needs.

4.2.5 Operational structure

The actual operations of a company may be organised on **project** basis or on a **production** basis, although the line separating the two may be vague.

A project is an activity that has specific objectives that have to be achieved within a fixed time period and with the expenditure of no more than some fixed quantity of resources. Every project is different from every other project. In some companies, nearly all the revenue-earning activities are project-based. This is particularly true of companies that produce bespoke software or companies that carry out system integration work.

Project-based activity is not restricted to operations. Most research and development is organised on a project basis and such administrative activities as introducing a new accounting system or transferring a company's head office are also to be regarded as projects, in that they last for a fixed length of time, after which they should be complete.

Projects last a comparatively long time but the team carrying out the work only stays together for the length of the project. Production activities are comparatively short but the team carrying them out stays in existence indefinitely. Classic examples of production activities are motor vehicle manufacturing, oil refining and dairy farming; each of them goes on year after year producing much the same outputs. The central data processing operations of a company are organised on a production basis. There is a schedule of programs – payroll, accounts payable, accounts receivable, and so on – that have to be run regularly on specific dates. It is the job of the operations team to ensure that these activities are completed on schedule. Although the individuals in the team will change from time to time, the team itself will continue to exist.

From the point of view of the employee, the difference between project-based and production structures is very marked. On the whole, if activities are structured on a project basis, employees will find their working environment – their colleagues, their clients and even the job they are doing – changing radically every few weeks or months, as they move from project to project. If they are working in a production environment, change will be slower and more gradual. One environment is not generally preferable to the other; much depends on the personality of the employee.

4.3 DEPTH OF STRUCTURE

The depth of an organisational structure is the number of layers in the structure – or, more precisely, the maximum number of layers, since not all parts of the structure will have the same number of layers. Organisational structures are often described as flat or, in contrast, deep or tall, according to whether the depth is small or large. For a given number of people, the depth of the structure will obviously depend on the number of people reporting directly to each manager; this is sometimes known as the manager's **span of control**. Figures 4.2 and 4.3 both show 12 people organised in a bureaucratic structure. In Figure 4.2, each manager's span of control is two and there are four layers in the structure. This means that the people at the bottom of the structure, such as H, have to pass through two managers (B and D in the case of H) before reaching the head of the organisation, A. Figure 4.3 shows a flatter structure for the same number of people. Each manager's span of control is six but the number of layers is reduced to three, meaning that people at the bottom of the structure only have to pass through one manager to reach A. It is generally accepted that, in a bureaucratic structure, managers should not be expected to have more than six people reporting to them directly.

Figure 4.2 Twelve people organised into a four-level structure

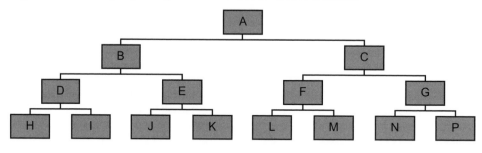

Figure 4.3 Twelve people organised into a three-level structure

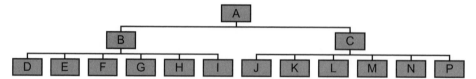

Obviously the structure of organisations with large numbers of employees is likely to be deeper than that of smaller organisations. Professional staff generally prefer to work with flatter structures.

4.4 CENTRALISATION

Organisations may be centralised or decentralised. In a centralised company, as much power as possible is kept at the top of the company, with delegation only when essential. In a decentralised company, as much power and control as possible is delegated to the lowest level. If we take a software company as an example, centralisation might mean that there were company-wide rules that all programming should be done in C++ and that, whenever a database package was needed, Oracle should be used. Such a policy has the obvious advantages that programmers could be easily moved from one part of the company to another and that it would be possible to build up a close relationship with Oracle. On the other hand, it might mean that C++ and Oracle were used for projects that would have been much better done using Java and MySQL, or Visual Basic and Access. Decentralisation would allow the most suitable tools to be chosen for each project but might mean that the staff were very inflexible. It could also lead to a maintenance nightmare in the future, with maintenance staff needing to be familiar with large numbers of obsolete tools.

Drawing the correct balance between centralisation and decentralisation is important but difficult. Decentralisation is commonly found in hi-tech companies, where there is plenty of talent at lower levels. Centralisation is commoner in large manufacturing companies and other long-established organisations. The ideal might be described as **flexible centralisation**, in which rules and practices are laid down centrally but it is accepted that reasonable arguments for modifying them in specific cases will be readily accepted. Unfortunately, putting this into practice often proves difficult.

4.5 SETTING UP A STRUCTURE IN PRACTICE

In most cases, an organisation of any size will have a structure that includes elements of several of the different types of structure described above.

Consider the case of a medium-sized UK-based company providing bespoke software development and consultancy in the UK and operating in several other western European countries through subsidiary companies there.

At the top level, the company is faced with a choice. It could adopt a market sector structure, with divisions corresponding to each market sector in which it operates. Each division would be responsible both for sales and marketing in that sector and operations, that is, carrying out projects for that sector. Alternatively, it could adopt a functional structure with a sales and marketing department and an operations department. In either case it seems sensible to have a finance and administration department, probably under the management of the Finance Director.

The functional structure would have the advantage of bringing together all the programmers, analysts, designers and project managers in one group and all the sales and marketing staff in another. This offers great flexibility and should enable the head of each group to deploy its staff efficiently. If this is done, however, it will probably be necessary to structure the sales and marketing division according to market sector, because sales and marketing activity is usually only effective if aimed at specific sectors.

In order to sell in a country, it is almost essential to speak the language and to be familiar with the culture. Furthermore, despite the gradual harmonisation of business regulations in the European Union, each country has its own laws, its own bureaucratic procedures and its own way of producing accounts. All these factors suggest a need for a country-based organisation. The best way of doing this may be to set up a subsidiary company in each country, with a small office, responsible for sales and marketing, and administration in that that country. The subsidiary will be able to call on the sales and marketing division in the UK for specialist help.

The organisational structure within the operations division presents other difficulties. Although a project structure will obviously be used for carrying out individual contracts for customers, some higher level structure is required. Do we group projects by market sector or by technical characteristics? It may be that both are appropriate, that is, projects where the risks and problems are technical are grouped into one or more units, depending on the technology required, while projects where application considerations are more important are grouped into units depending on market sector.

Figure 4.4 shows an example of the sort of structure that such a company might adopt.

Figure 4.4 An organisational structure for a bespoke software house

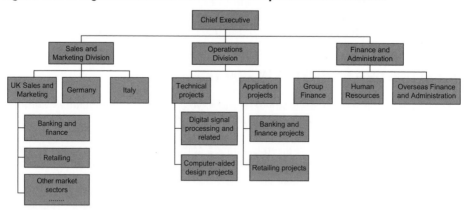

4.6 JOB DESIGN

Setting up an organisational structure implies designing jobs. As soon as a one-person organisation becomes a two-person organisation, it has to decide who does what; in other words it has to design jobs. In project-based organisations, jobs get designed when the project team is set up and when the project plan is produced. The jobs are ephemeral – they last only as long as the project – and the technical nature of the project determines exactly what tasks the jobs have to cover. Nevertheless, this job design is done within an established framework: a project-based organisation will have (or should have) procedures that lay down the way in which project teams are to be structured; such procedures may mandate the use of chief programmer teams in certain circumstances or specify the maximum span of control and the responsibilities of team leaders and project QA staff in a hierarchically organised project. The tasks to be carried out will probably be defined by the development methodology that the company uses.

In many large organisations structured along bureaucratic lines, job specialisation leads to very narrow and tightly defined jobs. As a result, the people carrying out those jobs find them dull and unsatisfying. This in turn leads to poor performance and high turnover. In an effort to alleviate this problem, companies have tried three different ways to provide more interesting and satisfying jobs: job rotation, job enlargement and job enrichment.

Few jobs in the IT industry suffer from the extremes of job specialisation that are found in production line jobs, for example. Nevertheless, the manager should bear in mind that a software engineer who is expected to spend a full year on testing a system may well be moved to apply for other jobs and that efforts to reduce staff turnover are unlikely to be successful if staff are expected to spend most of their time carrying out tasks that they find dull or distasteful.

The basic ideas of job design become of major importance when we are designing information systems. The introduction of the system can have a considerable impact on the jobs of its users. Very often this may involve an element of deskilling, that is, the jobs under the new system demand fewer skills or less knowledge from the people doing them; this tends to reduce job satisfaction. The way in which the system is designed can ameliorate this situation or exacerbate it. Information systems engineers should be concerned with the effect the system they are building will have on the work of its users.

Job rotation, that is, rotating staff through a series of jobs, is the most obvious way of preventing employees from becoming bored with a very narrow and specialised task.

Consider the handling of creditors' invoices in a large accounts department with a very specialised regime, An analysis of the process might identify the following tasks, which then might be allocated to the individuals named:

1. receive incoming invoice and match to purchase order (Freda);
2. confirm price calculations and despatch to receiving department for confirmation that goods or services have been received (Gareth);
3. receive confirmation from department and pass for payment (John);
4. produce payment (Peter);
5. handle queries arising at any of the above stages (Julie).

Job rotation could be introduced very simply by arranging that in week 1, Freda does task 1, Gareth, task 2, and John, task 3; in week 2, Freda moves to task 2, Gareth to task 3 and John to task 1; and in week 3, Freda moves to task 3, Gareth to task 1, and John to task 2; and in week 4 they return to the tasks they carried out in week 1. Some extra training would be required but any cost would be more than balanced by the added **resilience** of the department, that is, by its increased ability to handle absence through sickness or holiday. Including tasks 4 and 5 in the cycle is not so easy. The principle of separation of responsibility as a means of reducing fraud means that the payment function should not be given to anyone who is involved at any point in authorising payment. Task 5 is inherently a more sophisticated task requiring both greater intelligence and more experience.

Job enlargement means redesign of a job so that it includes more tasks which require essentially the same level of skill and responsibility. Thus, in the case of the example cited in the previous paragraph, Freda, Gareth and John might each be asked to handle all three of tasks 1, 2 and 3. This might be done by allocating each of them responsibility for invoices from certain suppliers or perhaps for orders from certain departments. In this way, they would see more of the whole process and would be more likely to build up relationships with the departments or suppliers with which they deal; this, in turn, is likely to encourage them to take a pride in their work.

Job enrichment means redesigning jobs so that the amount of responsibility, discretion and control required of the employee is increased. In the accounts office example, this might mean encouraging Freda, Gareth and John to try to handle simple queries themselves, rather than refer them all to Julie. Care is necessary here. Some staff may be reluctant to take on extra responsibility, either because they fear that they may not be competent to handle it or because they like a simple and quiet life.

JOB DESIGN IN THE IT INDUSTRY

In the context of professional jobs in the IT industry, job enlargement and job enrichment usually turn out to be synonymous. Since almost all tasks involve an element of discretion, judgement and decision making, adding an extra task will always increase the extent of the job holder's discretion. However, whichever term we use, the idea can be an important and valuable one. Software maintenance is a notoriously unpopular task; it is common for an analyst to analyse and specify users' requests for changes, while a programmer implements them. The job can be made much more attractive, and also valuable from the point of view of staff development, if the job is enlarged so that one individual analyses user requests for changes, specifies the changes and obtains change control board approval, as well as implementing the changes and retesting the system.

FURTHER READING

There is an enormous amount of literature on organisations and management. At one end of the spectrum are the popular but superficial books to be found on airport bookstalls. The biggest weakness of such books is not that they are wrong nor that their prescriptions are often imprecise. It is that their authors' experience is usually restricted to one type of company, typically in the retail sector, and that this limitation is reflected in their text. At the other extreme, there are jargon-filled books of great length, usually written by those who have little experience of business or management, which present elaborate theories that are applicable, if at all, only to very large organisations.

Nevertheless, there is a great deal to be learned about the subject from books and this chapter has barely scratched the surface. One writer who avoids the two extremes mentioned above and writes in a thought-provoking way about the topics discussed in this chapter is Charles Handy. Two of his books are strongly recommended:

Handy, C. (1993) *Understanding organisations.* 4th ed. Penguin Books, London.
Handy, C. (1995) *Gods of management.* 3rd ed. Arrow, London.

Microsoft's annual report for 2012 gives a good picture of the way the company is organised:

www.microsoft.com/investor/annualreports

The CGI website is not as informative as Microsoft's but is still contains useful information about the company structure:

www.cgi.com/en

5 FINANCING A START-UP COMPANY

After studying this chapter, you should:

- *understand why start-up companies need capital;*
- *be able to produce a simple business plan;*
- *understand the different ways in which capital can be raised and the advantages and disadvantages of each.*

5.1 WHY CAPITAL IS NEEDED

It is very difficult to start any commercial venture without having some money in hand, because your customers will not be willing to pay you until you have provided them with the service or the product they are buying. You, however, have to buy the things you need to make the product or to provide the service, and you have to live while you are making or doing it.

To take a very simple example, suppose that you are setting up in business painting houses. You need to buy paint brushes, paint, ladders and so on. It may take you two weeks to paint a house and during this time you have to live. You will only get paid when you've finished painting your first house. Indeed, you may well find that your customers don't always pay immediately but take another two or three weeks to pay. The amount of money you need may not be very large but you will find yourself in difficulties if you haven't got it.

If you are setting up a company to build websites, you are likely to need much more money. First, because your customers are likely to be other companies, it will take you longer to get paid. In normal commercial practice, invoices for services are issued at the end of a month to cover the work that has been done during the month. A client is unlikely to pay an invoice within less than one month of receiving it. Two months is more likely with commercial clients and three months is not uncommon; some large companies are notorious for not paying invoices for as much as six or even 12 months. The result is that you need enough cash in hand to be able to live for at least three months. Additional money will be needed for the expenses of starting the company.

If you intend to develop a package, the sum of money needed is likely to be even larger. While the package is being developed, there will be no revenue coming into the company. For this period cash will be needed for:

- salaries, however small, for the founders and for any other staff they may need to employ;

- rent, rates, heating and lighting of the premises used;

- equipment and consumables;

- costs of advertising and marketing the products;

- miscellaneous expenses, ranging from company stationery to travelling expenses for any trips that may be necessary;

- interest on any money borrowed.

Although it is often possible to carry out the early stages of development in the founders' spare time, working from their homes, this is not usually satisfactory once commercial sales have started. However successful the development of the packages, it will take some months before sales reach a level sufficient to cover the company's ongoing costs, so, even after development is complete, more cash will be needed.

5.2 THE BUSINESS PLAN

The first step in raising the money is to produce a **business plan**. This is a document that explains your plans to potential funders and tries to convince them that these plans are well thought out and realistic, and that the venture is likely to be successful. It should contain:

- a description of what the company will be doing, together with information to show that it is technically feasible and that the founders of the company have the necessary expertise;

- a description of the market the company is aiming at, an estimate of its size, and an assessment of the competition. It might contain statements like the following: 'The company's target market will be small firms providing repair and maintenance services to householders, within a radius of 15 miles of the centre of Llanafan. So far as can be estimated from the data provided by the Llanafan Chamber of Commerce, there are around 1,200 such firms in the area, only 16 of which have websites. There are two other companies offering website design and hosting services in the area but neither appears interested in this market.'

- a prediction of the financial performance of the company. This will include budgets, cash flow predictions, and projected balance sheets and profit and loss accounts. These are dealt with in the following chapters.

Armed with the business plan, you are in a position to approach people who might be willing to lend you money, invest money in your company, or even give you money.

It is a mistake to think of a business plan as a prediction of what will happen when and if you succeed in starting your company. It should be seen much more as a scenario that demonstrates that your company has a reasonable chance of success. The attempt to produce a business plan will often show that what a new company is trying to do has very little chance of succeeding. This should have been true of many of the dot.com companies that failed in the crash of 2001. Their predictions of the size of their market were quite unrealistic and any shrewd investor might have seen this.

5.3 SOURCES OF FINANCE

Government policy in the UK has, over recent years, strongly encouraged the growth of small companies and, as a result, there are many possible sources of funding. However, they can all be grouped under three headings: grants, loans and sale of equity. Many other countries have similar policies but there are big differences between countries in the way that the policies are implemented, and policy within a single country can swing violently over time.

5.3.1 Grants

A **grant** is a sum of money given to the company; although the company is obliged to demonstrate that it has been used for the purposes for which it was intended, it is not intended that the grant should ever be paid back to the organisation which gave it. Not surprisingly, grants are only available from government (local or national) and EU sources or, very occasionally, from charities. Very often, grants are limited to a certain proportion of the money spent on a particular development and are conditional upon the remainder being raised from other sources.

The availability of grants and other help for new companies depends very much on where the company is located, how many people it expects to employ, and on government policy at the time. Typically, in the UK, a new company, setting up in an area where maximum assistance is available, might expect to be provided with premises rent free or at half rent for the first 12 months; it might also expect a grant of £15,000 to £20,000, once it is employing five or six people, and a second similar grant when the number of employees reaches ten or a dozen. (Very much larger grants are available to established companies intending to make substantial investments that will lead to the creation of many jobs.)

These grants are usually:

- intended to assist with capital investment, typically investment in premises and equipment;
- subject to a number of conditions, in particular the raising of capital from other sources;
- limited to a certain proportion of the capital investment that the company can prove it has made.

This means that they are often of limited usefulness to small software companies, whose investment more usually takes the form of employees' time.

A variety of programmes, both national and European, offer grants to assist in the development of high technology products. These are likely to be particularly helpful to start-up companies aiming to develop new packages. Examples are the EU's Framework 7 and Horizon 2020 programmes, and the Smart scheme (previously known as Grants for Research and Development) run by the UK government's Technology Strategy Board. The Smart programme offers funding of up to £25,000 over nine months to small and medium-sized enterprises, providing up to 60 per cent of the cost of R&D projects in science, engineering and technology, from which successful new products, processes and services could emerge. For other programmes, it may be a requirement that the proposed development is collaborative, i.e. involves more than one company, and, in the case of European programmes, that the collaboration involves companies from at least two member states of the European Union. The assistance is almost invariably limited to 50 per cent of the cost of the development and often to less.

5.3.2 Loans

Although grants are undoubtedly very helpful, their effect on company finance is short term. The major sources of finance are loans and the sale of equity.

A loan is a sum of money lent to the company; interest is payable on it, at a rate that may be fixed or variable, and the loan is usually for a fixed period. The company has to pay back the loan eventually and, if it goes into liquidation, the lender is entitled to recover the loan from the sale of the assets of the company. In most cases, security (in this context sometimes known as collateral) is required for the loan. In other words, the company agrees that if it fails to make repayments, the lender is entitled to sell some of the company's assets in order to make up for the shortfall, rather in the same way that, if you borrow money to buy a house and then fail to keep up the repayments, the lender can sell the house to recover the loan.

It often happens that small companies do not have sufficient assets to cover the loan they are looking for. In this case, the lender may ask for personal guarantees from the directors of the company; this may mean that the directors have to use their own homes or other property as security for the loan.

It is usual to divide loans into overdrafts and long-term loans. An overdraft is the most flexible form of loan. Overdrafts are offered by banks; they allow a company (or an individual) to spend more money than is in its account, up to a specified maximum. Interest is only payable on the amount actually owned and the rate is normally comparatively low; it is usually fixed at a certain number of points above the bank base lending rate, the precise figure depending on the bank's view of the credit-worthiness of the borrower. Although overdrafts are the most flexible and usually the cheapest way to borrow, there is a price to be paid. A bank can withdraw overdraft facilities without warning, possibly for reasons of general policy that have nothing to do with the borrower. Many small companies have been forced into liquidation unnecessarily as a result of such action by banks.

In contrast, long-term loans are usually made for a fixed period at a fixed rate of interest. The borrower receives the capital (the amount of the loan) at the start of the period of the loan and is committed to paying interest on that amount throughout the period of the loan. Provided the borrower pays the interest on time, the lender cannot call in the loan. The borrower must repay the capital at the end of the period.

As a result of various government initiatives, a 'soft loan' may be available; this is a loan on terms which are less onerous than those that prevail for commercial loans. Soft loans are usually only available to start-up companies; the interest rates may be lower than commercial interest rates and security is not demanded.

Public limited companies can raise loans through stock exchanges by issuing what are known as **corporate bonds**. For private companies, however, loans are usually provided by banks or similar institutions. Even if a soft loan is available as part of a government initiative, it will usually be channelled through a commercial bank. In some instances, start-up companies are able to borrow money from relatives or friends of the founders – or, indeed, the founders may be able to lend the company money themselves. In such cases, it is important that the loan is put on the same sort of formal basis as a commercial loan. If it is not, and things go wrong for the company, there is real danger that confusion will lead to bitter arguments and will end up by spoiling personal relationships.

5.3.3 Equity capital

Equity capital is money paid to the company in exchange for a share in the ownership of the company, as described in the previous chapter.

The founders of a new company often find the initial capital from their own resources or from friends and family, but few are able to continue raising capital in this way. If a company looks to have good prospects but needs to raise more capital, it will usually need to resort to business angels or venture capitalists.

Business angels are wealthy individuals who provide equity capital for start-up companies and small firms that are seeking to grow rapidly. They are usually interested in investing in firms operating in areas of which they have some experience and, as well as providing capital, they will usually expect to offer advice on management and other business issues. Business angel networks are organisations that bring business angels together and provide mechanisms to assist small companies to find suitable business angels and vice versa. The networks usually operate at national or regional (i.e. sub-national) levels.

Venture capitalists are companies whose business is investing in small companies with high growth potential. They are usually only interested in fairly substantial investments, from, say, £500,000 upwards.

If the company is already operating, the shares issued to business angels or venture capitalists will usually be new shares, taken from the difference between the issued capital and the authorised capital. The new investors will probably be paying substantially over the par value of the shares.

Both business angels and venture capitalists aim to make money by helping the company to expand and become successful and then selling their shares at a profit. Of course, many of their investments will not be very successful and a significant number may fail completely. They aim to offset these losses by very substantial gains in the most successful cases; often this may happen when the company has grown enough to be floated on a stock exchange, so that its shares become publicly traded.

5.4 GEARING

The relationship between loan capital and equity capital in a company is important. It is known as **gearing** or **leverage**. Shareholders are at a much greater risk of getting a poor return on their capital or even losing it completely than are lenders but, in compensation for this, they stand to make a greater profit than lenders if all goes well.

Suppose a company is started with a share capital of £100, owned by its two founders, and that it has a fixed-term loan of £100,000, at an interest rate of 10 per cent. If in its first year the company makes an operating profit of £10,000, the interest charges will consume all the profit and the shareholders will receive nothing. If the company's operating profit doubles, to £20,000, the lender will still receive £10,000 but, neglecting taxation and assuming that all the profit is distributed to the shareholders, the shareholders will receive £10,000, a very handsome return on an investment of £100. Furthermore, as the profits increase, the value of the company, and hence the value of the shares, increases. If the company is sold, the shareholders will get much more than their original £100 investment, but the lenders will still only be entitled to their original £100,000, plus interest. If, on the other hand, the company is unsuccessful and goes into liquidation, the lenders will be at the front of the queue of people to whom money is owed, whereas the shareholders will get nothing until everyone else has been paid in full.

Such high levels of gearing are undesirable both from the point of view of the shareholders, because so much of the company's income is committed to interest payments, and from the point of view of the lenders, because shareholders may encourage the company to trade recklessly in the knowledge that they have little to lose and a lot to gain. Most lenders will be reluctant to lend money if a company seems too highly geared.

FURTHER READING

The UK government has a website that includes financial and other advice on setting up a business and gives valuable guidance on producing a business plan:
www.gov.uk/browse/business

The website of the Technology Strategy Board, which runs the Smart programme and various other programmes intended to encourage technological innovation:
www.innovateuk.org

Information about the UK Business Angels Association can be found at:
www.ukbusinessangelsassociation.org.uk/
and there are a number of regional networks of business angels in different parts of the UK. There is also a European Business Angels Network:
www.eban.org
as well as a World Business Angels Association, based in Brussels:
http://wbaa.biz

There are innumerable books on accounting and finance that will take the reader beyond what is covered in this book; most of them are, however, intended for budding accountants. A good treatment for non-specialists will be found in:

Atrill, P. and McLaney, E. (2012) *Accounting and finance for non-specialists*. 8th ed. Pearson Education.

This covers the material in this chapter and the next three.

6 FINANCIAL ACCOUNTING

After studying this chapter, you should understand the nature and purpose of the three most important elements of a company's annual report:

- *the balance sheet;*
- *the profit and loss account;*
- *the cash flow statement;*

and you should be able to interpret them in straightforward cases.

6.1 DISCLOSURE REQUIREMENTS

The proprietors of limited liability companies are privileged, precisely because their liability is limited – they can lose no more than the money they invested in the company. In return for this privilege, the law requires that, every year, the company produces an **annual report**, which must be filed at Companies House. The annual report contains information about the company and its activities during the preceding year. In particular, it contains information about its financial health so that those who are considering dealing with the company can judge whether it is likely to meet its obligations. If the company is a public one, that is, if its shares are available for purchase by the public, through trading on a stock exchange, the stock exchange will impose additional **disclosure requirements**. In other words, it will require the company to make more information public. In recent years, a series of scandals has led to calls for greater openness and more extensive disclosure of companies' activities, which has, in turn, led to the inclusion of further statements and more extensive notes in companies' annual reports. Some are required by stock markets and some have simply become regarded as good practice. On the whole, but by no means universally, software companies set good examples in this regard.

6.2 THE BALANCE SHEET

The purpose of the balance sheet is to show what the company owns – its **assets** – and what it owes, its **liabilities**. It is a snapshot of the state of the company at a particular point in time, normally at the end of the last day of the company's financial year.

6.2.1 Balance sheet for a student

Perhaps the easiest way to get to understand the idea of a balance sheet is to look at the balance sheet not of a company but of an individual. We take an imaginary student called Jemima Puddleduck and, as is usual, we show her present position side by side with the position a year ago, so that it is easy to make a comparison. Notice also the common accounting convention of putting a number in parentheses to indicate that it is negative, rather than using a negative sign as is normal in science or mathematics. Her balance sheet is shown in Table 6.1.

Table 6.1 Balance sheet for a student

Jemima Puddleduck Balance Sheet As at 31 October 2013	2013	2012
ASSETS		
Cash in hand	25	40
Cash at bank	361	240
Pre-paid accommodation	300	180
Debts owed by friends	18	0
Computer	240	360
Guitar	160	180
Total assets	1,104	1,000
LIABILITIES		
Credit card bill	174	64
Student loans	4,800	1,900
Total liabilities	4,974	1,964
NET WORTH	(3,870)	(964)

Jemima's most obvious asset is money. She has, let us say £25, in cash in her purse and another £361 in her bank account.

The next two items are less obvious. The accommodation item refers to the fact that Jemima has paid a term's fees to the hall of residence in advance; since the balance sheet refers to the position on 31st October, some 60 per cent (six weeks out of ten) of this accommodation has not been used. Depending on the regulations of the hall, if the accommodation is no longer required, the student may be able to get a refund on the unused period or sell it to another student; in other words, the student has paid for the right to live in hall for a further six weeks and this right can be converted into cash and is therefore an asset. In a similar way, the debt of £18 owed by friends can be turned into cash and is also therefore an asset.

The next two items are more complex because they represent capital items. Jemima owns a computer, which cost £480 including the software when her parents bought it for her, two years ago. She also owns a guitar, which she bought for £200 in 2012. These are examples of fixed assets, that is, assets that she will continue to own and to use for a fairly long period.

Standard accounting practice is to reduce the value of fixed assets each year to reflect the likely lifetime of each asset; the fall in the value of the asset from one year to the next is called the **depreciation**. Thus, Jemima will probably keep her computer for four years before it becomes obsolete and she has to replace it with a new one. The simplest and commonest way of calculating the depreciation is to assume that it falls in value uniformly, that is, that it loses value at a rate of £120 per year. Hence after one year, it is worth £360, after two years £240, after three years £120, and at the end of the fourth year it no longer has any value. Musical instruments typically have a longer life than computers. We have assumed that the guitar will have a life of 10 years, so that its value drops by £20 each year.

The figure given for 'other assets' covers the many personal items that everyone owns, including clothes, books and CDs. We simply take an approximate figure for these, because the calculations involved in dealing with them precisely would be far more extensive than the value of the items justifies.

The valuation of assets can be a contentious issue. For the moment we shall simply accept the figures given in the balance sheet but we shall have more to say on this topic when we come to look at a commercial balance sheet.

Jemima's liabilities are more straightforward. She owes money on her credit card and she has a student loan. The credit card debt is an example of a short term debt; she is expected to repay it fairly quickly, although she may incur other debts against it. The student loan is a long-term debt, which does not need to be repaid until she graduates and is earning a reasonable salary.

As its name suggests, a balance sheet must balance: the total assets and total liabilities should be equal. To achieve this we need to include a **balancing item** on one side or the other; it is often labelled 'excess of assets over liabilities' but in this case we have chosen to call it 'net worth' because it represents the amount of cash which Jemima would have if all her assets were sold and all her debts paid off – in other words, how much, in financial terms, she is 'worth'. The net worth plus the liabilities together equal her total assets. In her case, as with many students, her net worth is negative.

6.2.2 Commercial balance sheets: assets

Commercial balance sheets are prepared on precisely the same basis as we have just described but the assets and liabilities are grouped into various categories and a single figure is given for each category. There will be several 'notes' to the balance sheet describing the basis of the accounts and giving more detail about certain items; such items will cross reference the notes. Table 6.2 shows an example of such a balance sheet for an imaginary software services company.

Table 6.2 Balance sheet for a services company

XYZ Software Ltd Balance Sheet As at 31 October 2013	2013 £'000	3012 £'000
Fixed assets		
Intangible assets	475	–
Tangible assets	960	770
Investments	50	82
Total fixed assets	1,485	852
Current assets		
Work in progress	550	621
Debtors	3,400	2,580
Cash in hand and at bank	2,491	1,770
Total current assets	6,441	4,971
Creditors: amounts falling due within one year	(3,210)	(2,601)
Net current assets	3,231	2,370
Total assets less current liabilities	4,716	3,222
Creditors: amounts falling due after one year		
Borrowings	(154)	(61)
Provisions for liabilities and charges	(7)	(16)
Net assets	4,555	3,145
Capital and reserves		
Called up share capital	318	308
Share premium reserve	350	145
Profit and loss account	3,887	2,692
Shareholders' funds – equity	4,555	3,145

Assets are classified as current assets and fixed assets. The essential difference between the two is that fixed assets contribute to the company's productive capacity and are held primarily for the purpose of creating wealth, while current assets are items which are bought and sold in the course of its day to day trading activities. The fixed assets are further subdivided into investments (e.g. shares in other companies), tangible assets (assets which have some physical existence) and intangible assets (assets such as copyright in software or ownership of brand names, which have no physical existence).

In most cases the difference between fixed assets and current assets is easily perceived. A new file server bought to support program development facilities in a software house or a machine tool used to produce satellite dishes are clearly examples of fixed assets; a stock of paper for the laser printer is equally clearly a current asset. It should be borne in mind, however, that the treatment of the same item may vary from organisation to organisation or even within the same organisation. Thus, if a company buys a car to enable one of its sales staff to operate more effectively, this is a fixed asset but, if a car dealer buys a car in order to resell it as part of the business, this is a current asset. If the software house buys a computer on which it will implement special software before delivering the whole system to a client, the computer is a current asset, not a fixed one.

The rules of accounting state that current assets are shown on the balance sheet with a value that is the lower of what they cost and what it is expected they could be sold for. Suppose a company has a stock of 1,000 user manuals for a piece of software that it sells. The manuals sell at £10 each but cost £2 each to produce. Then they will appear on the balance sheet as worth £2,000, the cost price, rather than £10,000, the resale price. On the other hand, a stock of printer paper that cost £5,000 would only be saleable for a lower figure, say £2,000. It would therefore appear on the balance sheet at the resale price, because this is lower.

In contrast to current assets, fixed assets are not expected to be sold in normal trading operations and their resale value is irrelevant; what is needed is a measure of their value to the company. In practice, this is done by reducing their value each year in accordance with the company's depreciation policy. Much the commonest way of doing this is the so-called straight line method we described in connection with Jemima's computer. We first decide how many years the asset will continue to be useful for. We then divide its initial cost by that number to get the annual depreciation. Each year, we reduce (or **write down**) the value of the asset by the amount of the annual depreciation until the value of the asset reaches zero. Suppose a company buys a large database server costing £100,000 and expects to use it for five years. Then the annual depreciation will be £20,000 (£100,000/5) and the values shown in the balance sheet will be £80,000 at the end of year 1, £60,000 at the end of year 2, £40,000 at the end of year 3, £20,000 at the end of year 4, and zero at the end of year 5. It is customary to depreciate all items of the same type over the same period and this will be stated in the notes to the accounts, which might include statements such as 'It is the company's policy to write off all computer equipment over a period of three years and office furniture over a period of ten years.'

Assets are generally valued on the basis of historic cost, that is, their original monetary cost. In times of high inflation, this can be seriously misleading. The value of certain types of fixed assets, in particular land and buildings, may increase rather than decrease.

Some companies therefore arrange to have their property re-valued from time to time and include this valuation in the balance sheet.

Tangible fixed assets have to be recorded in the company's fixed asset register and, from time to time, their presence will be physically checked. Each year, depreciation must be calculated and, if a fixed asset is sold for a sum higher than its depreciated value, the company must show the difference as income. Because of these complicated procedures, it is usual to treat all purchases of less than, say, £1,000 as expenses in the year in which they are incurred.

There are some items which are difficult to classify. Software is one example. Consider a payroll package. A company buys such a package because it will help it to carry out part of its day-to-day operations more efficiently. The package will be bought with the intention of using it for some time, at least five years and probably 10 or 15. Logically, the package should be treated in the same way as a piece of machinery. It should be treated as a fixed asset and the initial cost depreciated over its useful lifetime. The rules of accounting allow this to be done. But, because software is intangible, many companies treat the cost of buying it as current expenditure.

The treatment of research and development is a particular problem. Logically, resources spent on developing new products should be regarded as an investment that will produce a fixed asset, that is, something that will allow the company to operate more effectively. However, the results of research and development are always uncertain and often prove to be worth very little; to treat all the costs as investment would be misleading. In practice, most software companies in the UK treat expenditure on research and development as current expenditure rather than as investment, although the accounting rules allow for more flexible treatment. In the USA, there are strict rules regarding the capitalisation of software that is developed for sale; these rules are based on a rather unrealistic model of the product life cycle.

Intangible fixed assets are the source of much discussion in the accounting profession. Software is generally regarded as an intangible asset but it is more tangible than many items, brand names, for example, which are often shown as intangible assets. An item that frequently appears under intangible assets on the balance sheets of software product companies is **goodwill**. This might arise, for example, if XYZ Software Ltd purchased another company, PQR Ltd, that owned the rights in a profitable package. If, as is likely, the package was not shown as an asset on PQR's balance sheet, XYZ would probably have paid much more to buy PQR than the value of its net assets. The difference between the price paid for PQR and the value of its net assets represents XYZ's estimate of the value of the rights in that package (and, possibly, other things such as the value of PQR's name). This needs to be shown on XYZ's balance sheet. Although it would be preferable for the value of the package to be shown explicitly, this is not normal practice and the whole of the difference between the purchase price and the value of PQR's net assets is normally shown under the heading of goodwill. It will then, of course, need to be depreciated over a fixed period. The notes to a company's accounts will normally itemise any acquisitions and give details of the goodwill arising from each one. When internet companies change hands a similar situation occurs but, in this case, the intangible assets may be much more difficult to identify; they are certainly less tangible than the rights to a package.

Readers who are football fans may be interested to know that football clubs that are organised as public companies – Manchester United, for example – include among their intangible assets the rights to the services of players whom they have bought.

6.2.3 Commercial balance sheets: liabilities and owners' equity

The entry under 'current liabilities: amounts falling due within one year' refers to debts that the company has and is committed to repaying within one year. These will include trade creditors, that is, outstanding invoices that the company has received but has not yet paid, in just the same way that the 'debtors' item refers to invoices that the company has issued but which have not yet been paid. They will also include any bank overdraft, as opposed to a long term loan.

The figure obtained by subtracting the current liabilities from the current assets, referred to as net current assets in the example, is also known as the **working capital**. It represents the amount the amount of money invested in the day-to-day operations of the company, as opposed to its infrastructure.

'Creditors: amounts falling due after one year' refers to long term debts. These may be long term borrowings or they may be liabilities, that is sums that the company expects to have to pay at some time in the future.

When the total liabilities are subtracted from the total assets, we arrive at a figure called the 'net assets'. These are balanced by items under the heading of 'Capital and reserves'. There are a number of ways in which these may be shown. First, there is the item labelled 'Called up share capital'. This is the amount raised from the par value of the shares that the company has issued. When a successful company decides to issue more shares, these are often sold at more than there par value. The extra is known as the share premium and the money raised from this is shown under the next heading, as the 'share premium account'. In our example the remainder is labelled as 'profit and loss account', indicating that it results from the accumulated surplus on the profit and loss account over the life of the company.

The total under the heading of 'Capital and reserves' is often known by names such as shareholders' equity, owners' equity, or owners' claim. It notionally represents the value of the company to its shareholders.

6.3 THE PROFIT AND LOSS ACCOUNT

The **profit and loss account** shows how much money has been received and how much has been spent in a given period – usually the organisation's financial year. In the USA it is usually known as an income statement and in the case of non-profit-making organisations it is usually called an income and expenditure account. Table 6.3 shows such an account for our imaginary student. It does not include money borrowed or received from the sale of equity nor does it include expenditure on acquiring fixed assets.

Table 6.3 Income and expenditure account for a student

Jemima Puddleduck Income and Expenditure Account Year ended 31 October 2013	2013	2012
INCOME		
Contribution from parents	1,500	1,300
Income from summer job (net)	1,840	1,682
Total income	3,340	2,982
EXPENDITURE		
Course fees	1,050	1,025
Hall fees	2,100	1,980
Books	30	25
Clothes and personal items	179	120
Transport	134	112
Food	1,400	1,247
Entertainment	1,303	840
Depreciation	140	140
Total expenditure	6,336	5,489
EXCESS OF INCOME OVER EXPENDITURE	(2,996)	(2,507)

It is important to observe that the excess of expenditure over income, that is, the amount that the student has overspent, is the same as the difference in her net worth between 2012 and 2013. This will usually be the case in simple situations where there has been no capital investment. In more complicated cases, particularly with commercial organisations, other items enter into the relationship.

Just as in the balance sheet, there is a certain arbitrariness about the way in which items have been aggregated. We could, for example, have lumped together 'Food' and 'Entertainment' under the heading 'Living expenses' or have split 'Transport' into 'Road' and 'Rail'. We have chosen to show the income from the summer job net (i.e. the take home pay) rather than show it gross (i.e. before deductions) with tax and national insurance on the expenditure side.

Some explanation of the depreciation item is required. The net figure at the bottom of the profit and loss account should reflect the extent to which the organisation – or, in this case, the individual – is better or worse off at the end of the year than at the beginning. Clearly, a fall in the value of the assets tends to make it worse off. Depreciation, although it is not an expenditure in the sense that cash is paid out, reflects this decline and is therefore shown as an expenditure. The figure of £140 arises from the depreciation on the computer and the guitar.

A commercial profit and loss account looks very different from Jemima's income and expenditure account, even though precisely the same ideas underlie it. Table 6.4 shows an example for a fictitious computer services company. Just as with the balance sheet, we see that items have been aggregated into very broad categories; the notes to the accounts will usually provide more detail. A package company, for example, might show in the notes how much of its income came from sales of packages, how much from training and consultancy, and how much from maintenance contracts.

Table 6.4 Profit and loss account for a services company

XYZ Software Ltd Profit and Loss Account Year ending 31 October 2013	2013 £'000	2012 £'000
TURNOVER		
Continuing operations	14,311	11,001
Acquisitions	407	
Total turnover	14,718	11,001
Cost of sales	(11,604)	(8,699)
Gross profit	3,114	2,302
Other operating expenses	(1,177)	(805)
OPERATING PROFIT	1,937	1,497
Interest payable	(23)	(27)
Profit on ordinary activities before taxation	1,914	1,470
Tax on profit on ordinary activities	719	480
Retained profit for the year	1,195	990

A number of points about this statement need to be explained. First, the turnover for a company acquired during the year is shown separately from the turnover from continuing operations, that is, operations that were carried on in 2012 and 2013. This is to facilitate the comparison between the two years. In the same way, if part of XYZ Software Ltd had been disposed of in 2012, its turnover would have been shown under the heading 'discontinued operations'.

A second point is the distinction between 'cost of sales' and 'other operating expenses'. This distinction is an uncertain one and some companies do not show the items separately. However, for a package software company, there is a real difference between, on the one hand, expenditure on selling, printing documentation, installing software, and so on, all of which are the costs of sales, and expenditure on the development of new versions of existing packages or on new products, which would come under the heading of other operational expenses.

The bottom line shows the retained profit, that is the profit not paid out in tax or dividends to shareholders; this is added to the retained profit in the previous year's balance sheet to give the value of the retained profit that shown in the new balance sheet.

The profit and loss account itself gives very little information about where the company's revenue during the year has come from or how it has spent its money. Such information is normally given in the notes to the accounts. The Notes to the Accounts in the 2012 Annual Report of The Sage Group plc, for example, give a breakdown of turnover by both by geographical area and by market sector. It shows numbers of staff and expenditure on wages and salaries, on social security costs, and pension costs and other costs are also broken down into a number of categories. (Sage is one of the largest suppliers of accounting software in the world.) Package companies will often also show a breakdown of revenue into licence fees, maintenance charges, and consultancy fees. On the whole, software companies are fairly open in revealing information in the notes to their accounts but the level of detail provided in other sectors varies enormously from company to company.

6.4 THE CASH FLOW STATEMENT

As we have already pointed out, the income and expenditure account does not show expenditure on capital items, only their depreciation; capital expenditure affects the balance sheet but the balance sheet does not give sufficient information to deduce how much this expenditure amounts to and how it was funded. The link which ties the balance sheet and the profit and loss account to the capital expenditure is the cash flow statement. A moment's examination of our student's financial statements will reveal that, because there is no cash flow statement, there is no explanation of where the money to purchase her CD player came from.

Cash is defined as 'cash at bank and in hand and cash equivalents less bank overdrafts and other borrowings repayable within one year of the accounting date'. In Jemima's case, this means £361 (the money in her bank account) plus £25 (the notes and coins in her possession) less £174 (her credit card debt), that is, £212. The previous year the figure was £(220 + 40 – 64) = £196. One function of the cash flow statement is to explain this difference of £16.

The most obvious source of a change in the amount of cash Jemima holds is her profit and loss account. She appears to have spent £2,996 more than she received. This is her major cash outflow. In fact, not all of this sum is a cash outflow. The item of £140 for depreciation corresponds to a reduction in the value of her capital assets but not to any outflow of cash. To take this into account, we add the depreciation back in as a cash inflow. The only other cash outflow is the £18 that she has lent to a friend. This is not expenditure, because it repayable. Nevertheless, it represents cash that has paid out. If she had bought her guitar during the year, its cost would also appear as a cash outflow.

We see from her balance sheet that Jemima's student loan increased by £2,900 from 2012 to 2013. This means that she received £2,900 in cash from that source. Although it is an inflow of cash, it is not income, because it will have to be repaid; hence it does not appear as income on the income and expenditure account.

These changes are summarised in Table 6.5, which shows Jemima's cash flow statement.

Table 6.5 Cash flow statement for a student

Jemima Puddleduck Cash Flow Statement Year ended 31 October 2013	2013	2012
Cash inflow		
Addition to student loan	2,900	1,900
Add back depreciation	140	140
Total cash inflow	3,120	2,120
Cash outflow		
From income and expenditure account	2,996	2,507
Loans made to friends	18	0
Total cash outflow	3,014	2,507
Increase/(decrease) in cash over the year	106	(387)

Jemima Puddleduck's cash flow statement tells us very little more than we could deduce from her other financial statements. In the case of a company, however, the cash flow statement has much more to tell us, because there are many more sources of cash flows.

Figure 6.1 shows the cash flows that are captured in the cash flow statement of a typical company. The arrows show the **normal** direction of the flow in a profitable company but it is always possible for the flows to be in the opposite direction. Table 6.6 shows the cash flow statement for our example company.

Figure 6.1 Sources and destinations of cash flows

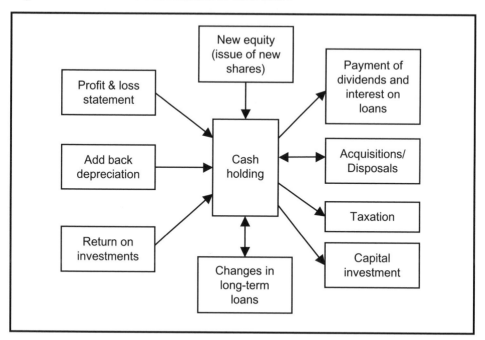

The first source of cash is the operating profit before tax generated during the year. This needs to be adjusted for certain items which may appear in the profit and loss account but do not involve the movement of money in or out of the company. The most obvious of these is depreciation. This was entered in the profit and loss account to reflect the extent to which the life of the fixed assets was consumed during the year; in no way did it reflect the movement of money out of the company and so it must be added to the profit.

Following the adjusted figure for the operating profit, there are a number of items that may lead to cash flowing out of the company for reasons that are nothing directly to do with its operations. Taxation, interest payable and dividends paid are obvious examples. Capital investment in equipment or premises is another reason for which cash may flow out of the company, as is the purchase of another company. In some circumstances, e.g., the disposal of a subsidiary company, these items can give rise to an inflow of cash. When all these items are added together and subtracted from the operating profit, we arrive at a total figure for the inflow or outflow of cash into or out of the company before taking into account any changes in the financing of the company. The final section of the cash flow statement shows the effect on the cash position of changes in the financing of the company. The company has issued new shares and raised £215,000 through this; it has also paid off £50,000 of long term debt. Both of these, of course, affect its cash position and the bottom line of the cash flow statement reflects this; it gives the overall change in the company's cash position over the year.

Table 6.6 Cash flow statement for a software company

XYZ Software Ltd Cash Flow Statement Year ending 31 October 2013	2013 £'000	2012 £'000
Net cash inflow from operating activities	2,105	1,620
Returns on investments and servicing of finance	(23)	(27)
Capital expenditure and financial investment	(320)	(265)
Taxation	(719)	(480)
Acquisitions and disposals	(380)	
Equity dividends paid		
Cash outflow before financing	(1,342)	(772)
Net cash inflow before financing	763	848
Financing		
Issue of share capital	215	100
Repayment of long term loan	(50)	
Net cash inflow from financing	165	100
Increase in cash in the year	928	948

The alert reader will recall that XYZ's balance sheet shows that, despite the fact that a loan of £50,000 has been paid off, the long term debt has increased from £61,000 to £154,000 and that there is nothing in the cash flow statement to account for this. It almost certainly arises from the acquisition of another company. The statement shows that £380,000 was spent on acquisitions; the likelihood is that the company bought substantial debts, which were taken over by XYZ as part of the deal. This would be explained in the notes to the accounts.

At this point we should make clear that the financial statements for XYZ Software Ltd show a vigorous company growing very rapidly in an expanding market; they are typical of some young and successful IT services companies but not typical of many other industries.

6.5 THE OVERALL PICTURE

The balance sheet, the profit and loss account and the cash flow statement cannot be understood or interpreted in isolation. Their relationship to each other needs to be understood and they need to be looked at together when assessing the financial state of a company.

The balance sheet shows a snapshot of the financial position of a company at the end of an accounting period (usually the company's financial year), while the profit and loss account and the cash flow statement describe what has happened during the accounting period and thus explain the relationship between successive balance sheets. This is illustrated in Figure 6.2. The profit and loss account explains the relationship between the owners' equity in the two balance sheets, while the cash flow statement explains the relationship between the cash item shown in the two balance sheets. This is illustrated in Figure 6.3.

Figure 6.2 The relationship between the three financial statements

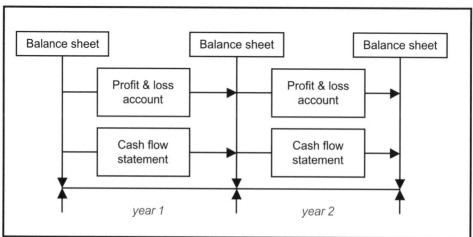

Figure 6.3 How the cash flow statement and the profit and loss account affect the items in the balance sheet

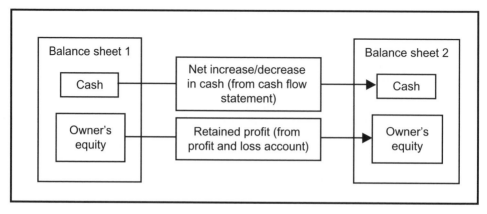

FURTHER READING

To get a feeling for company accounts and for the way the IT industry works, it is worth reading the annual reports and accounts of software companies. Many of them are available directly from the companies' websites. As a starting point we suggest looking at CGI, the Sage Group and Microsoft, all of which are readily available on the web at the following addresses:

www.cgi.com/en/investors/annual-reports
www.microsoft.com/investor/reports/ar12/index.html
www.investors.sage.com/reports_presentations/reports

The book by Atrill and McLaney recommended at the end of Chapter 5 also covers the material in this chapter.

7 MANAGEMENT ACCOUNTING

After studying this chapter, you should:

- *understand how to produce a budget and a cash flow forecast, and know how to monitor them;*
- *be able to calculate the unit cost of labour;*
- *understand the concept of overheads and the different ways in which they may be distributed;*
- *be able to determine how much it costs to produce a particular product or provide a specific service.*

7.1 PLANNING AND MANAGEMENT INFORMATION

The last chapter was concerned with financial accounting, that is, with reports about the financial state of a company as a whole. Such reports are public and are required to meet standards set by the law and by stock exchanges. The information they contain is intended primarily for potential investors and trading partners. It is historical, that is, it is concerned with what has happened in the past.

The reports produced by financial accounting are not very useful in the day-to-day running of the company. Managers need plans and accounting information that will help them to make good business decisions; this means, above all, up-to-date information about costs and sales so that the company's actual progress can be monitored against the plans, as contained in its budget and its cash flow forecast. It is these documents that are the main subject of this chapter.

7.2 BUDGETS AND OVERHEADS

A budget is a financial plan showing the expected income and expenditure for an organisation over a specific period, typically one year. In order to produce a budget for the company we have to make some more assumptions about what it will be doing. We shall illustrate the idea of a budget by considering a small company that sells desktop computers that it assembles from bought-in components and basic software. We suppose the owner runs the company and it employs three technicians and a part-time secretary. It owns a van that it uses for delivering computers to customers.

The company makes three models of computer, the Basic, the Advanced and the Professional. Table 7.1 shows the cost of the components for each model, the number of hours of technician time it takes to build one and the expected sales of that model over the next year.

Table 7.1 Direct costs and expected sales

Model	Cost of components	Technician timesales	Expected
Basic	£200	10 hours	200
Advanced	£300	12 hours	100
Professional	£400	15 hours	50

A possible budget for the company is shown in Table 7.2; it contains an estimate of the company's costs and its income over the next year of operations.

The costs under the heading 'Overhead expenditure' are costs that the company will have to pay regardless of how many computers it sells. For this reason, they are sometimes known as 'fixed costs'. Most of these costs are obvious enough but three items may require some explanation. We have said that the company is run by its owner. For many reasons, to do particularly with taxation and social security, the owner should be treated as an employee and pay himself or herself a salary, rather than attempt to live on the company's profits. This accounts for the item labelled 'Owner's payroll costs'. Unless the owner is an experienced accountant, the services of an accountant will be necessary to help prepare the annual accounts and possibly to give advice from time to time. The advice of a lawyer may also be necessary from time to time. These items are covered under the heading 'Professional fees'. Finally, employers are legally required to carry insurance to cover any claim against them for injuries suffered by employees during the course of their employment; other insurance, against theft from the company's premises for example, may also be necessary. This explains the heading 'Insurance'.

The total figure of £63,500 for overheads is money that the company has to pay out and which it therefore needs to recover from its sales.

Unlike the overheads, the figures under the heading 'Operating costs' depend on the number of computers the company sells. For this reason they are known as 'variable costs'. The cost of components is directly connected to the number of computers sold, while the cost of the technicians can be adjusted to match the sales volumes, though less easily, by recruiting another technician or making a technician redundant.

Table 7.2 An example budget

Overhead expenditure

Owner's payroll costs	42,000
Secretary's payroll costs (part time)	8,000
Costs of van (including depreciation)	3,500
Internet connection, telephone, postage, etc.	1,000
Advertising	2,000
Premises (heating and lighting, rent, rates, etc.)	4,500
Professional fees	1,000
Insurance	500
Total overheads	63,500
Operating costs	
Technicians' payroll costs	66,000
Bought-in components	90,000
Total operating costs	156,000
Total costs	219,500
Sales income	
Basic model (200 @ £595)	119,000
Advanced model (100 @ £795)	79,500
Professional model (50 @ £895)	44,750
Total income	243,250
Profit	24,750

The sales income is based on the company's best estimate of how many computers it can sell and at what price. We note that the prices are not directly related to the costs (by whatever method of calculation).

Once a budget has been agreed, it should be used to monitor the company's financial progress. The first step is to break it down to show monthly income and expenditure – a budget broken down in this way is sometimes called a **profiled budget**. At the end of each month, the management then compares what has actually happened during the month with what was planned in the budget. Where income or expenditure differ significantly from what was planned, the management will investigate the reasons for the exceptions and decide what action, if any, to take. If, for example, sales income is 30 per cent lower than predicted, managers might decide to mount a further advertising campaign or they might decide to cut costs by reducing staff. The point is that they will be made aware of the problem as soon as it appears and can take appropriate action quickly.

7.3 COST OF LABOUR

The cost of employing someone is more than just the cost of their salary. In most countries, employers are required to pay a tax for every employee. This tax usually goes by a name such as employers' National Insurance contribution (the UK name) or social security contribution; it is proportional to the employee's salary. In some countries, this contribution may be as large as 60 per cent of salary while in others it is very much smaller. In the UK, the rules for calculating the National Insurance contribution are complicated and change frequently but for the purposes of this chapter we shall take it as simply 10 per cent of salary.

There may be other costs associated with an employee, depending on the law and the practices of the individual country. In the UK, it is common for larger companies to operate a pension scheme of their own, to which the company makes a contribution on behalf of each employee. The company may pay for medical insurance for its employees. Senior employees may be provided with a car or other benefits. The total cost of employing a person, that is, the salary plus employers' social security contributions plus any other costs associated directly with the employee, is sometimes known as the employee's **payroll cost** or **direct cost**.

Consider one of the technicians who is employed to assemble the computers and suppose that they are paid an annual salary of £20,000. To calculate the cost of the time the technician spends assembling a computer, the annual payroll cost is not very helpful. What we need to know is the cost per hour. This is harder to calculate than one might expect. First, we need to calculate how many days we can expect the technician to work. There are 52 weeks in the year. Assuming the company works a five-day week, there will be 260 week days. However, the company will be closed for public holidays and the technician will not be working. The number of public holidays varies from country to country and even within a country. In England and Wales there are eight public holidays a year; there are also eight in Scotland but they are different; in Northern Ireland there are 10.

In addition to public holidays, employees are generally entitled to a certain amount of paid leave. Within the EU, most employees are by law entitled to 20 days of paid annual leave in addition to public holidays. (This is generous by international standards. Indeed, in many countries there is no requirement to grant paid annual leave.)

In addition to their annual leave, employees may miss some working days because of sickness. Although we cannot predict accurately how much time will be lost in this way, it is usual to guess at a reasonable average of, say, five days per employee. Finally, it may well be that there are some days in the year when, because of scheduling difficulties, there will be no revenue-earning work available for the employee. Finally, we assume that employees work for seven hours per day. Table 7.3 shows how all these factors can be taken into account to obtain a figure for the number of revenue-earning working hours that can be expected from an employee over the period of one year.

Table 7.3 Calculation of the number of revenue-earning hours in a year

---

Total number of weekdays (1)	260	
Public holidays (2)		10
Annual leave (3)		20
Sick leave (4)		5
Unproductive time (5)		10
Total non-revenue-earning time = (2) + (3) + (4) + (5) = (6)	45	
Total number of revenue earning days = (1) − (6) = (7)	215	
Total number of hours available (7) × 7	1,505	

Assuming the technician gets no non-salary benefits such as pension contributions, the direct cost of their time will be £20,000 plus 10 per cent National Insurance, i.e. £22,000 per year, so that the direct cost of an hour of their time is £22,000/1,505 = £14.62.

7.4 ALLOCATION OF OVERHEADS

In a large business, there are many ways in which overheads can be spread over the different activities the business performs; there is no single 'right' way of doing this.

In the next section we shall show how this scenario might lead to annual overheads of £63,500, which the company has to recover from its sales. There are at least three commonly used ways that we might spread these overheads over the computers sold.

The simplest way is to allocate the same overhead to each computer sold, regardless of the cost of the components or the amount of labour involved. Since we expect to sell 350 units, this means £181.43 per computer. This means that the Basic model, would cost:

$$£181.43 + £200 + 10 × £14.62 = £527.63.$$

The Advanced model would cost:

$$£181.43 + £300 + 12 × £14.62 = £651.83$$

and the Professional model would cost:

$$£181.43 + £400 + 15 × £14.62 = £802.23.$$

The second way of allocating the overhead is to make it proportional to the number of hours of labour involved. This means adding an overhead component to the cost of an hour of a technician's time. Since we have three technicians, each supplying 1,505 hours of productive labour per year, we need to add:

$$£63,500/(3 × 1,505) = £14.06$$

to the cost of an hour's labour, making it up to £14.62 + £14.06 = £28.68. Now the cost of the three models comes out at:

$$£200 + 10 × £28.68 = £486.80 \text{ (Basic)}$$

$$£300 + 12 × £28.68 = £644.16 \text{ (Advanced)}$$

$$£400 + 15 × £28.68 = £830.20 \text{ (Professional).}$$

Finally, we can distribute the overhead in proportion to the total cost, that is, taking into account the cost of components as well as the cost of labour. This means that we take the direct cost (components and labour) and add on a fixed percentage. To calculate this percentage we divide the total overhead by the total direct cost of all the units we expect to sell, that is, 63,500/(200 × 346.20 + 100 × 475.44 + 50 × 619.30) = 0.43. This means the cost of the Basic model is £346.20 × 1.43 = £495.06, of the Advanced model, £679.88 and of the Professional model, £885.60.

Table 7.4 summarises the cost (to the nearest pound) of the three different models according to the three different ways of distributing the overheads.

Table 7.4 Effects of different overhead calculations

	Fixed overhead	Overhead proportional to labour content	Overhead proportional to total direct cost
Basic	528	487	495
Advanced	652	644	680
Professional	802	830	886

The costs calculated in this way can form the basis for pricing the computers. Certainly, computers should not normally be sold at prices that are lower than the costs. More commonly, the prices will be set on the basis of 'what the market will bear', that is, how much customers will be willing to pay, and this depends very much on the competition. The cost calculations will, however, show us where our costs lie and how to go about reducing them so that we can sell our products more cheaply.

7.5 CASH FLOW FORECAST

A company may be very profitable but unable to pay its bills. For that reason, it may be forced into receivership. This apparent paradox typically arises because bills have to be met – in particular, staff have to be paid – before the income they generate is received. In order to avoid this difficulty, businesses need to prepare cash flow forecasts, that is, estimates of the amount of cash that will flow into and out of the company each month.

Table 7.5 shows a cash flow forecast for our example company's operations. In order to keep the overall picture clear, we have only shown a six month forecast. In practice

Table 7.5 A six-month cash flow prediction

Month	Jan	Feb	March	April	May	June
Cash outflow						
Rent and property taxes	500			500		
Energy costs		400	400	300	200	200
Payroll costs	9,666	9,666	9,666	9,666	9,666	9,666
Communications		83	83	83	83	83
Insurance	500					
Components		4,000	7,000	10,000	10,000	10,000
Advertising		500		250		500
Road tax and insurance on van	700					
Professional fees			300			
Van operating costs	100	100	100	100	100	100
Monthly cash outflow	11,466	15,349	17,549	20,899	20,049	20,549
Cash inflow						
Income from retail sales	5,000	5,000	5,000	5,000	5,000	5,000
Income from trade sales		5,000	7,000	10,000	15,000	18,000
Monthly cash inflow	5,000	10,000	12,000	15,000	20,000	23,000
Net monthly cash flow	(6,466)	(5,349)	(5,549)	(5,899)	(49)	2,451
Cumulative cash flow	(6,466)	(11,815)	(17,364)	(23,263)	(23,312)	(22,861)

companies normally try to forecast twelve months ahead. We have also made the rather unrealistic assumption that the company is launching into its operations at full stretch from day 1. Finally, because sales and energy costs are both seasonal, we have assumed that the company is starting operations on 1st January.

The figures in each cell show the amount of cash entering or leaving the company during that month, under the heading given at the left-hand end of each row. Thus the figure of £500 given in the January column and the Insurance row means that an insurance premium of £500 will be paid sometime in January. The figure of £7,000 in the March column and the 'Income from trade sales' row means that £7,000 will enter the company's bank account in March as a result of trade customers paying invoices.

The timing of the payments is important and it depends on commercial practice. Thus rents are normally paid quarterly, in advance. Hence the rent payment will be made at the beginning of January and the beginning of April. Components will probably be bought against credit accounts with one or more suppliers. Under such arrangements, invoices for components delivered in one month will be issued at the end of that month and customers will be expected to pay the invoice within 28 days of its being issued. Similar arrangements will probably apply to energy costs but these will reduce as we move from the cold winter months into the warmer season.

We have assumed that retail sales, that is, sales to individuals, are paid for immediately and that these run at a steady level of £5,000 per month throughout the period. Trade sales, that is sales to businesses, are typically paid for in the month following delivery. We expect these sales to increase steadily during the period. The total cash received for the six month period is estimated to be £85,000. Since trade sales made in month 6 will not appear in this figure, it looks as though the sales for the period are estimated to be around £105,000. The budget (Table 7.2) is based on total sales of £243,250, leaving £138,250 to be earned in the second six months. This is not unreasonable; demand both from consumers and from businesses is traditionally at its highest in September, October and November.

Assuming that the estimates are realistic, this forecast shows that, at no time during the period, will the cash received come close to balancing the cash paid out. At the worst point, at the end of month 5, the cash paid out will be £23,312 more than the cash received. This has nothing to do with the company's profitability; it could well be that the company is on track to meet the budget in Table 7.2 and make a respectable profit. Nevertheless, the company will need to have at least £23,312 available in cash if it is to keep operating through this period. Prudence suggests that it should plan on requiring £30,000 to allow for things going wrong.

The amount of cash required to allow the company to continue to operate over a period is known as its **cash requirement**. It is also often referred to as working capital, although, as we have seen in Chapter 6 on liabilities and owners' equity in commercial balance sheets, this term is more correctly used to refer to the difference between current assets and current liabilities. The two concepts are related but they are not identical. The traditional way of funding a company's cash requirement is through a bank overdraft but banks are not always eager to lend to small companies and loans from other sources may be necessary.

An initial cash flow forecast is an essential part of a business plan but a well-run company will maintain a rolling twelve-month cash flow forecast. That is, each month it will produce a new cash flow forecast for the next twelve months, the first eleven months of which will be an updated version of the figures in the previous month's forecast. Such forecasts will provide early warning of any prospective cash shortage and banks will generally respond well to a request for an increase in overdraft facilities that is made well in advance and based on detailed cash flow predictions.

At first sight, cash flow forecasts and budgets seem very much the same thing. It is important to understand the difference. Cash flow forecasts deal with the flow of cash or its equivalents in and out of the company. Budgets deal with income and expenditure. If our company delivers computers worth £100,000 to a large corporate customer today and sends it an invoice, this will immediately appear as income when we are monitoring the budget. However, many large companies are very slow to pay their bills and it may be three or four months before the invoice is paid and the corresponding sum appears as cash. The difference can be crucial.

FURTHER READING

The book by Atrill and McLaney recommended at the end of Chapter 5 also covers the material in this chapter.

8 INVESTMENT APPRAISAL

After studying this chapter, you should:

- *understand what is meant by the time value of money;*
- *be able to carry out a discounted cash flow analysis to assess the viability of a proposed investment proposal;*
- *be able to interpret a discounted cash flow analysis in commercial terms.*

8.1 INVESTMENT PROPOSALS

Successful companies are always looking at ways in which they can change and develop. The senior management will be faced with a number of different proposals, ranging perhaps from the development of a new product to establishing a company presence in a new part of the world. The company will only have a limited amount of money of its own available and lenders and investors will only be prepared to offer limited amounts. The management is therefore faced with the need to decide which of the proposals to support.

There is no single way of assessing and comparing the different proposals; factors that must be taken into consideration include, for example:

- the extent to which the proposals are consistent with the company's long-term plans;
- the risk attached to the proposals;
- the availability of the necessary resources even if the money is available.

One important criterion, however, is the financial one: which of the proposals will give the best return on the investment? The usual way of determining this is to use the method known as **discounted cash flow** (DCF) and this is what we shall describe in this chapter.

It is important to realise that DCF is a tool that is used for many different purposes, for example:

- by investors on the stock market to assess whether the share price of a company reflects accurately its financial prospects;
- to assess whether it is better to purchase capital equipment or to lease it;

- to decide which of several possible projects is the most financially appealing;
- to decide whether a proposed capital project will be worthwhile.

In this book, however, we are concerned almost exclusively with the third and fourth of these.

8.2 THE TIME VALUE OF MONEY

Advertisements for cars often make offers like the following:

New Wolseley Hornet
£8,995 or
only £500 down and £400 per month for 24 months

Suppose that you have £8,995 available so that you could pay cash if you decided to. Would you be better off at the end of two years paying cash at the beginning or taking the easy payment terms? We shall show how to answer this question a little later. For the moment, we consider a simpler situation.

Suppose that you have £100. You can choose to deposit it with a bank or some other savings organisation. If the rate of interest is 3 per cent, then in a year's time you will have £103. In other words, the promise of £103 in a year's time is worth the same as £100 now. This simple example illustrates what is known as the **time value of money**. It forms the basis of discounted cash flow analysis.

In general, if the interest rate is r (expressed as a fraction such as 0.03, not a percentage), then the present value of a sum of money X due in t years' time is

$$\frac{X}{(1+r)^t}$$

The quantity $1/(1+r)^t$ is known as the **discount factor**. Table 8.1 shows the discount factors for periods up to five years for a range of interest rates:

To use this table, we look for the cell in the row corresponding to the discount (interest) rate and the column corresponding to the time period. The value in this cell gives the discount factor. Thus the discount factor for a discount rate of 8 per cent over a period of four years is 0.7350. This means that, if the discount rate is 8 per cent, the present value of a sum of £1,000 payable in four years' time is £1,000 × 0.7350 = £735.

We are now in a position to tackle the question of buying the car. The easy terms on offer mean we pay £500 now, £400 at the end of the first month, another £400 at the end of the second month, and so on until the end of the 24th month. Using the idea of discount factors, we can calculate the present value of each of those monthly payments. If we add the present value of all those payments to the £500 that we have to pay immediately, we shall obtain the present value of the total of the payments we have to make. If this is more than £8,995, we shall be better off buying the car outright immediately.

Table 8.1 Discount factors for periods up to five years

Interest rate	1	2	3	4	5
3%	0.9709	0.9426	0.9151	0.8885	0.8626
4%	0.9615	0.9246	0.8890	0.8548	0.8219
5%	0.9524	0.9070	0.8638	0.8227	0.7835
6%	0.9434	0.8900	0.8396	0.7921	0.7473
7%	0.9346	0.8734	0.8163	0.7629	0.7130
8%	0.9259	0.8573	0.7938	0.7350	0.6806
9%	0.9174	0.8417	0.7722	0.7084	0.6499
10%	0.9091	0.8264	0.7513	0.6830	0.6209
15%	0.8696	0.7561	0.6575	0.5718	0.4972
20%	0.8333	0.6944	0.5787	0.4823	0.4019

The discount rate that we need to use in doing our calculations is the rate of interest that we would receive on our £8,995 if we left it in our savings account. Let us assume that this is around 3 per cent per year. We, however, need the equivalent monthly rate and this is 0.2466 per cent per month. (The equivalent monthly rate is not simply 1/12th of the annual rate because the interest is compounded. The monthly equivalent of a rate of r (as a fraction) is $(1+r)^{\frac{1}{12}}-1$.) With this discount rate, the discount factors at the end of the months 1 to 3 are 0.9975, 0.9951 and 0.9926. The present values of the first three £400 payments are thus £400 × 0.9975 = £399.02, £400 × 0.9951 = £398.03 and £400 × 0.9926 = £397.05. The necessary calculations are tedious but, fortunately, spread sheets such as Excel have a built-in function for calculating the net present value of a series of payments at a given discount rate. The result of applying this function (NPV) to a sequence of 24 payments of £400 with a discount rate of 0.2466 per cent is a net present value of £9,310.30. To this we must add the £500 down payment. This shows that the net present value of the payments on easy terms is £9,810.30. Clearly we shall be much better off by buying the car outright for £8,995 if we have the money available.

8.3 APPLYING DCF TO A SIMPLE INVESTMENT PROJECT

The essence of investment is that money is spent now so as to produce benefits in the future; assuming those benefits can be quantified in monetary terms, we need to ask what their present value is. To do this, we calculate the net cash flows that the project will generate over each year of its life and convert these to a present day value. Then we add these up to get the net present value (NPV) of the project as a whole.

As an example of simple DCF analysis, consider a small computer maintenance company. The company has one van that it uses for transporting computers that cannot be repaired on site to and from its workshop. When things are busy, the one van is not enough and the company often has to rent a second van. It is considering whether it is worthwhile to buy a second van.

A new van will cost £10,000. There will be annual costs of £500 for insurance and £150 for road tax. The cost of maintenance is estimated to be £200 in each of the first two years, £300 in year 3, £400 in year 4 and £500 in year 5. At the end of the fifth year, it is expected that the van will be sold for around £2,000. The interest rate that the company pays on its borrowings is 10 per cent. Van hire costs £30 per day and it hires a van for about 100 days a year. All the costs are subject to inflation, which is judged to be around 5 per cent over the period but the resale value of the van is the cash figure expected at the time.

Table 8.2 shows the cash flows in the two cases. Most of the figures are in brackets, indicating negative cash flows, because the flows of cash are out of the company.

Table 8.2 DCF analysis of van purchase v. leasing

	Year 0	Year 1	Year 2	Year 3	Year 4
Buying a van					
Van purchase/sale	(10,000)				2000
Tax and insurance	(650)	(683)	(717)	(752)	(790)
Maintenance	(200)	(210)	(331)	(463)	(608)
Annual cash flow	(10,850)	(893)	(1,048)	(1,215)	602
NPV of annual flow	(10,850)	(812)	(866)	(914)	412
	(13,030)				
Continuing to rent					
Annual costs	(3,500)	(3,675)	(3,859)	(4,052)	(4,254)
NPV of annual costs	(3,500)	(3,341)	(3,189)	(3,044)	(2,906)
Total NPV	(15,980)				

The NPV of the cost of continuing to rent is £15,980, while the NPV of the cost of buying a van is £13,030. We conclude that the company will be better off by buying a van. This conclusion depends, of course, on the validity of the assumptions. The main uncertainty is in the number of days for which a van would have to be rented. If the company's business expands, so that it would have to rent a van more often, the cost of the rental option would increase so that buying would have more of an advantage. If, however, business declined or the company were able to use the existing van more efficiently, the cost of the rental option would decrease and the advantage of buying would be reduced or even disappear.

8.3.1 Timing of the cash flows

The analysis assumes that the cash flows take place at the start of each period, so that the discount factor for year 0 is 1. In other words, the first payments are at the start of project so that their net present value is their actual monetary value. This is realistic for the costs involved in buying the van; the cost of the van itself is due when it is bought, which is effectively the start of the project, while the insurance and the road tax are both due at that point and on the same date in succeeding years. Only the comparatively small maintenance costs occur at different points during the year.

This assumption about the timing of the cash flows is not, however, valid for the rental option. The maintenance company is likely to have an account with the rental company so that it receives monthly invoices for the rentals in the previous month, so that the cash flows are distributed throughout the year. If we assume that 'on average' the rental costs are paid half way through the year, we can correct for the result of assuming that the cash flows take place at the beginning of the period by applying a further six month discount factor to the NPV. This factor is the square root of the annual discount factor, 0.9091, that is, 0.9535. The resulting NPV is £15,237. The advantage of buying the van is thus slightly less than in the original calculation but is still significant.

8.3.2 Cost of capital

We said that the company pays 10 per cent interest on its borrowings and we assumed that it would have to borrow the money to buy the van. This is an over-simplification.

Even if the company has the cash available to buy the van outright, there is still a cost because the company will lose the income it could have received by investing the money somewhere else, in a suitable interest bearing account for example. Such a cost is known as an **opportunity cost**. If the company is able to pay cash for the van, this is the interest rate it would be appropriate to use in the DCF analysis.

As we have seen in Chapters 4–6, large companies raise money by taking loans, the rate of interest on which may be fixed or variable, by the issue of shares, on which dividends may be paid, or by retaining profits. When a large company invests in new projects, the money required is likely to come from a combination of these. The company's financial director is expected to carry out arcane calculations to balance the cost of money from these different sources and come out with a single figure for the cost of capital, which the company will use in appraising all investment proposals.

8.3.3 Handling inflation

Inflation in a financial context means the fall in the value of money over time. It is usually expressed as an annual percentage. Thus, for example, an inflation rate of 5 per cent means that in a year's time goods that today cost £100 will cost £105. In two years' time, they will cost £100 × 1.05 × 1.05 = £110.25. The inflation rate can vary very much from time to time and from country to country. Typically, in countries with a stable economy it will be under five per cent while in countries where the economy is disintegrating and out of control it can rise to several thousand per cent.

The presence of inflation means that the 'monetary' rate of interest, that is, the rate that is normally quoted is something of a delusion. £100 invested at a quoted interest rate of 10 per cent, will be worth £110 in money in a years' time. However, if the rate of inflation is 5 per cent, this £110 will only buy as much as £110/1.05 = £104.76 would buy today. Thus the real rate of interest is only 4.76 per cent.

In the example, we initially estimated all costs in today's pounds. We then assumed an inflation rate of five per cent and adjusted the cash flows for future years to take this into account. We used the 'monetary' rate of interest rather than the 'real' rate. In normal economic conditions this is the simplest way to carry out a DCF analysis. It is perfectly possible, however, to carry out a DCF analysis ignoring inflation and using the 'real' rate of interest as the discount factor.

8.3.4 Financial cash flows

It is not necessary to include the cash flows associated with borrowing the money to buy the van, that is, the cash inflow when the bank loan is received and the interest payments made to the bank. The DCF analysis automatically takes these into account so that the same result is obtained whether or not they are included.

8.4 ASSESSMENT OF A SOFTWARE PRODUCT PROPOSAL

As a more sophisticated example, we consider a company that is assessing a proposal for the development of a software product. It is estimated that three people will be required for development in the first year and a further person and a half in the second year; suitable staff cost £35,000 per year, including the employer's pension and National Insurance costs. The product will be released in the second year. After the second year, maintenance is expected to require one person, full-time. Sales and marketing costs are estimated to be £20,000 in the first year, rising to £30,000 for each of the next four years. The product itself is a fairly high value but specialised product. It is expected that about 100 copies will be sold over this period, at around £5,000 a copy. Table 8.3 shows the DCF analysis of the project over a five year period, using 10 per cent as the (monetary) cost of capital.

In Table 8.3, we have shown additional entries for the **cumulative present value**. This is the NPV at the end of the first year, the NPV at the end of the second year (that is, the present value of the cash flows for the first two years), and so on. The NPV of the project over its five year life is the cumulative present value at the end of year 4, shown in the bottom right hand entry, £52,993, but there are other measures of a project's attractiveness which can be deduced from this table. One is the **pay-back period**; this is the time required for the project to achieve a positive net cash flow. For the project in the table, this is a little over four years, since the cumulative cash flow at the end of year 3 (£3796) is close to zero, and the cumulative cash flow is firmly positive by the end of the year 4. (The term **simple pay-back period** is sometimes used to refer to the pay-back period calculated without taking into account the time value of money.)

Table 8.3 DCF analysis of a proposed software package development

	Year 0	Year 1	Year 2	Year 3	Year 4
Development cost	105,000	55,125			
Maintenance			38,588	40,517	42,543
Sales and marketing	10,000	21,000	22,050	23,153	24,310
Number of sales		10	20	40	30
Revenue		50,000	100,000	200,000	150,000
Net cash flow	(115,000)	(26,125)	39,363	136,331	83,147
Discount factor	1	0.9091	0.8264	0.7513	0.6830
Present value	(115,000)	(23,750)	32,529	102,425	56,789
Cumulative present value	(115,000)	(138,750)	(106,221)	(3,796)	52,993

The pay-back period is important in a project like this one because predicting the sales of a software product three or four years ahead is a very uncertain activity. A project that promises a pay-back within two years will therefore usually be preferred to one whose pay-back period is four or five years. The same thing would not necessarily be true of a project in a more stable industry such as electricity generation, where it is quite normal to look 20 years ahead and to accept projects whose pay back periods are 10 years.

It is also possible to calculate the **internal rate of return** (IRR) on the project. This is the cost of capital which would lead to the NPV being precisely zero. The calculation involves some difficult mathematics but, fortunately, most spread sheets provide a function to calculate it. The IRR is the maximum cost of capital at which the project would be viable. For the figures in the table, it is 23 per cent. The term **accounting rate of return or simple return on investment** is used to denote the average annual benefit as a percentage of the average investment.

There are times when interest rates can fluctuate quite violently, even in basically stable economies. This happened, for example, in the UK in the mid-1970s and again in the late 1980s. The IRR is a useful guide to the viability of a project in such an environment. An IRR of 23 per cent at a time when the company's cost of capital is 10 per cent means that the viability of the project will not be affected by any likely increase in interest rates.

A proposal will normally be rejected out of hand if its NPV is not positive, if its pay-back period is greater than some pre-set threshold or if its IRR is less than the current cost of capital. If there still remain projects between which a choice must be made, the organisation should probably choose those which have the highest positive NPV. This, however, usually reflects a long-term view and other pressures may cause companies to accept the projects with the highest IRRs or the shortest pay-back periods.

8.5 PITFALLS OF DCF

Because of its apparently precise nature, there is a tendency to put too much trust in DCF analysis. However precise the calculations, the cash flow predictions are inherently uncertain. An example of the case where uncertainty is comparatively low, is the replacement of plant or equipment in the manufacturing or process industries. If the new plant is installed and functioning correctly by the scheduled date and if market conditions do not change dramatically, the cash flow predictions should be reasonably accurate and the major source of uncertainty is the cost of capital; there are, of course, plenty of occasions when the assumptions about installation of the plant and market conditions will prove false but this is likely to be the exception rather than the rule.

If we use DCF analysis to assess a proposal for developing a software product, as we have done above, then the sources of uncertainty are very much greater. Although a net present value of £52,993 and an IRR of 23 per cent look attractive, we must take into account that:

- most software projects take more effort than expected;
- most software doesn't work very well when it's first released;
- we may not manage to sell as many copies as we expected;
- there is a considerable risk that a competitor will launch a similar product before ours is ready.

We need to assess how sensitive the project is to such risks. The way to do this is to carry out a series of DCF analyses with different estimates of the cash flows and the discount rate and see how the results change. If the project remains attractive under the different sets of assumptions, it is comparatively low risk; if it becomes unattractive under small changes, then it is high risk and should probably be rethought. In the given example, if the sales in year 3 drop from 40 to 20, the cash flow never becomes positive. Predicting sales this far ahead is very uncertain, so the project should be regarded as high risk. On the other hand, if the price is increased to £6,000, the NPV rises to £117,420 and the pay-back period falls to two years. This sensitivity to changes in sales volumes and selling price is characteristic of software product developments.

FURTHER READING

The following book is highly recommended. It contains a lot of more detailed material specifically concerned with the assessment of IT investment proposals, as well as some material covering other aspects of finance and accounting:

Blackstaff, M. (2012) *Finance for IT decision makers: a practical handbook.* 3rd ed. British Informatics Society, London.

The book by Atrill and McLaney recommended at the end of Chapter 5 also covers the material in this chapter.

Much of the other literature on discounted cash flow is aimed at investors on the stock market or in other financial markets. It is not therefore directly relevant to the appraisal of alternative investment proposals within a company.

9   HUMAN RESOURCES ISSUES

The purpose of this chapter is to explain some of the most important human resources issues that affect companies in the IT sector. After studying it, you should:

- *appreciate the complexity of the law in this area;*
- *understand the constraints under which management and human resources staff act;*
- *understand why and to what extent managers need to be aware of general human resources issue.*

9.1 WHAT ARE HUMAN RESOURCES?

The term 'human resources' (HR) emphasises the fact that the people who work for an organisation are an indispensable part of the organisation's resources and, very often, the most important part. For this reason, the organisation will try to ensure that it always has available the appropriately skilled, qualified and experienced staff that it needs in order to exploit its other assets. This must be done without wasteful over-staffing and within the constraints of what is lawful. The cost of recruiting new staff is high and the loss of continuity when staff leave can also be very expensive. Accordingly the organisation will want to keep staff turnover low. Many organisations (though by no means all) want to behave as a 'good' employer and will therefore try to follow the best of current employment practice.

Any organisation that employs staff will be faced with the need to handle administrative issues relating to their employment. When the number of employees grows to, say, a dozen, one person will have to devote a significant proportion of their time to this. By the time the number of employees reaches around 30, a full-time personnel officer or HR manager will be required. However, managers cannot hand over all responsibility for personnel matters to specialists. This is especially the case in the information systems industry, where staff have high expectations and staff turnover is particularly high.

9.2 THE LEGAL CONTEXT

HR management is practised in an environment beset by legislation. Furthermore, since it is an area in which it is often difficult to legislate clearly, the practical effect of much of the legislation can only be assessed in the context of subsequent decisions by the courts and by tribunals. To make the situation worse, it is a political battleground so that changes in the legislation occur frequently – four Employment Acts and three Trade Union Acts between 1980 and 1993. There was a consolidating act – the Employment Act 1996 – that was intended to bring all the employment legislation together but there have since been further substantial changes, most recently in the Enterprise and Regulatory Reform Bill 2013. Anything one reads on the subject is thus in danger of being out of date, which makes it very much a field for experts.

Throughout the 20th century, up to the end of the 1970s, industrial relations in Britain were based on collective bargaining and were conceived very much in terms of relations between trades unions and employers. In particular, the rights of trade unions received much more prominence than the rights of individual employees. The situation could be characterised by the following features:

- Industrial disputes leading to damaging strikes were common.

- Such strikes were often fomented by politically motivated left-wing members of the trade unions, against the wishes of the majority of members.

- Strikes were supported by aggressive picketing, that is, by large numbers of strikers gathering outside workplaces to 'persuade' other employees to join the strike.

- Secondary action was common, so that companies that had nothing to do with a dispute could find themselves subject to strike action or intimidatory picketing.

- The closed-shop (the system by which, through agreement between the employer and a trade union, all employees had to be members of that trade union) meant that expulsion from the trade union would cause the employee to lose his job. This meant that trade unions could discipline their members very effectively and made workers very reluctant to disobey their union's instructions, whatever their feelings.

- Nearly all trade unions imposed a 'political levy' on all their members, which was passed on to the Labour party, whatever the political views of the individual member.

- Elections for trade union officials were often rigged.

- Over-manning was preventing British industry from taking advantage of modern equipment, because trade unions insisted that the same number of people continue to be employed to carry out a task, whether or not they were required.

- Trade unions were effectively immune from legal action.

There had been attempts at reform through the 1960s and 1970s, most notably the plans put forward in the white paper *In Place of Strife* by Barbara Castle under the Labour government elected in 1966, but they had all failed because of the strength of the opposition from the trade unions.

The trade unions were to pay dearly for their opposition to the moderate reforms proposed by Mrs Castle. In 1979, a Conservative government under Margaret Thatcher was elected with a mandate for root and branch reform of the law relating to industrial relations and trade unions. The popularity of this policy was an important factor in the victory of the Conservative party at the next three general elections. The legislation passed under these four successive Conservative governments completely broke the power of the trade unions, aided, it must be said, by economic conditions that led to the decline of the heavy industries that were the stronghold of trade union power. None of the nine bulleted statements above would any longer be regarded as true, although the trade unions continue to hold significant power in the Civil Service, the National Health Service, education and local government.

The erosion of the collective power of employees through the limitations on the rights of trade unions has been balanced by a significant increase in the rights of individual employees. This started in the 1960s with legislation to ensure equal pay for women. This is an example of anti-discrimination legislation; this topic is so important we shall deal with it in a chapter of its own (Chapter 10). Industrial or employment tribunals were introduced in 1964. These are special courts designed to handle cases concerning employment rights and related matters. They provide a cheap and comparatively speedy way for employees to take action if they consider that their rights have been breached. The concept of unfair dismissal was introduced in the Industrial Relations Act 1971. There has been a steady stream of legislation outlawing discrimination of various kinds, which was brought together in the Equality Act 2010.

RESPONSIBILITIES OF THE HR DEPARTMENT

The greater attention paid to the rights of individual employees and the need to comply with anti-discrimination legislation have very considerably increased the work load of HR departments in the UK. The following list is a summary of the responsibilities they are expected to take on within the overall aim of ensuring that the organisation has the workforce that it needs:

- ensuring that recruitment, selection and promotion procedures comply with anti-discrimination legislation;
- staff training and development;
- setting up and monitoring remuneration policy;
- setting up and monitoring appraisal procedures;
- administering dismissal and redundancy procedures;
- contracts of employment;
- workforce planning;
- designing and administering grievance procedures;
- being aware of new legislation affecting employment rights and advising management of what the organisation must do to comply with it;
- health and safety;
- administering consultative committees.

The need to comply with so much new legislation has forced HR departments to adopt formal, bureaucratic procedures that are often felt to be irrelevant and unwelcome by those staff that see themselves as carrying out an organisation's core functions. At the same time, comparatively junior staff in HR may find themselves having authority over some decisions that more senior staff elsewhere in the organisation regard as their prerogative. Tact, wisdom and administrative efficiency are needed to handle such situations and these are qualities that are not easy to find together, whether in HR departments or elsewhere.

9.3 RECRUITMENT AND SELECTION

HR managers often make a distinction between the two terms recruitment and selection, using recruitment to mean soliciting applications and selection to mean selecting the applicants to whom offers will be made. Increasingly, the two are seen as separate activities and recruitment, particularly at professional level, is being outsourced to specialised agencies. Such agencies handle the advertising and, often, carry out initial screening of applicants, before presenting their clients with a short list of suitable applicants. They charge a fee that is normally based on the salary of the person appointed, typically something like 25 per cent of the first year's salary.

The best of these agencies are thoroughly professional and offer an excellent service but the world of recruitment agencies is murky and some of them indulge in very questionable practices.

Before you employ a recruitment agency you need a description of the job to be filled and the type of qualifications or experience you expect in the successful applicant; a good agency can help draw this up. Note that there are two clearly different situations: it may be that you need to fill a specific post, such as Manager of Feline Rodent Elimination Agents, or it may be that you are looking for as many good staff with experience of programming in Python as you can find. In the latter case, the job description is likely to be much less precise, specifying simply a range of activities that people appointed may be expected to carry out.

Selection is kept in the hands of the employer, although a member of the recruitment agency staff may sometimes be invited to advise. A wide range of selection techniques is available and is used in making professional appointments:

- A series of one-to-one interviews with senior management and senior technical staff. This can be a very reliable method of selection, particularly if records are kept so that you can look back and see how effective each individual's judgement has been. Unfortunately, this approach does not make it easy to demonstrate that equal opportunities legislation has been complied with.

- Interview by a panel. Despite extensive research evidence demonstrating its unreliability, this technique is widely used, particularly in the public sector. It tends to favour applicants who are smooth talkers. The panel may well contain a majority of people who are neither professionally competent nor operationally involved in the appointment. Such 'independent' members are commonly used, for example, in appointing school teachers and university staff; they are thought to help prevent nepotism and other forms of corruption but the evidence suggests that they are often responsible for bad appointments.

- Assessment of references. In appointments in the public service, great importance is usually attached to references, especially for academic posts. In contrast, commercial employers usually pay little heed to them and use them only as a final check that candidates are who they say they are. Legislation in many countries is making it possible for job applicants to demand to see references written about them and even to sue for damages if they consider the reference unfair. Employers, or others, who feel that they have been misled by a reference could also sue if they can show that the reference was written without proper care. Because of these legal dangers, references are being used less and less.

- Psychometric tests. These are of three types. **Ability tests** measure an individual's ability in a general area, such as verbal or numerical skills. **Aptitude tests** measure a person's potential to learn the skills needed for a job. Such tests can be fairly effective, provided that the ability they are assessing is well correlated with the ability you are looking for. In the past, these were widely used for recruiting trainee programmers. However, results can be spoiled if the candidates have had the opportunity to practise, and this is usually the case nowadays. It is difficult to design satisfactory tests for higher level skills. **Personality tests** attempt to assess the characteristics of a person that significantly affect how they behave in their relationships with other people. Unfortunately, there are several competing theories of personality and, although the tests are widely used, their value is far from clear.

- Situational assessment. This is much used in selecting military officers and by prestigious multinational companies when recruiting new graduates. The short-listed applicants are brought together and put into a variety of situations where their performance is observed and assessed by the other participants in the situations. It is expensive and is only suitable for use when a number of candidates for jobs can be brought together. However, the use of situational questions in interviews is valuable. The interviewer describes a scenario to the candidate and asks him or her what they would do in such circumstances.

- Task assessment. Candidates are asked to carry out some of the tasks that they will be required to do in the job, for example ask them to write a program. This works very well, provided that the tasks the successful candidate will be expected to undertake lend themselves to being assessed in this way. The trouble is that, where a job involves some skills that can be assessed in this way and some that can't, the former will tend to be overemphasised. Thus the ability to write a short program can be easily assessed in this way but the ability to write a 2,000 statement program cannot – it would take too long. Unfortunately, there are many people who can write short programs but not long ones.

The comments above apply to professional appointments; selection of, say, bar staff or cleaners is likely to be done just using a single interview, backed up by references.

To these formally recognised methods of staff selection we should add **nepotism** (choosing cousins, children or other family members) and **cronyism** (choosing friends or former colleagues). The latter, in particular, should not be rejected as unfair or ineffective. If one has worked with a person in the past and seen that they are effective in the role that one is now looking to fill, then to offer them the job is a low risk way of filling it.

As described in the next chapter, the need to comply with anti-discrimination legislation and with codes of good practice associated with it is of great importance and, in a large organisation, the HR department is likely to spend a good deal of effort in ensuring this compliance.

9.4 STAFF TRAINING AND DEVELOPMENT

UK management is frequently criticised for its lack of interest in staff training. By and large, these criticisms seem fair and they reflect also the comparative lack of concern for qualifications. In the USA, employers commonly encourage staff to undertake part-time masters degrees by paying the fees and buying the books needed for the course – and, most importantly, by not promoting people who don't have masters degrees. Such behaviour is rare in Britain.

Successive British governments have been well aware of this problem and there are a number of initiatives that provide positive encouragement and support to firms to invest in staff training. Some of these, such as the Modern Apprenticeships programme, are intended to give young employees the opportunity to acquire skills and obtain qualifications.

It is important, however, to ensure that employees are able to keep their skills up to date throughout their working lives and this falls under the Investors in People programme. This is a programme run by the UK Commission for Employment and Skills, a public body that provides advice on skills and employment policy to the UK government and the devolved administrations in Northern Ireland, Scotland and Wales. It usually falls to the human resources department to establish and administer a policy for staff training and development, particularly if government support is to be received through one of the programmes mentioned.

In general, these programmes are not aimed primarily at professional staff although there is no reason in principle why continuing professional development (CPD) should not be supported. Furthermore, unless the company is a specialist IT company, it is unlikely that internally organised courses will contribute very much to the CPD of the information systems engineer. For this reason, it may be up to individuals themselves, and their managers, to identify specific needs and seek out conferences or external courses through which these needs can be addressed. In this context, it is worth noting that the BCS Code of Conduct not only requires members to maintain their own professional knowledge but also to encourage their subordinates to do so. This means that managers are expected to take some responsibility for the CPD of their staff.

Staff training and development are of particular importance in hi-tech companies, where failure in this respect can threaten the company's raison d'être. It is unfortunate that, when money is tight, it is often the first thing to be cut.

9.5 REMUNERATION POLICIES AND JOB EVALUATION

One of the major sources of discord and staff dissatisfaction in organisations both large and small is perceived disparities in remuneration. (We use the term 'remuneration' rather than salary to indicate that other things, such as private health insurance or a company car, may be included.) It is the difficult task of HR management to provide a framework for fixing remuneration that will avoid giving rise to such disparities.

In the public services, this is achieved by using fixed scales which employees move up by annual increments. The financial effect of a promotion is that you are moved to another, higher scale. Regular negotiation with trade unions leads to the scales as a whole being increased from time to time, possibly to reflect inflation and possibly to reflect increases in the aspirations of the employees involved or changes in the esteem in which the public or the government hold them. Some systems also include provision for allowances for specific responsibilities, for example being dean or being in charge of keeping school premises tidy. By and large, as might be expected, any discord that arises under such systems arises from the allocation of jobs to grades. This is now often done by bureaucratic job evaluation schemes; these require the preparation of elaborate job descriptions that are then painfully compared against sets of criteria for each grade.

The trouble with such systems is that they have difficulty in coping with market conditions. Thus, the Civil Service has always had difficulty in recruiting and retaining good software staff because the grading system always lands up by paying them much less than they could get in private industry.

Formal bureaucratic systems of this type are also employed in some of the larger companies, albeit with, in most cases, much more flexibility to cope with market conditions. However, automatic annual progression up a fixed scale is uncommon. In professional environments it is more usual to fix salaries individually, within broad guidelines. Ensuring that these guidelines are adhered to is always difficult. The author knows of a case where someone threatened to leave, whereupon his annual salary was increased from £25,000 to £40,000. Either he was underpaid before or he was overpaid afterwards; in any case it is very likely that this increase breached whatever guidelines the HR department was trying to maintain.

Job evaluation is a technique that is often used for comparing the relative worth of jobs and allocating jobs to specific grades. Job evaluation must always involve an element of individual judgement but the aim is to be as objective as possible.

Anti-discrimination legislation has led to the need for organisations to be able to demonstrate that they comply with the doctrine of 'equal pay for work of equal value'. Job evaluation has a valuable role to play here. In the private sector, mergers and acquisitions of one company by another also lead to a need to harmonise remuneration policy and job evaluation is a valuable tool in these circumstances. It also has a place in younger, rapidly growing companies, where it is used to underpin the reward system to provide clarity and consistency, while flexibility is maintained.

Many organisations are now using job evaluation as the basis for flatter, broad-banded pay structures. Having extended pay ranges means that the emphasis moves away from promotion as the only way of progressing, with an expectation that lateral movement between functions may be more common. It has often been the case in the IT industry that the only way in which highly competent designers could be rewarded adequately was by promoting them to managerial positions for which they were unsuitable – turning good designers into bad managers. Broad-banded pay structures allow the salaries of such staff to be increased without changing their roles.

To further facilitate career management, some companies are establishing generic role profiles, which follow the factors measured during the job evaluation exercise. This allows roles to be compared across the organisation. Some companies seek to strengthen the links between job evaluation and other HR activities by using competency frameworks as a unifying factor.

JOB EVALUATION SCHEMES

Job evaluation schemes may be **analytical** or non-analytical. **Non-analytical** schemes involve comparing whole jobs without considering the individual elements and skills that go to make up the job. There are a number of fairly simple non-analytical techniques in use. One technique that has been widely used in the public sector is known as job classification. Using this technique, the number of grades is decided first and descriptions of the characteristics of jobs in each grade are then produced.

Analytical job evaluation schemes assess each job on the basis of the different elements that are involved. Such elements might include financial responsibility, supervisory responsibility, degree of autonomy, decision making powers, IT skills, linguistic skills, and so on. Each of these elements is given a weight to reflect its importance relative to the others. Each job is then assessed for each of the elements on a scale, typically of 0 to 4, with the criteria for each level specified as objectively as possible. Thus, for linguistic skills, one might ask which of the following statements most accurately describes the job, and award the score shown

There is no requirement or opportunity to speak a language other than English	0
Situations occasionally occur when it is helpful that the holder can speak a second language.	1
The holder of the post regularly has to use a second language in informal situations and the ability to do this is a requirement of the job.	2
The holder of the post is required to speak and read a second language fluently.	3
The holder of the post is required to be completely fluent in a second language, including being able to write it correctly and to act as an interpreter when required.	4

A score for the job is then calculated by adding the scores for each element, multiplied by the weight assigned to that element.

Analytical job evaluation is usually preferred because its (spurious) objectivity is considered to make it more likely to be successful against a claim for 'equal pay for work of equal value'.

It is always stated that job evaluation schemes are intended to evaluate the job and not the person currently doing the job. This is reasonable when there are a large number of people doing a more or less identical job. It does not make sense in an organisation where every individual is doing a different job and where individuals are valued for their own individual contribution.

When job evaluation schemes are first introduced, it is usual to ask each employee covered by the scheme to complete a fairly lengthy form describing their job. The questions on the form are often worded in ways that are open to more than one interpretation. Thus, a person whose job includes looking after petty cash may reply 'No' to the question 'Does your job carry any financial responsibility?', on the grounds that they make no decisions about what the money is spent on, or 'Yes' because it's their job to make sure that all petty cash is correctly accounted for. The cumulative effect of such misinterpretations can be very great and lead to significant differences in remuneration between people doing identical jobs in different parts of the organisation.

9.6 APPRAISAL SCHEMES

It is astonishing and contrary to all common sense that people should be able to spend 30 years in a professional job without anyone, colleague or superior, giving them any indication of how well they are doing the job or how they might improve. Yet, until recently, this was commonly the case for school teachers, university lecturers, many civil servants, and not a few managers in commercial and industrial organisations. It is still true of many doctors, solicitors, architects and others. To be more precise, there are or were no procedures or regulations that ensured that there was any such feedback. In practice, many senior practitioners in these fields would try to keep an eye on new entrants to the profession and help and advise them; equally, the newcomers would commonly seek such help from their more senior colleagues. Nevertheless, there was no requirement that this should happen and very often it did not. Even when it did happen, it would probably cease to happen by the time the practitioners reached the age of, say, 35, and they would continue to practise for the next 30 years, with no feedback, unless they were disastrously incompetent.

It falls to HR management to design procedures to avoid this undesirable situation. Appraisal schemes are the usual formal way of doing this. They derive from the idea of Management by Objectives (MBO). This idea was developed by Peter Drucker, one of the most distinguished of management theorists, in the 1970s, and it rapidly became popular in industry. It was seized on by government in the 1980s as a way of dealing with what they saw as poor performance and indolence in many state-funded jobs.

The essence of MBO is that managers and their subordinates agree on a set of objectives for the subordinate to achieve over the next period, typically six months. These objectives should be precise, objectively verifiable and, ideally, quantifiable. In other words, objectives like 'increase the turnover of your division by 10 per cent while maintaining its present level of profitability' are preferable to objectives like 'improve the public image of your products'. At the end of the period, they meet and discuss the extent to which these objectives have been achieved. If the objectives have not been achieved, they will discuss the obstacles that have prevented them from being achieved and how these might be overcome. They then agree a revised set of objectives for the next period. The process filters down from the highest level of management, where the overall objectives of the organisation are set. At each level, managers take their objectives and break these down into more specific goals. From these goals, they delegate tasks by negotiating goals for their subordinates.

The strength of MBO is that it makes managers and others aware of what the organisation's objectives are and how they are expected to contribute towards achieving them. Its main weaknesses are as follows:

- Not all legitimate objectives can be easily specified in precise and quantifiable terms. Such objectives are often therefore ignored when using MBO. This is particularly a problem in the public sector.

- The insistence on quantifiable objectives can distort behaviour. For example, setting specific targets for cutting the length of waiting lists in the British National Health Service can lead to doctors choosing patients for treatment on the basis of the effect on the waiting list rather than on their clinical needs.

- MBO tends to emphasise short-term objectives at the expense of long-term strategic objectives.

Modern management practice has moved away from the idea of setting rigid, formal objectives, while maintaining the general principles of MBO. The emphasis is now on **empowerment**, that is, telling employees at all levels what is expected of them but then leaving it to them to decide how to achieve this.

Appraisal schemes usually involve an appraiser and an appraisee meeting regularly (every six months, every year, even every two years) to discuss the employee's performance and career development under a number of headings. The result is a report signed by both parties; if they cannot agree on certain points this will be recorded in the report. There is an obvious similarity to MBO, all the more so because many schemes seek to identify objectives to be achieved by the time of the next appraisal interview.

There is no doubt that such schemes are useful. Professional staff (in the widest sense) are usually willing to listen to ways in which they can improve their performance and will usually accept that someone else can throw new light on the way they do their job; they also provide a good opportunity to review career plans and ambitions and to assess training needs. A good appraiser will do all these things. (From an employee's point of view, it is worth noting that appraisal reports, assuming they are favourable, can provide valuable ammunition in unfair dismissal cases.)

However, the process has many weaknesses. It often seems artificial and appraisal interviews can be rather uncomfortable affairs. Appraisals are supposed to be non-judgemental but this may be difficult to achieve when the appraisee is not felt to be pulling their weight. The training typically given to appraisers is derisory and many of them prove unable to perform satisfactorily in the role. There is the difficult question about whether appraisals should have any link with promotion or salary increase. Too close a link may mean that they are not conducted with the openness and frankness that is essential if the participants are to get the best out of them; if there is no link – and perhaps the appraiser has no influence on the promotion procedure – then appraisees may regard the process as a farce: if your appraisals for the last five years have said that you are ready to become a project manager but you have never been given that opportunity, you can be forgiven for doubting the usefulness of the appraisal system.

9.7 REDUNDANCY, DISMISSAL AND GRIEVANCE PROCEDURES

It normally falls to the HR department to ensure that, when staff are made redundant or are dismissed, the proper procedures are followed. Failure to follow the proper procedures can lead to the organisation facing the embarrassment of actions for unfair dismissal in an industrial tribunal. This is expensive in terms of staff time as well as money and is bad for an organisation's image. Unless the dismissal or redundancies are seen to be fair as well as lawful, the effect on the morale of the remaining staff will be bad.

9.7.1 Unfair dismissal

In order for a dismissal to be fair, the reason for the dismissal must be a fair one and the dismissal procedure itself must have been carried out fairly. If either of these conditions is not satisfied, an employee can take action in an industrial tribunal alleging unfair dismissal. If the tribunal finds in favour of the employee, it will usually order the employer to pay compensation to the employee who has been unfairly dismissed. The amount of compensation awarded depends very much on the circumstances of the particular case; the Enterprise and Regulatory Reform Act 2013 imposes a limit of 12 months' salary or £74,200, whichever is lower. A tribunal can also order reinstatement of the employee, that is, order the employer to take the employee back. In practice, tribunals are reluctant to do this. Employees can only claim unfair dismissal if they have been working for the employer for two years or more. (This restriction does not apply if the dismissal is for reasons of political belief or affiliation.)

The law accepts a wide variety of reasons as justifying dismissal. Specifically, it accepts:

- lack of capability;
- misconduct;
- breach of the law – not by the employee (that would be covered by misconduct) but that the employer would be in breach of the law if he continued to employ the employee, e.g. because the employee is a foreign worker whose work permit has expired;
- redundancy (see next section).

Furthermore, it allows for 'any other reason'! However, there are many reasons that cannot be used to justify a dismissal. These include anything excluded by anti-discrimination legislation (see next chapter), taking legal action against an employer to enforce your employment rights, taking part in trade union activities, and so on.

Dismissals are **automatically** considered to be unfair unless the statutory dismissal procedure has been followed. In other words, no matter what the employee has done or has not done, if the employer has not followed the statutory procedure in dismissing them, an industrial tribunal will judge to have been unfairly dismissed and will award them compensation.

The statutory dismissal procedure is not, on the face of it, unreasonable. It requires the employer to give the employee a written statement of why dismissal is being considered; the employer must then arrange a meeting at which both sides can state their case. Following that meeting, the employer must inform the employee of the decision. If it is decided to go ahead and dismiss the employee, then the employee must be given the opportunity to appeal, with the appeal being considered by a more senior manager where this is practicable.

Until the regulations have been in operation for some time, it is difficult to know how tribunals will react to claims from employees such as:

- The statement of why dismissal was being considered did not provide enough detail or was not provided far enough in advance of the meeting for the employee properly to consider his or her response.

- The employer was too slow in following the procedures.The meeting was conducted in such a way that the employee did not have a reasonable opportunity to state his or her case.

For this reason, it is very important for HR departments to lay down detailed procedures to ensure that such claims are not successful.

Of course, the fact that the statutory procedures have been followed does not automatically mean that a tribunal will consider a dismissal to be fair. Most of the reasons for which an employer might reasonably consider dismissing an employee – inability to do the job, misconduct, persistent absenteeism, and so on – are, in principle, acceptable but the employer has to show that appropriate training was offered or warnings given, and so on.

9.7.2 Redundancy

Essentially, dismissal because of redundancy (retrenchment in the USA) occurs when employees are dismissed because the employer no longer needs people to do their jobs. In these circumstances, most employees will be entitled to compensation based on their age, salary and years of service. The law lays down a minimum level of compensation that must be paid. In practice, many employers pay more than this.

If the employer is intending to make 20 or more employees redundant over a period of 90 days or less, the employees or their representatives have a right to be consulted.

Rather confusingly, however, there are two definitions of redundancy used in British law and they are not equivalent. For the purposes of entitlement to compensation, redundancy occurs when an employee is dismissed because the employer no longer needs employees to do that job in that place. In determining the right to consultation, however, redundancy is defined as occurring when the dismissal is for a reason or reasons not related to the individual concerned.

In most cases of redundancy, the employer will be seeking to reduce the number of workers in a particular job category rather than dismiss all such workers. The question of how to select the employees to be made redundant therefore arises. It is common practice to use the 'last in, first out' principle, that is, the most recently recruited employees are the first to be made redundant. Although there are many reasons for feeling that this is not a desirable policy, it is acceptable to the trade unions and to the courts. Dismissal for redundancy can easily become unfair dismissal if individuals are selected for redundancy in some other way. There is a long list of criteria that are not acceptable in this context, ranging from participation in trade union activities to sex, racial or ethnic origin, sexual orientation, religion, and so on.

9.7.3 Constructive dismissal

It sometimes happens that an employer behaves towards an employee in such a way that the employee feels that he or she has no option but to resign. If the employer's behaviour amounts to a substantial breach of the contract of employment, the law may regard the employer's behaviour as tantamount to dismissal. This situation is known as constructive dismissal and can be the subject of unfair dismissal proceedings, although the fact that it is constructive dismissal does not automatically make it unfair dismissal.

The following are a few examples of circumstances that might lead to employees resigning in circumstances that would probably amount to constructive dismissal:

- The employer moves an employee's place of work to somewhere 400 km away, at short notice and without consultation.
- The employer requires someone who was employed as an accountant to spend their time acting as a receptionist.
- A senior manager repeatedly countermands instructions issued by a more junior manager.

The regulations regarding dismissal procedures also lay down statutory grievance procedures to be used if an employee has a grievance against the employer. Employees are required to make use of these procedures before they can claim constructive dismissal.

9.7.4 Takeovers and outsourcing

It frequently happens in modern commerce and industry that one company takes over another; this is particularly frequent in the IT industry. It also happens when an organisation outsources its IT activities (or any other activities). In these circumstances, staff involved are usually transferred to the new employer. This could mean a major change in their employment conditions. In particular, if IT activities are being outsourced from a government department to a private company, there are likely to be major changes affecting security of employment and pension rights.

There are specific regulations in the UK and other countries of the European Union governing what happens to employees when an undertaking or part of an undertaking is transferred from one employer to another. These are known as the Transfer of Undertakings (Protection of Employment) (TUPE) regulations. The original TUPE regulations dated back to 1981 but they were replaced by a new set of regulations in 2006, reflecting a change to the underlying EU directive. The purpose of the regulations is to maintain the employees' conditions of employment in these circumstances. The government leaflet *Transfer of Undertakings: a guide to the regulations* (PL699 rev 6) states:

> Employees employed by the previous employer when the undertaking changes hands **automatically** become employees of the new employer on the same terms and conditions. It is as if their contracts of employment had originally been made with the new employer. Thus employees' continuity of employment is preserved, as are their terms and conditions of employment under their contracts of employment (except for certain occupational pension rights).
>
> Representatives of employees affected have a right to be informed about the transfer. They must also be consulted about any measures which the old or new employer envisages taking concerning affected employees.

9.7.5 Public interest disclosures

Until comparatively recently, an employer could dismiss an employee for revealing publicly that, for example, the employer was consistently and wilfully breaking the law. There were a number of well-known cases in which senior employees revealed that their employers were breaking the law in areas such as price fixing or the disposal of toxic wastes. The employees (so-called **whistle blowers**) were dismissed and, furthermore, because of the high profiles of the cases, they found it impossible to get other jobs in the industry.

The Public Interest Disclosure Act 1998 (PIDA) is intended to protect employees who raise concerns about criminal behaviour, certain types of civil offences, miscarriages of justice, activities that endanger health and safety or the environment, and attempts to cover up such malpractice. Since it is closely tied to the law relating to confidential information, we shall postpone a fuller discussion to Chapter 11.

9.7.6 Wrongful dismissal

For the sake of completeness, we should mention wrongful dismissal. This is significantly different from unfair dismissal. An action for wrongful dismissal is an action for damages brought by an employee against an employer for breach of the contract of employment. It is an action under the common law and for this reason is not subject to the maxima laid down by statute for unfair dismissal. It is typically brought by very senior or highly-paid employees who can make a reasonable case for very substantial compensation resulting from their employer's breaking of the contract.

9.8 CONTRACTS OF EMPLOYMENT

Under British Law, every employee has a contract of employment, whether or not it is written down. What this means is that the agreement between an employee and his or her employer can be enforced in a court of law. The law requires that, if the contract is not written down, the employer must provide the employee with a statement of the major conditions of the employment, including grievance procedures.

A good contract of employment should be written in terms that are easily understood and should avoid legal jargon. Prospective employees should not need to consult a lawyer in order to understand it. They should, however, read it carefully before signing it. It is an important function of HR staff to ensure that contracts of employment are issued to all employees and that signed copies are retained.

An example of a contract of employment, with some explanatory comments, is included as an appendix.

9.9 HUMAN RESOURCE PLANNING

If the HR department is to ensure that the organisation always has available the staff it needs, it must be able to forecast the needs some time ahead. This is extremely difficult, particularly in software companies. As we move through the spectrum of organisations, from software houses through banking, manufacturing and retailing to policing, health care and the operation of lighthouses, the uncertainty, although always present, is reduced and it becomes possible to predict staff needs much more precisely.

In a software house, there are three inputs to the HR planning process:

- HR plans from existing projects, showing how many staff of each grade and with which specialised skills will be required in each of the following months.

- Sales forecasts. These are subject both to the whims of potential clients and the judgement, good or otherwise, of the sales staff. Sales staff are asked to identify all active sales situations, i.e. situations in which they are talking to potential clients about their actual needs, not just trying to establish the company's credentials. They then estimate the staff needs for doing this work, in terms of numbers of staff in the various grades and any special skills required, and assign a probability to winning a contract to carry out the work. The probabilities are carefully defined in something like the following manner:

0.9	negotiations concluded successfully but no signed contract yet received;
0.7	the company has been offered the business, subject to negotiation on price, contractual conditions, etc;
0.5	the company has submitted a proposal for the business and has been short-listed, or for other reasons, are in competition with no more than two other companies;
0.3	the company has been asked to submit a formal proposal;
0.1	the client has an identified requirement that is expected to be met by commissioning a software house.

- Forecasts of the likely staff losses in the coming months. In the software business this depends very much on the buoyancy of the market for software developers. This, in turn, seems to depend on the economic cycle, being, like other capital goods industries, sensitive to growth rates rather than to the overall production of the economy. However, it is also very strongly affected by events such as decimalisation in 1972 and the problems associated with the year 2000. Such events generate an enormous demand for staff in the year or two leading up to them, and are followed by an equally large fall, leading to much temporary unemployment, particularly among contractors.

From these inputs, we can try to predict how many staff will be required each month, with their grades, qualifications and experience, and how many will be available. We can then proceed to produce a plan for recruiting staff if necessary.

In practice, HR prediction in project-based companies never works very well and there are good statistical reasons why it never will. If we are summing 1,000 weighted predictions, the uncertainty in the sum will be quite small, even though the uncertainty in each prediction may be quite large; this follows from what is called the Law of Large Numbers. But if we are summing over only 20 predictions, the uncertainty will still be very large. This suggest that human resource planning should be easier in larger companies and to some extent this is so. However, few project-based companies, even large ones, ever have as many as 100 live sales situations referring to the same pool of staff at any one time. Furthermore, most such companies depend for their success on specialised skills; this means that you cannot treat every employee in a given grade as the same – the fact that you have a grade 5 expert on communications available does not help the project that needs a grade 5 expert on data modelling. And you cannot turn one into the other by sending them on a two week training course. As a result of all these difficulties, most project-based organisations find themselves see-sawing between being desperate to get new staff for the projects they've won and being desperate to get new projects for the staff they've got.

FURTHER READING

The ACAS advisory handbook *Discipline and grievances at work* and its advisory booklet *Redundancy handling* are the best sources of information on the material covered in the section on redundancy. Information about contracts of employment is also available from ACAS:

www.acas.org.uk

The Department of Business, Innovation and Skills publishes a comprehensive document covering the TUPE regulations, entitled *Employment rights on the transfer of an undertaking*, see:

www.gov.uk/government/organisations/department-for-business-innovation-skills

The website of the UK Commission for Employment and Skills:

www.ukces.org.uk

10 ANTI-DISCRIMINATION LEGISLATION

After studying this chapter, you will:

- *understand in general terms what anti-discrimination laws are trying to do;*
- *understand why employers need codes of practice that their staff are expected to follow in order to avoid breaching the legislation;*
- *know how legislation affects the design of information systems.*

10.1 THE DEVELOPMENT OF ANTI-DISCRIMINATION LEGISLATION

Three hundred years ago, the laws of the UK contained many specific statutes embodying discrimination on grounds of sex, religion and wealth. In order to vote, you had to be male and own property. In order to be admitted to either of the two universities, you had to be male and a member of the Church of England. If you were a woman, when you married all your personal property became the property of your husband.

From 1700 to the 1950s, all these explicit examples of discrimination enshrined in the law were slowly but surely abolished. With a very few exceptions, men and women, whatever their religion and however rich or poor they might be, were treated by the law in the same way. This did not, however, eliminate discrimination. There were, for example, golf clubs that would not admit Jews, medical schools that were very reluctant to admit female students and professions that it was difficult for anyone not from a wealthy background to enter.

Since the 1960s there has been a plethora of legislation outlawing discrimination and a number of bodies were established to help enforce the law. The Equality and Human Rights Commission (EHRC) came into being in 2007 to promote and enforce equality and non-discrimination laws in England, Scotland and Wales, replacing several existing bodies. There is a separate body for Northern Ireland. The Equality Act 2010 brought all the existing legislation together in a single act of parliament. It is, however, one thing to make a law giving women the vote, but quite another to legislate effectively to ensure they are treated on an equal footing with men in all matters concerned with employment, not to mention other matters such as getting a mortgage. Equally, it is one thing to make racial discrimination unlawful but quite another to eliminate racial prejudice. Even if effective legislation can be framed – itself a difficult task – legislation, of itself, is not enough; time is required to bring about the changes of attitude that are necessary if discrimination is to be eliminated.

Information systems engineers need to have an appreciation of anti-discrimination legislation for two reasons. First, as professionals, they will inevitably find themselves in managerial and supervisory positions and the law requires people in such positions to prevent the people they supervise from behaving in a discriminatory manner and to avoid such behaviour themselves. Secondly, the obligation to avoid certain sorts of discrimination, in particular discrimination on grounds of disability, should influence the way in which information systems are designed and constructed.

Although the Equality Act has done a great deal to bring about consistency in the way that the law deals with discrimination, it is a long, complicated and far-reaching piece of legislation. What is presented here is a very limited and simplified picture of the law as it is likely to impinge on the information systems professional.

10.2 WHAT IS DISCRIMINATION?

Discrimination means treating one person or one group of people less favourably than another on the grounds of personal characteristics. The Equality Act 2010 prohibits discrimination on any of the following grounds, known as **protected characteristics**:

- age;
- disability;
- gender reassignment;
- marriage and civil partnership;
- pregnancy or maternity;
- race, colour, ethnic origin or nationality;
- religion or belief;
- sex;
- sexual orientation.

Similar legislation applies across the EU, in the US and in many other countries.

Much of the law and much of the debate on discrimination issues relates to employment and related matters. However, the legislation relates to discrimination in other contexts as well – education, the provision of goods and services, letting of premises, and so on.

Discrimination can be **direct** or **indirect**. Direct discrimination occurs when one person is treated less favourably than another specifically because of one of the protected characteristics, such as his or her sex or race. Here are some examples that, on the face of it, would constitute direct discrimination:

- A woman does exactly the same job as a man but is paid less than he is.
- A doctor refuses to treat a Chinese patient on the grounds that he has no room for any more patients but then accepts an English patient.

- A company advertises for a secretary and automatically rejects all the male applicants.
- A landlord seeking to let a flat tells a black applicant that the flat is already let but next day lets it to a white applicant.
- A company advertises for 'a mature woman to act as the chief executive's personal assistant' or 'a strong young man to work as a trainee zoo-keeper'.

Industrial tribunals have increasingly taken the view that harassment and victimisation constitute direct discrimination and this was formalised under the Act. Harassment is defined as 'engaging in unwanted conduct related to a protected characteristic which has the purpose or effect of violating another person's dignity or is creating an intimidating, hostile, degrading, humiliating or offensive environment'. Victimisation is treating a person badly because that person has brought proceedings under the Act, alleged that someone has contravened the Act or given information or evidence in connection with proceedings under the Act.

Indirect discrimination occurs when general conditions are imposed that have a disproportionate effect on one group.

EXAMPLES OF INDIRECT DISCRIMINATION

Here are a few examples that might constitute indirect discrimination:

- A job is advertised with the requirement that applicants must be at least 180 cm tall. In the UK there are many men over 180 cm tall but very few women. The result is that few women can apply for the job.
- When allocating public housing, a local authority has a policy of giving priority to the children of existing tenants.
- An employer insists that all employees work on Saturdays. This might be held to be indirect discrimination against those who practice Judaism, since Saturday is their Sabbath. This would be discrimination on grounds of religion but, since the practitioners of Judaism are overwhelmingly of the Jewish race, it might also be regarded as racial discrimination.

The Equality Act permits discrimination in many cases where it is 'a proportionate means of achieving a legitimate aim'. Where it is associated with employment, indirect discrimination can also be justified if the employer demonstrates that there is a genuine occupational requirement that the offending condition be satisfied.

10.3 DISCRIMINATION ON GROUNDS OF SEX

Most people under 50 are surprised when they are told about the position of women workers in the 1960s. Where formal salary scales were in operation, there would either be separate, lower scales for women or there would be additional allowances for men, especially for married men. A female employee who got married might lose her job or might be transferred to the 'temporary' staff, making her ineligible for bonuses or additional holiday entitlement for long service. Women who had babies were not normally expected to return to work and had no legal right to do so. Outside a few professions such as nursing and teaching, promotion prospects for women were very poor and there were few women in senior positions. Indeed, it was very difficult for women to gain entry to academic and professional courses in fields such as medicine or the law which would have qualified them for senior positions. Discrimination also existed outside the field of employment. Some hotels would refuse to let rooms to unaccompanied women. Building societies applied much stricter criteria when considering whether to offer a mortgage to a single women than to a single man.

10.3.1 Employment

The most important features of the law can be summarised as follows:

- It is unlawful for an employer to discriminate against a person on grounds of their sex or marital status in terms of the arrangements made for recruitment and selection and the terms on which employment is offered (not just pay but also holiday entitlement, sick pay, notice period, and so on). The Act specifically makes unlawful advertisements that explicitly or implicitly suggest that only persons of one sex will be considered. The courts have interpreted the principal of equal pay for equal work as applying not just to men and women doing the same jobs but also to men and women doing jobs 'of equal value'.

- It is unlawful for an employer to discriminate against an employee on grounds of their sex or marital status in regard to opportunities for promotion, transfer or training or to any other benefits.

- It is unlawful for an employer to discriminate against an employee on grounds of their sex or marital status in regard to dismissal or redundancy.

- It is unlawful for an employer to victimise an employee for bringing a complaint of sex discrimination or for giving evidence in support of another employee's complaint.

- It is unlawful for any of the following to discriminate against a person on grounds of sex or marital status: a trade union, a professional body, a registration authority (e.g. the Architects Registration Board; see section in Chapter 2 on royal charters), an employment agency or a provider of vocational training.

Contract workers are also covered by the legislation.

There are a few exceptions to these provisions. The most important is where there is a genuine occupational requirement for a person of a specific sex, as for example in the case of recruiting actors to play roles of a specific sex. There is also a provision that specifically allows political parties to use procedures for selecting candidates for parliament that ensure that women will be selected.

10.3.2 Education

It is unlawful for a provider of education (public or private, school, college or university) to discriminate against a person on the basis of their sex, in offering admission to the establishment or to specific courses, and in providing access to the other benefits and facilities it offers.

The main exceptions to this are that allowance is made for single-sex establishments and that provision for physical education may be different for the two sexes.

10.3.3 Provision of goods and services

It is unlawful to discriminate on grounds of sex:

- in the provision of goods, facilities or services. This covers accommodation in a hotel, facilities for entertainment, recreation or refreshment, banking and insurance services and so on;
- in selling or letting property.

The main exception to these provisions are for charities that have been founded with the purpose of helping a specific group of people who are all of the same sex, for example, single mothers.

Two consequences of this part of the legislation are that it is unlawful to offer:

- car insurance to women at a lower price than to men because women are statistically less likely to be involved in car accidents;
- offer better pensions to men of a given age than to women of the same age because men are statistically likely to die sooner.

10.3.4 Remedies

A person who believes that they have been discriminated against in their employment because of their sex – whether by being refused a job, refused promotion, paid less, not given training opportunities or anything else – can take the matter to an employment tribunal. If the tribunal finds in favour of the complainant it can award damages and make recommendations to the respondent. If the respondent fails to act on the recommendations, the amount of the damages may be increased.

An individual who feels that they have been the victim of sexual discrimination in the other areas covered by the legislation – education, the provision of goods and services – can take action in the civil courts for damages.

The EHRC provides advice and assistance to complainants who feel that they have been subjected to discrimination on grounds of their sex, whether in their employment or elsewhere. Anyone considering a formal complaint of sex discrimination is well advised to start by consulting the Commission.

10.4 DISCRIMINATION ON RACIAL GROUNDS

The first race relations legislation in the UK was the Race Relations Act 1965, which made it unlawful to discriminate on grounds of race or colour by banning people from using public services or entering places such as bars, cinemas or theatres. It also created a new criminal offence of incitement to racial hatred by inflammatory publications or speeches. In 1968, a further act was passed making it unlawful to refuse housing, employment or public services to people because of their ethnic background.

The specific provisions of the law relating to discrimination on racial grounds are now very similar to those already described, relating to discrimination on grounds of sex and the EHRC has the same responsibilities for providing advice and assistance to complainants.

There is one major difference, however, that makes the implementation of racial discrimination legislation much more problematic than that of sex discrimination legislation. With a very few exceptions, the human race is divided into two sexes; a person can only belong to one sex at one time; and it is clear to which sex any given person belongs. (The Act does, in fact, make specific provision for persons who change their sex.) The same is very much not true of race, colour, ethnic origin or nationality. The Act does not define these terms. Are the English, the Irish, the Scots and the Welsh to be regarded as different racial groups? Is a person whose parents were Afro-Caribbean but who was born and brought up in Cardiff to be regarded as belonging to the Welsh, British or Afro-Caribbean racial groups, or perhaps to all three? Does the requirement that candidates for a job speak a specific language (e.g. Urdu or Welsh) constitute indirect discrimination? These considerations go far beyond what it is relevant to consider here but they illustrate the difficulty of legislation in this area.

10.5 DISCRIMINATION ON GROUNDS OF DISABILITY

From the 1970s onwards, government had been encouraging the recruitment of disabled employees into the Civil Service and encouraging employers to take on disabled workers by withholding government contracts from companies that could not demonstrate a commitment to offering opportunities to the disabled. It was not, however, until 1995 that anti-discrimination legislation was extended to cover discrimination on grounds of disability, in the Disability Discrimination Act. This was followed in 2001 by the Special Educational Needs and Disability Act, which extended the provisions of the earlier act to cover education. The provisions of these acts are now included in the Equality Act 2010 and the EHRC is responsible for advising and assisting complainants.

The Act makes it unlawful to treat a disabled employee or applicant less favourably because of their disability without justification. The justification must be serious and substantial. Thus it would be justified to reject a blind applicant for a job as a bus driver or a paraplegic for a job as a lifeguard, and it would probably be justified to reject a dyslexic applicant for a job as a copy editor. However, the Act requires the employer to make reasonable adjustments to meet the needs of disabled applicants or employees. This might include adapting a bus so that a disabled applicant could drive it safely or providing a work station with special hardware and software to make it suitable for use by a partially-sighted employee.

The Act also makes it unlawful for businesses and organisations providing goods and services to treat disabled people less favourably than other people, for a reason related to their disability, and service providers are required to make reasonable changes to make it possible for disabled people to use their services.

The requirement to make reasonable adjustments could certainly include adapting information systems so that they can be used by a blind or partially-sighted employee, provided this can be done at reasonable cost. The requirement for service providers to make reasonable adjustments certainly requires that reasonable adjustments should be made to the way that services are provided over the web. The legislation thus has a direct effect on information systems professionals in a way that other anti-discrimination legislation does not: it directly influences – or should influence – the way in which information systems are designed. In practice, for the ordinary information systems developer (as opposed to specialists working in areas such as text to speech conversion) this translates into the need to make systems usable by the blind, those whose vision is impaired, those whose hearing is impaired, those suffering from lack of manual dexterity (and so unable to use a mouse, for example), and those suffering from dyslexia. This need is most apparent, and most likely to be enforceable, when the system includes publicly accessible web pages.

Just a few of the ways accessibility can be improved include:

- Do not rely on subtle colour contrasts such as yellow text on a green background.

- Provide a textual alternative for non-text content such as diagrams or pictures.

- Make all functions available from the keyboard – some users may have difficulty using a mouse.

- Do not impose time constraints on users, some of whom may only read slowly.

- Ensure that the page can be read satisfactorily by a screen reader (i.e. software that converts text on the screen to speech output).

- If you use speech to convey information, ensure that the information is also available as text.

- Make it easy to avoid or correct mistakes.

In 1997, the World Wide Web Consortium (W3C) established the Web Accessibility Initiative (WAI), with the specific aim of improving the accessibility of the web for disabled users. In 1999, it published version 1.0 of its Web Content Accessibility Guidelines (WCAG) to help developers produce accessible web pages. In 2008, WCAG version 2.0 was published and in 2012 the International Organization for Standardization (ISO) adopted these guidelines as an international standard ISO/IEC 40500:2012.

The guidelines specify three levels of compliance:

- Level A is the lowest level of compliance. If a web page is not compliant at this level, one or more groups of disabled people will be unable to access the page.
- If a web page is not compliant at level AA, some groups of disabled people will have difficulty in accessing the page.
- Compliance at level AAA will make it easier for some groups to access the web page.

Several pieces of software are available to test whether a web page complies with the W3C guidelines.

Many of the guidelines are likely to make it easier for non-disabled users to use the internet. In 2004, the Disability Rights Commission (one of the predecessors of EHRC) commissioned a study of web accessibility for the disabled, which resulted in a report entitled *The web: access and inclusion for disabled people*. The study included a survey of 1,000 homepages and found that 81 per cent, including many government sites, failed to comply with even the lowest level of the W3C guidelines. Among the commonest reasons why disabled users experienced difficulty were:

- Page layout was unclear and confusing.
- The navigation mechanisms were confusing and disorienting.
- There was poor contrast between the text and the background and colours were used inappropriately.
- Graphics and text were too small.
- Links and images were poorly labelled.
- The web pages were incompatible with the software designed to assist disabled users (screen readers, magnification software).

It is striking that the first four of these, and possibly the fifth, are a source of difficulty for all web users. Eliminating these faults would not only improve the accessibility of the internet to disabled users but would also enhance its usability for everyone. Although many web pages are much improved since the report was produced, many others are still poor.

W3C also produces accessibility guidelines for authoring tools. As stated in version 1 of these guidelines, they are intended to ensure 'that the authoring tool be accessible to authors regardless of disability, that it produces accessible content by default, and that it supports and encourages the author in creating accessible content'. Because most of the content of the web is created using authoring tools, they play a critical role in ensuring the accessibility of the web. Since the web is both a means of receiving information and communicating information, it is important that both the web content produced and the authoring tool itself be accessible.

Quite apart from the ethical and commercial reasons for making web pages accessible to the disabled, there are legal requirements. In 2012, the Royal National Institute for the Blind served legal proceedings against low-cost airline bmibaby over its failure to ensure web access for blind and partially sighted customers. This case and several others have been settled out of court but similar cases have been brought in other countries. The requirement laid down in the Act is to make reasonable adjustments to allow access by the disabled. In practice, this probably means that a small company can claim that it does not have the necessary resources to make significant adjustments but no such defence is available to larger organisations.

10.6 DISCRIMINATION ON GROUNDS OF AGE

The Equality Act 2010 makes it unlawful to discriminate on grounds of age. In the field of employment this has meant the end of compulsory retirement ages. It also means that it is probably unlawful for employers to seek specifically to recruit new graduates. (This would be indirect age discrimination because a much smaller proportion of over-50s fall into the category of 'new graduates' than of under-25s.)

The test that discrimination can be justified if it represents 'a proportionate means of achieving a legitimate aim' means, however, that examples such as the following might well be considered lawful:

- special treatment of different age groups in order to protect them (but note that the age discrimination provisions of the Act do not, anyway, apply to persons under the age of 18);

- different premiums for life insurance policies, depending on the age of the person at the time the policy is taken out, and different pension rates depending on the age of retirement (but these must not amount to sex discrimination);

- fixing a maximum age for recruitment based on the need for a reasonable period of employment after training and before retirement;

- fixing a minimum age, a minimum amount of professional experience or a minimum number of years with the company before a person will be regarded as eligible for a given post or eligible for certain employment benefits (e.g. additional annual leave).

The IT industry has traditionally been a youthful one and many companies have discriminated against older job applicants, albeit unconsciously or unintentionally, As the industry itself has grown older, the average age of its employees has been increasing, so this phenomenon has become less marked. Legislation against age discrimination will probably have little direct effect on the industry beyond accelerating this tendency.

10.7 AVOIDING DISCRIMINATION

It is not enough for an employer to support anti-discrimination legislation and resolve to comply with it. In an organisation of any size, it is necessary to ensure that all members of the organisation share the employer's resolve. Even if this is achieved, the organisation may have to deal with such problems as unlawful harassment from its customers or unjustified accusations of discrimination.

Effective compliance with anti-discrimination legislation in the workplace requires three things:

- a suitable written policy, well publicised and freely and easily available;
- a training programme for new and existing staff, to ensure that they are all aware of the policy and its importance;
- effective procedures for implementing the policy.

It is a sad fact that an employer's ability to rebut an accusation of unlawful discrimination will often depend as much on their ability to demonstrate that proper procedures have been followed as on whether any discrimination took place.

FURTHER READING

The Equality Act:
    www.legislation.gov.uk/ukpga/2010/15

The EHRC website contains much information and guidance about the Equality Act 2010. In particular, it publishes a Statutory Code of Practice covering the Equality Act 2010 as it applies to employment:
    www.equalityhumanrights.com

ACAS (Arbitration, Conciliation and Advisory Service) also provides much helpful advice relating to equality issues at work:
    www.acas.org.uk

The Disability Rights Commission report referred to in the section on discrimination on the basis of disability:
    www-hcid.soi.city.ac.uk/research/DRC_Report.pdf

11 INTELLECTUAL PROPERTY RIGHTS

After studying this chapter, you should:

- *be familiar with the different types of intellectual property that are relevant to information technology and understand their applicability;*
- *understand the rights attached to the different kinds of intellectual property and the way in which these rights can be enforced;*
- *be aware of the issues that are at the root of current debates about intellectual property rights.*

11.1 INTELLECTUAL PROPERTY

If someone steals your bicycle, you no longer have it. If someone takes away a computer belonging to a company, the company no longer has it.

This seems very obvious. In fact, it hides an important and subtle point. If you invent a drug that will cure all known illnesses and leave the formula on your desk, someone can come along, read the formula, remember it, and go away and make a fortune out of manufacturing the drug. But you still have the formula even though the other person now has it as well. This shows that the formula – more generally, any piece of information – is not property in the same way that a bicycle is.

The legal definition of theft involves taking away a piece of someone's property with the intention permanently to deprive them of it. As we have just seen, this cannot apply to a piece of information.

Property like bicycles or computers is called tangible property, that is, property that can be touched. It is protected by laws relating to theft and damage. Property that is intangible is known as **intellectual property**. It is governed by a different set of laws, concerned with **intellectual property rights**, that is, rights to use, to copy or to reveal information about intellectual property.

Intellectual property crosses national borders much more readily than tangible property and the international nature of intellectual property rights has long been recognised. The international law relating to trade marks and patents is based on the Paris Convention, which was signed in 1883. The Berne Convention, which lies at the basis of international copyright law, was signed in 1886.

Rapid changes in technology and the commercial developments that follow them present the law with new problems. The law relating to intellectual property rights is evolving very rapidly and most of this evolution is taking place in a global or regional context. For the UK, European Community law regarding intellectual property rights is critically important, but this law is itself much influenced by developments elsewhere, particularly in the USA.

Software can be very valuable, as the accounts of companies such as Oracle, IBM or Microsoft show. But software is intangible property. The industry can only therefore protect its assets by using intellectual property rights. Hence the importance of the topic for information systems engineers and hence the length of this chapter. Similar considerations apply to films, television programmes and recordings of musical performances.

There are several different rights that relate to intellectual property. In this book, we shall primarily be concerned with those that are relevant to software and the information systems industry. These rights should be looked on as a package; different rights may be used to protect different aspects of a piece of software.

Copyright is, as the name suggests, concerned with the right to copy something. It may be a written document, a picture or photograph, a piece of music, a recording or many other things, including a computer program.

Confidential information is information that a person receives in circumstances that make it clear he or she must not pass it on.

Patents are primarily intended to protect inventions, by giving inventors a monopoly on exploiting their inventions for a certain period.

Trade marks identify the product of a particular manufacturer or supplier.

Any or all of these rights can be used to protect a piece of software. Suppose for example that a company has developed an innovative computer game called Spookcatcher. The game is marketed in packaging that features the name superimposed on the image of a ghost. It comes with an add-on device that the company has invented called a wailer. This attaches to the computer and emits very convincing ghostly wails at suitable points in the action. The software uses some clever data structures developed within the company that make it possible to achieve very high performance.

The law of copyright automatically protects the source code and all documentation of the package from copying. The company might be able to patent the wailer, in which case no one else would be able to produce a similar product. The law relating to confidential information could be used to prevent any employee who left to join a competitor from passing on details of the clever data structure. Also, the name and the logo could be registered as a trade mark to prevent other companies from using it on their products.

In the following sections we shall discuss each of these rights separately and explain the conditions under which they come into existence and what their effects are. The use of internet domain names can conflict with trade marks and, arguably, domain names are themselves a special type of intellectual property right. We therefore discuss them in the last section of this chapter.

11.2 COPYRIGHT

As the name suggests, copyright is associated primarily with the right to copy something. The 'something' is known as the **work**. There are three categories of work protected by copyright law:

1. original literary, dramatic, musical and artistic works;
2. sound recordings, films, broadcasts and cable programmes; and
3. the typographical arrangement of published editions.

So far as software is concerned, we are primarily concerned with the first category, because the 1988 Copyright Design and Patents Act states that the term 'literary work' includes a table or compilation, a computer program, preparatory design material for a computer program and certain databases. Note the use of the adjective original. Copyright only protects work that is **original** so, even if you did copy the statement $i := i+1$ from someone else's program, you will not have infringed their copyright because there is no element of originality in the statement. However, the development of the internet has made the issue of copyright in recordings, films and other media into a controversial topic that we shall return to in Chapter 14.

As a general rule, the copyright in a work in the first category belongs initially to its author. If the work is jointly written by several authors, they jointly own the copyright. Copyright comes into existence when the work is written down or recorded in some other way. It is not necessary to register it in any way although some jurisdictions, such as the US, provide a mechanism for registering copyright that may make it simpler to take action against any infringement. Although it is not strictly necessary, the copyright symbol (©), followed by the name of the owner of the copyright holder and a year, is very often placed on copyright works (e.g. © Frank Bott 2013). The purpose of this is to draw the copyright status of the work to the attention of anyone who might be contemplating copying the work.

There is one important exception to the rule that the copyright belongs to the author of the work. If the author is an employee and has written the work as part of their job, then the copyright belongs to the employer, unless there is an explicit, written agreement to the contrary. Note that the copyright nevertheless extends to 70 years after the author (or the last of the joint authors) dies, even though it is very improbable that it will be possible to trace their names!

The employer owns the copyright only if the author is legally an employee. If the author is an independent contractor, they will own the copyright unless there is an agreement to the contrary. For this reason, if a company commissions an independent contractor (freelance programmer) to write software, it is important to have a formal agreement regarding ownership of the copyright in the resulting software.

The rights of the copyright owner

Copyright law gives the owner of the copyright certain exclusive rights. The rights that are relevant to software and, more generally, to written documents, are the following:

- the right to make copies of the work. Making a copy of a work includes copying code from a disc into RAM in order to execute the code. It also includes downloading a page from the internet to view on your computer, whether or not you then store the page on your local disc;

- the right to issue copies of the work to the public, whether or not they are charged for;

- the right to adapt the work. This includes translating it – whether from English to Chinese or from C to Java;

- the right to rent or lend the work to the public;

- the right to perform, play or show the work in public;

- the right to broadcast the work or include it in a cable programme service.

In other words, no one can do any of these things without the copyright owner's permission. In some cases, the permission may be implied rather than explicit. The act of making a document available on the web implies that people are allowed to view it over the internet, which involves copying it into the memory of their own computer; however, it does not necessarily extend to allowing people to store copies on their local disc or to print it. The last three of the rights listed above are primarily relevant to books, plays or music but they would be relevant, for example, to any attempt to set up a library of computer games or to making software available in an internet café.

In general, these rights last for 70 years after the death of the author; there are, however, many exceptions and special cases. In the case of joint authors, it lasts until 70 years after the death of the last of them to die. This is far longer than is likely to be commercially relevant for software, even though there is software still in use that was written over 40 years ago.

It is very important to realise that copyright law does not give the owner of the copyright any power to prevent someone else using or publishing identical material, provided they can show that they did not produce it by copying the copyright work. (This is in marked contrast to patent law.) This means that programmers do not need to worry that they will be breaching copyright if they inadvertently produce code that is identical to that produced by another programmer somewhere else – something that can easily happen.

11.2.1 What you can do to a copyright work

The law specifically permits certain actions in relation to a copyright work and some of these are of particular relevance to software.

First, it is explicitly stated that it is not an infringement of copyright to make a backup of a program that you are authorised to use. However, only one such copy is allowed. If the program is stored in a filing system with a sophisticated backup system, multiple backup copies are likely to come into existence.

Secondly, you can 'decompile' a program in order to correct errors in it. You can also decompile a program in order to obtain the information you need to write a program that will 'interoperate' with it, provided this information is not available to you in any other way.

Thirdly, you can sell your right to use a program in much the same way that you can sell a book you own. However, when you do this, you sell all your rights. In particular, you must not retain a copy of the program.

11.2.2 Databases

Copyright subsists in a database if 'its contents constitute the author's own intellectual creation'. There are many databases that do not satisfy this criterion but which, nonetheless, require a lot of effort and a lot of money to prepare. Examples might include databases of hotels, pop songs or geographic data. In order to encourage the production of such modest but useful databases, regulations were introduced in 1997 to create a special intellectual property right called the database right. The database right subsists in a database 'if there has been substantial investment in obtaining, verifying or presenting the contents of the database'. It lasts for 15 years and prevents anyone from extracting or reusing all, or a substantial part of, the database without the owner's permission. Fifteen years is much less than the protection given by copyright but is, in practice, likely to be longer than the commercially valuable life of the database, unless it is updated. If it is updated, however, a new 15-year period will start.

11.2.3 Copyright Infringement

Anyone who, without permission, does one of the things that are the exclusive right of the copyright owner is said to infringe the copyright. There are two sorts of infringement. Primary infringement takes place whenever any of the exclusive rights of the copyright owner is breached. It is a matter for the civil courts and the usual remedies are available: a claim for damages or an injunction to refrain from the infringement are the most likely. Secondary infringement occurs when primary infringement occurs in a business or commercial context. In the case of software, this could involve trading in pirated software or it could involve using pirated software within a business. This is a much more serious matter and may result in criminal proceedings leading to a substantial fine or imprisonment and the confiscation of the copying equipment, as well as civil damages.

Software and other material distributed in digital form is now often protected against copying by some sort of technical device. Inevitably, information about how to circumvent this protection has appeared on the internet and ready-made devices to do it are available from certain sources. The 1988 Act provides that anyone who publishes such information or makes, imports or sells such devices will be treated in the same way as if they were infringing the copyright in a protected work.

There are some cases in which it may be difficult to demonstrate that copying has taken place. One technique that is sometimes used to overcome this problem is to insert the occasional statement that had no functional effect. If the code were copied, the present of such statements would be convincing evidence of the fact. So also would be the presence of identical comments, particularly if the comments included a few deliberate spelling errors.

11.2.4 Licensing and assignment

It is very common for the owner of the copyright in a piece of software to license other people or organisations to carry out some of the activities that are otherwise the exclusive right of the copyright owner. The copyright remains the property of the owner but the **licensees** (the people to whom the software is licensed) acquire certain rights. We shall look at this topic in more detail in the next chapter.

The owner of the copyright can transfer ownership to someone else completely. This is known as assignment of the copyright and must be done in writing. In this case, the new owner of the copyright has all the rights that the previous owner had.

11.2.5 Where does copyright law come from?

The primary source of law relating to copyright in the UK is the Copyright, Design and Patents Act 1988; important amendments to the Act were made by the Copyright (Computer Programs) Regulations 1992, the Copyright and Rights in Databases Regulations 1997 and the Copyright and Related Rights Regulations 2003. Many of these amendments were made in order to comply with European Union (EU) legislation and the description of copyright given here is broadly valid throughout the EU. A much larger number of countries (121) have signed the Berne Convention, last revised in 1979. Countries that sign the Berne Convention agree to establish national laws protecting copyright along the lines described above. In practice, details such as the length of time for which protection is provided may vary, as may the enthusiasm with which cases of copyright infringement are pursued.

11.3 EXAMPLES OF COPYRIGHT CASES INVOLVING SOFTWARE

Copyright infringement is one of the commonest reasons for litigation in the IT industry. It is instructive for practitioners, therefore, to look at a number of typical cases in order to avoid inadvertently exposing themselves to such litigation.

11.3.1 Perreira and Oroyan versus US Federal Government

A straightforward but widely reported case of software copyright infringement occurred in Hawaii. (Hawaii is a part of the United States.) The two defendants had been buying Microsoft X-box game consoles, which are normally sold without any game or other software, the purchaser being expected to buy or rent games software, DVDs and so forth, separately. The defendants were installing hundreds of games, as well as music videos and feature length movies, without the permission of the copyright owners, and selling the resulting modified X-boxes at a considerable profit. The defendants could have faced a penalty of five years in jail and a fine of $250,000. In the event, when they were arrested in 2006, they chose to cooperate with the FBI's investigators and as a result the penalties were comparatively light: one defendant was sentenced to four months imprisonment, four months of home confinement and three years of supervised release; the other defendant escaped a prison sentence but was sentenced to 300 hours of community service, three months of home confinement and five years' probation.

11.3.2 Cantor Fitzgerald versus Tradition (UK) Ltd and Others

This action, which was heard in the High Court of England and Wales in 1999, concerns a system for inter-dealer bond broking, a somewhat esoteric financial activity in which both Cantor Fitzgerald (CF) and Tradition (UK) are involved. The managing director of CF, Michael Howard, was dismissed and obtained employment with Tradition, taking with him Christopher Harland, a senior member of the team that had worked on CF's system, as well as two very capable junior members of staff, who were formally employed as trainees. It took them less than three months to develop a system for Tradition that was a significant improvement on the CF system but had many features in common with it. The claimants alleged that this must have been a copy of their system. They therefore brought an action for copyright infringement (and breach of confidence – see next section) against Tradition itself and against Howard and Harland.

There are many complicating factors in this action and a great deal of effort was needed to establish the facts of the case. In essence, however, it appears that:

- When the staff left CF, they took a copy of the source code of the system with them.

- After he had left CF, Harland logged into CF's system and took a copy of a substantial data file.

- Howard and Harland initially expected to implement a system for Tradition that would have been very largely a copy of CF's system and intended to conceal this copying.

- The system eventually implemented was very different from CF's system in internal structure and substantially better but contained a comparatively small amount (no more than 4 per cent) of code copied from the CF system.

- The programmers used the copy of the CF system that they had taken both for reference and for testing.

The judge ruled that Howard, Harland and the programmers (who were not sued individually) had infringed copyright and that Tradition, as their employer, was also liable. The extent of the liability was, however, very much limited by the fact that only a small proportion of the system had been copied. Many of the claims made by CF were unjustified.

When CF started the action against Tradition, Howard denied that there had been any copying. This led Tradition to spend a great deal of money on a line of defence that ultimately had to be abandoned. The judge ruled also that, by not telling Tradition about the copying while the system was being developed, he had failed in his duty to his employer. For these reasons, therefore, Howard was obliged to indemnify Tradition against its costs and damages.

The circumstances of this case are not unusual and it serves to demonstrate how easily behaviour which may seem only marginally dishonest can result in expensive litigation.

11.3.3 Navitaire Inc. versus easyJet and Bulletproof Technologies Inc.

In November 1996, easyJet, a successful UK budget airline, purchased a licence from Open Skies Inc to use its 'OpenRes' ticketless airline booking system. The OpenRes system consists of some 780,000 lines of COBOL. In October 1998, Open Skies Inc was acquired by Hewlett Packard who, in November 2000, sold it on to PRA Solutions, a subsidiary of Accenture, one of the world's largest management consulting companies. It was subsequently rechristened Navitaire Inc. By 1999, relations between the two companies had deteriorated, allegedly because of Navitaire's slowness in responding to maintenance requests and a considerable increase in maintenance charges following its takeover by Accenture. As a result, easyJet commissioned Bulletproof to write a replacement system with essentially identical functionality, including the user interface. This new system, known as 'eRes', went live in December 2001.

Although Navitaire did not allege that either easyJet or Bulletproof had had access to the source code of OpenRes, it was alleged that copyright in a number of aspects of the system had been infringed:

- user keyboard commands (both individually and as a complete set of commands). The judge ruled that these were not protected by copyright.

- screen layouts and icons. The judge ruled that the GUI screens and the icons were subject to copyright and that this copyright had been infringed. However, Navitaire had suffered no loss as a result of the infringement.

- the 'business logic' of the OpenRes system, that is, aspects of the system such as the relationship between the commands and the screens. The judge ruled that all of these had been copied but that they were not protected by the copyright in the source code. Rather, they were features that were commonplace in airline reservation systems.

- the OpenRes database structure. The judge ruled that although a few instances of direct copying of low-level aspects of the OpenRes database structure were infringements, they did not influence the design of the eRes database. Most of what might be regarded as copying was covered by the interoperability right (see subsection above on what you can do to a copyright work).

- that for the purpose of data migration, various infringing interim copies of the OpenRes database structure were made. The judge found these were either covered by the interoperability right or were infringements that caused no loss.

The judge's rulings in this case were important. Navitaire's action was an attempt to lock customers into using its system by making it very expensive to change. A customer who was dissatisfied with Navitaire's service would have been forced to change to a system that used a completely different approach, creating very heavy training costs, and would have been faced with great difficulties in migrating data.

11.3.4 Oracle Corp versus SAP AG

The interest of this case, a suit between the Oracle Corporation and SAP AG, two of the top four software and services companies in the world, is that it demonstrates how large the sums involved in corporate copyright infringement cases can be.

Oracle alleged that SAP's subsidiary, TomorrowNow, which provides support for older Oracle products at a discount, had infringed Oracle's copyright by downloading documentation and software from its customer support site, using the credentials of Oracle's customers whose support credentials had just expired or were about to. Oracle took its complaint to the US District Court in the Northern District of California in March 2007. Initially SAP argued that it was entitled to download the material, because TomorrowNow had been contracted by those customers to provide third-party support for their Oracle products. SAP subsequently admitted the infringement and the suit was brought in order to determine the damages payable. Oracle argued that the damages should be based on the amount that a customer would have had to pay in licence fees and support charges to be able to access legally all the material downloaded by TomorrowNow. This amounted to some $2 billion. SAP argued that Oracle had not suffered any financial loss through TomorrowNow's actions and that the damages should be limited to a very much smaller figure, somewhere between $28 million and $409 million. In November 2010, the jury in the case awarded damages of $1.3 billion to Oracle, essentially accepting Oracle's argument that the damages should be based on hypothetical licence fees. Following further procedural wrangling, however, the judge ruled that the jury was wrong to accept the basis of hypothetical licence fees and adjusted the damages to the much smaller figure of $272 million.

11.4 CONFIDENTIAL INFORMATION

As we have already explained, information cannot be 'stolen'. Nevertheless, it is possible to take action in a civil court to prevent someone from using or revealing information that they have received in confidence. The critical point is that the information must have been given to that person in circumstances that give rise to what is known as an **obligation of confidence**.

There is an implicit obligation of confidence on employees restraining them from revealing confidential information relating to their employer and his business. In many, if not most, instances this obligation will be reiterated in the contract of employment in order to make sure that the employee is aware of this obligation.

It is common for an obligation of confidence to come into existence as a result of a specific clause in a contract. Contracts for consultancy services or the provision of bespoke software will invariably include specific clauses binding each party to keep confidential any information it obtains about the operations or products of the other.

A non-disclosure agreement (NDA) is an agreement that is specifically intended to set up an obligation of confidence. For example, when two companies are discussing possible collaboration, each side will sign such a non-disclosure agreement to protect the information that they exchange.

Where there is no specific contractual term that creates an obligation of confidence, such an obligation may still exist if a reasonable person, placed in the position of the recipient of the information, would reasonably understand that the information was being given to them in confidence.

The term **trade secrets** refers to novel and effective techniques that companies develop to enable them to produce goods efficiently or perhaps to produce goods that are uniquely attractive to their customers. Secret ingredients in soft drinks or cat foods fall into this category, as might the use of a novel data structure in the implementation of a database management system. Such trade secrets are, obviously, likely to be protected by an obligation of confidence, as are ideas that might be the subject of a patent application. Because the application may be rejected if it can be shown that the ideas had already been made public, it is important that the inventor only discusses them in conditions where an obligation of confidence exists, whether this is through the signing of a non-disclosure agreement or otherwise.

Allegations of breach of confidence were made in the Cantor Fitzgerald v. Tradition case discussed in the previous section. It was alleged by the claimants that a novel inter-process communication technique, which the programmers had developed while working for the claimants, constituted a trade secret and that the defendants had breached confidence by using this in their system. The judge ruled that the mechanism was a programming technique of general application. Since it had been developed by the programmers while they were working for the claimants, its disclosure at that time would have been a breach of the employment contract and a breach of confidence. However, it was not a true trade secret, but the kind of useful technique which an ex-employee could not be prevented from using after the cessation of his employment unless there was an explicit agreement to this effect. He also ruled that the use of the Cantor Fitzgerald source code as a reference was a breach of confidence.

In practice, not many software companies have the type of trade secrets the disclosure of which would cause them serious damage. However, at any time, nearly all of them will be engaged in sales negotiations with a range of prospective customers and a knowledge of the content of these negotiations could certainly enable a competitor to gain a considerable advantage. If a member of the sales staff of company X gives notice of the intention to leave and join a competitor Y, it would be unwise to rely purely on the obligation of confidence, however clearly this is spelt out in the contract of employment. This is because it might be very difficult to prove that he or she had revealed crucial information that subsequently enabled Y to win a contract that X was expecting to win. For this reason, it is common for sales staff, and other staff who are likely to have sensitive knowledge about sales negotiations, to be employed on contracts of employment that specify comparatively long periods of notice – typically three or six months. When such employees give notice, they are immediately removed from the sensitive work and assigned to such important and worthy tasks as reorganising the company's technical library.

Confidential information is not at all the same thing as professional skill and expertise. If, as part of your employment, you learn to program in Perl or to design using UML you take these skills with you and you are entitled to use them in your new employment.

11.4.1 Public interest disclosure

An obligation of confidentiality is not absolute. A court may rule that it is in the public interest that certain confidential information is disclosed. Although this rules out an action for breach of confidence, it does not prevent an employee who discloses such information from being dismissed. Over the years, there have been a number of well-publicised instances in which employees have disclosed confidential information about malpractice on the part of their employer; they have done this because they felt strongly that the malpractice – be it illegal price fixing or serious environmental damage – should be stopped. For a long time there was nothing to protect such employees, who are often known as 'whistle-blowers', from being fired by their employers, often in such circumstances that it was difficult or impossible for them to get another job. Surprisingly, there are also many instances in which employees have been victimised for drawing their employer's attention to matters that the employer would rather not be told about. The author knows of one instance in which an employee was effectively dismissed for drawing his employer's attention to a systematic fraud going on in the organisation.

In 1998, Parliament passed the Public Interest Disclosure Act (PIDA), which amends the Employment Rights Act 1996 so as to provide some protection for employees in these circumstances. First, the Act defines what sort of disclosure of information is covered. A 'qualifying disclosure', that is a disclosure to which the Act applies, means any disclosure of information which the person making the disclosure reasonably believes shows that one or more of the following has occurred or is about to occur:

- a criminal offence;
- failure to comply with a legal obligation;
- a miscarriage of justice;
- danger to health and safety;
- environmental damage;
- information showing that any of these has been concealed.

A worker making a qualifying disclosure will only be protected against victimisation if the disclosure is made in the right circumstances. In this case, the disclosure is known as a protected disclosure. The rules defining the circumstances in which a disclosure become protected are complicated but they encourage the worker first of all to raise the matter internally – many employers have produced Codes of Practice on Public Interest Disclosure, which specify who the worker should make the disclosure to and the procedures for handling it. In more serious cases, or if the internal route has proved ineffective, it may be appropriate to disclose the information to a professional body or to a public official. Only in the most serious of cases will disclosure to the media be protected.

The Enterprise and Regulatory Reform Act 2013 added the requirement that a disclosure is only protected if the employee reasonably believed that it was made in the public interest. Further, if an employee is harassed or otherwise victimised by a co-worker for making a protected disclosure, the employer is made liable.

Despite support from government ministers, PIDA has proved ineffective, particularly in the public sector, most notably in the National Health Service. The final report into the care provided by Mid Staffordshire NHS Foundation Trust (the Francis Report, 2013) makes it clear that many staff had been reluctant to voice their concerns about poor standards of care because they had seen how badly staff who did voice such concerns were treated.

Anyone who is considering relying on PIDA when disclosing confidential information would be well advised to consult a lawyer specialising in the area, because the law is confusing and complicated.

11.5 PATENTS

11.5.1 What is a patent?

A patent is a temporary right, granted by the state, enabling an inventor to prevent other people from exploiting his invention without his permission. Unlike copyright, it does not come into existence automatically; the inventor must apply for the patent to be granted. Applying for a patent is expensive and requires a significant amount of effort. However, the protection it gives is much stronger than copyright, because the grant of a patent allows the person owning it (the **patentee**) to prevent anyone else from exploiting the invention, even if they have discovered it for themselves.

Patents were originally intended to encourage new inventions, and in particular to encourage the disclosure of those new inventions. Inventors are often hesitant to reveal the details of their invention, for fear that someone else might copy it. A government-granted temporary monopoly on the commercial use of their invention provides a remedy for this fear, and so acts as an incentive to disclose the details of the invention. After the monopoly period expires, everyone else is free to exploit the invention. And because of the disclosure made by the inventor, it is very easy to do so.

The temporary monopoly also gives inventors a chance to recoup the investments they made during the development of their invention. They could for instance use the patent to monopolize the market, excluding possible competitors by enforcing their patent. They could then set a high price and make a nice profit. They could also request money from others in return for a license to use the invention. The licensing income then provides extra income. Licensing a patent can be a very lucrative business.

11.5.2 What can be patented?

In Europe, the law relating to patents is based on the European Patent Convention. This was signed in 1973 by 27 European countries, and came into force in 1978. The UK's obligations under the Convention were implemented in the Patents Act 1977, although thus has now been superseded by the Copyright Design and Patents Act 1988, itself the subject of later amendments. The Act states that an invention can only be patented if it:

- is new;
- involves an inventive step;
- is capable of industrial application;
- is not in an area specifically excluded.

Similar criteria apply in all the countries that are signatories to the Convention.

The requirement that the invention must be new means that it must not have been disclosed or used publicly before the date on which the patent application was made. This applies as much to publication or use by the inventor as by anyone else. Thus if Alexander Graham Bell had demonstrated the telephone or written an article about it before he applied for his patent, the patent would not have been granted.

When a patent application is filed, officials at the Patent Office will search existing patents as well as the literature in the area to see whether the invention has been described before. The searches will not be limited to the literature published in the country where the application is made and they may go back many years. Provided it is publicly available (even if only with great difficulty) any publication describing the invention, no matter how obscure the source, will lead to the rejection of the application.

The requirement for an 'inventive step' means essentially that the invention should not be obvious. In other words, it must not be something that anyone reasonably competent in the field would have produced if faced with the same requirements. Thus, leaving aside any other considerations, a program to print invoices for a company is unlikely to satisfy the requirement for an inventive step, even if no one has ever written precisely the same program before, because any competent programmer would have written very much the same program.

The requirement that the invention is capable of industrial application is simply a requirement that the invention must have a practical application (sometimes referred to as a 'technical effect').

Following the European Patent Convention, the 1988 Act excludes the following:

- scientific theories. The theory of gravity cannot be patented although a machine that uses it in a novel way could be.

- mathematical methods. This means, for example, that the methods used for carrying out floating point arithmetic cannot be patented. A machine that uses the ideas can however be patented.

- a literary, dramatic, musical or artistic work or any other aesthetic creation: as we have already seen, these are protected by copyright.

- the presentation of information: again this is covered by the law of copyright.

- a scheme, rule or method for performing a mental act, playing a game or doing business, or a program for a computer.

The last of these exclusions is the one that is by far the most important for the readers of this book and we shall discuss it at length in the section below on software patents.

11.5.3 Obtaining a patent

Unlike copyright, which comes into existence automatically when the protected work is recorded, whether in writing or otherwise, a patent must be explicitly applied for. Applying for a patent can be an expensive and time-consuming business.

Patents are granted by national patent offices. Inventors who want protection in several different countries must, in principle, apply separately to the patent offices of each country. In practice, there are schemes run by the European Patent Office and the World Intellectual Property Organization (WIPO) that provide some assistance by simplifying the process of applying for patents in several countries simultaneously and by reducing its cost.

The requirement that an invention must be new if a patent is to be granted means that the date at which the patent application is first filed is critical, because it is at this date that the invention must be new. If someone else filed a similar application the day before, then that one will have priority. An initial application to one national patent office is enough to establish priority, provided it is followed within 12 months by the submission of a full patent specification to the national patent offices of all the countries in which a patent is sought, possibly through the European Patent Office or through WIPO.

The full patent specification needs to be prepared by a specialist patent attorney and it can take up to four years for the process of obtaining patents to be completed.

Because computing is a global industry, any patents relating to computing need to be taken out in enough countries to make sure that the market in which the invention is not protected is too small to attract a competitor.

11.5.4 Enforcing a patent

The grant of a patent is not a guarantee that it can be effectively enforced. If you own a patent and you find that someone is infringing the patent you may have to go to the courts to enforce your rights. In the court hearing, the offender can challenge your patent on the grounds that it does not satisfy the criteria listed above. The commonest challenge is on grounds of 'prior art', that is, that the invention is not new. The other likely challenge is that it does not involve an inventive step, in other words, that anyone of reasonable competence in the field could have produced the invention simply by following established practice.

The problem is that enforcing a patent that you own or challenging a patent held by someone else is a time-consuming and expensive process. This means that if a large company finds that a small competitor is producing a product that successfully competes with one of its products, it can threaten action for patent infringement which, although it is unlikely to be successful, the smaller rival cannot afford to fight in court. It also means that if an individual or a small company owns a patent, a large company can challenge that patent or even blatantly infringe it, knowing that the holder of the patent cannot afford to contest the challenge effectively.

11.5.5 Software patents

As we have seen, the European Patent Convention and the Copyright, Designs and Patents Act 1988 both state unequivocally that a patent cannot be granted for a computer program. Despite these provisions, the European Patent Office has been granting patents for software since 1998, as has the UK Patent Office. Patent offices in the different European countries have adopted different policies towards the patenting of software, with the result that there is much confusion about what is and what is not patentable. The result is that there is a conflict between the law and practice, a very undesirable situation. Attempts by the European Commission to create a legal basis for software patents in limited circumstances were rejected by the European Parliament.

It should be said that some large companies have a policy of defensive software patenting. This means that they take out large numbers of software patents, which they have no intention of enforcing. They do this in order to prevent other, unscrupulous companies from taking out similar patents and then suing for infringement.

The question of software patents has proved to be extremely controversial. There are many websites and many organisations dedicated to opposing the idea of software patents. The arguments for and against the patenting of software can be summed up as follows:

On the one hand, it is illogical and unfair that something that would be clearly patentable if implemented completely in hardware should not be patentable if implemented in software. Furthermore, patents encourage investment because:

- A patent is a well-defined asset that allows shareholders and, in particular, venture capitalists to be confident that their investment is producing something of value.

- Patents ensure that the benefit of research and development accrues to the people who financed it.

On the other hand, the IT industry has been immensely productive and successful. Much of its success is due to the efforts of small companies. Patents are not helpful to small companies, which, even if they can afford to file for patents, cannot afford to defend their patents or defend themselves against invalid claims for patent infringement coming from large companies. Anyway, the industry has done well enough without patent protection.

Many of the patents granted are 'bad' patents because they are not new or because there is no inventive step. A very great deal of software was written before software patents were thought possible. This means the records of prior art are very patchy. Although such patents could not be successfully defended in court, the threat of patent litigation, which is always likely to be both expensive and protracted, could restrict the activities of many smaller companies or even force them out of business.

Although patent law is more or less harmonised across the EU, there are important differences between EU patent law and the patent law that operates in the USA, in Japan and in many other countries.

For many years, the US Patent and Trade Mark Office (PTO) refused to grant patents for any invention that involved a computer program. In 1981, however, it was ordered by the Supreme Court to grant a patent on a method for 'curing rubber', the novel element of which was a computer program to calculate the optimal way of heating the rubber. Following this ruling by the Supreme Court, more and more software patents were granted, many of which did not involve any physical process and many of which should have failed the test for novelty. From the 1990s onwards, US patents were also granted for 'business methods', for example, novel ways of conducting auctions. However, a decision of the US Federal Circuit on 30 October 2008 in the case *In re* Bilski called into question the validity of most of these patents; this decision was partially reversed by the Supreme Court in June 2010. The situation remains confused.

Attempts to harmonise the law more widely have been going on since the end of the 1990s, under the auspices of WIPO, a United Nations organisation established in 1970. Little progress has so far been made, although the passing of the Leahy-Smith America Invents Act in 2011 has made major changes to US law and thus removed a number of obstacles to the harmonisation process.

11.6 TRADE MARKS

The law regarding trade marks in the UK is based on the Trade Marks Act 1994, which consolidated and updated existing legislation. The Act defines a trade mark as:

> ... any sign capable of being represented graphically which is capable of distinguishing goods or services of one undertaking from those of other undertakings. A trade mark may, in particular, consist of words (including personal names), designs, letters, numerals or the shape of goods or their packaging.

Some of the best known examples of trade marks include the name Coca Cola, the characteristic shape of the Coca Cola bottle, and the large M that serves to advertise McDonalds hamburger outlets. Microsoft is a trade mark as are the names of many Microsoft products such as Outlook.

Provision is made for registering trade marks and most trade marks are now registered. In the UK this is done through the UK Intellectual Property Office (UKIPO). The UKIPO maintains a database of registered trade marks and their owners that can be searched over the internet. Trade marks are associated with particular classes of products so that it is quite possible for the same trade mark to belong to several different owners because each has registered it for a different class of product. They are also specific to the jurisdiction in which they are registered, so a trade mark registered in the UK is not protected in the USA unless it is also registered there. There are comprehensive rules limiting what can be registered as a trade mark. For example, trade marks must not describe the service or product being sold nor must they be offensive.

The primary purpose of trade mark legislation is to stop the sale of bogus or counterfeit goods, that is, goods that claim to have been produced by someone other than the actual producer. There is, for example, a flourishing trade in luxury goods that imitate the products of such well-known houses as Gucci or Rolex.

The 1994 Act makes it an offence to

- apply an unauthorised registered trade mark (that is, a registered trade mark that you do not own or do not have the owner's permission to use) to goods;

- sell or offer for sale (or hire), goods or packaging which bear an unauthorised trade mark;

- import or export goods that bear an unauthorised trade mark;

- have in the course of business, goods for sale or hire goods (or packaging) which bear an unauthorised trade mark.

In other words, anyone who sells or imports goods bearing an unauthorised trade mark, such as Gucci or Rolex, will be in breach of the Act. In most circumstances, the offence will be criminal and punishable by a fine or up to two years imprisonment. However, the trade mark owner can also bring civil proceedings to claim for the financial damage he may have suffered.

Under the General Agreement on Tariffs and Trade (GATT), to which most countries are signatories, countries that do not have suitable laws to protect trade marks (or intellectual property rights more generally) or where such laws are not effectively enforced will face trade sanctions. It is hoped that this will stamp out the flagrant piracy that exists at present.

Trade marks are an effective way of protecting retail package software from piracy. Given, however, that pirated software can be distributed over the internet with no physical packaging, it is desirable to display the trade mark prominently when the software is loaded, as well as displaying it on the packaging. This means that anyone who sells pirated copies of the software will be in breach of the Act and subject to its penalties, since the software will display the trade mark without authorisation. It also means that anyone who applies someone else's trade mark to software they have written will also be in breach of the Act.

Even where a trade mark is not registered, action can be taken in the civil courts against products that imitate the appearance or 'get up' of an existing product. This is known as 'passing off'. However, it is usually better to register the trade mark than to rely on protection under civil law, because the legal action involved in defending it will be much more straightforward.

11.7 DOMAIN NAMES

Internet domain names are ultimately managed by the Internet Corporation for Assigned Names and Numbers (ICANN). ICANN is an internationally organised, non-profit making corporation, with headquarters in Los Angeles; it was founded in 1998. Its main responsibility is ensuring the 'universal resolvability' of internet addresses, that is, ensuring that the same domain name will always lead to the same internet location wherever it is used from and whatever the circumstances. In practice, ICANN delegates the responsibility for assigning individual domain names to other bodies, subject to strict rules.

Domain names were originally meant to be used just as a means of simplifying the process of connecting one computer to another over the internet. However, because they are easy to remember, they have come to be used as a way of identifying businesses. Indeed, they are frequently used in advertising. Conversely, it is not surprising that companies should want to use their trade marks or their company names as their internet domain names.

The potential for conflict between trade marks and domain names is inherent in the two systems. Trade marks are registered with public authorities on a national or regional basis. The owner of the trade mark acquires rights over the use of the trade mark in a specific country or region. Identical trade marks may be owned by different persons in respect of different categories of product. Domain names are usually allocated by a non-governmental organisation and are globally unique; they are normally allocated on a first come, first served basis. This means that if different companies own identical trade marks for different categories of product or for different geographical areas, only one of them can have the trade mark as domain name, and that will be the first to apply.

The inconsistencies between the two different systems of registration have made it possible for people to register, as their own domain names, trade marks belonging to other companies. This is sometimes known as **cyber squatting**. They then offer to sell these domain names to the owner of the trade mark at an inflated price. It is usually cheaper and quicker for the trade mark owner to pay up than to pursue legal remedies, even when these are available.

In 1999, WIPO published a report entitled *The management of internet names and addresses: intellectual property issues*. WIPO is an international organisation with 177 states as members. The report recommended that ICANN adopt a policy called the Uniform Domain Name Dispute Resolution Policy (UDRP), which includes specific provisions against cyber squatting. This policy has proved reasonably effective. Within two years, over 3,000 complaints had been dealt with by one of the arbitration centres alone, with 80 per cent being resolved.

In 2001, WIPO published a second report, *The recognition of rights and the use of names in the internet domain system*. This addresses conflicts between domain names and identifiers other than trade marks. Examples of such conflicts are the use of personal names in domain names or the use of the names of particular peoples or geographic areas by organisations that have no connection with them. These conflicts are more difficult to deal with than conflicts between trade marks and domain names because the international framework that underlies trade marks is missing in these other cases.

FURTHER READING

The UK Intellectual Property Office contains a great deal of information about intellectual property in a readily accessible form, including the Hargreaves Report:
www.ipo.gov.uk

The two reports on domain name issues produced by WIPO can be found at:
http://wipo2.wipo.int

Fairly comprehensive discussion of the cases described in the section on copyright can be found at the following addresses:

Cantor Fitzgerald v. *Tradition (UK)*
http://rpc.oxfordjournals.org/content/117/4-5.toc

Access to the full text is only available through subscribing institutions. A summary of the judgement can be found at:
www.humphreys.co.uk/articles/software_1.htm

Navitaire Inc. v. *easyJet and Bulletproof Technologies Inc.*
www.5rb.com/docs/Navitaire-v-Easyjet%20Airline%20Co%2030%20Jul%202004.pdf

Oracle Corp v. *SAP AG*
http://en.wikipedia.org/wiki/Oracle_Corporation_v._SAP_AG

The report of the Mid-Staffordshire NHS Foundation Trust Public Enquiry (the Francis report):
www.midstaffspublicinquiry.com/report

Intellectual property rights in software are highly controversial and it is very easy to be misled by material found on the web. Much of this material, on both sides of the argument, is biased, selective, misleading or just plain wrong. Even when an article is objective and accurate, it will often be misleading because it fails to state explicitly to which jurisdiction it is referring or to what point in time.

A clear statement of the position regarding software patents in the USA can be found at:
www.bitlaw.com/software-patent/index.html

In particular, the following page gives an excellent description of the confused situation as it stood at the beginning of 2012:
www.bitlaw.com/software-patent/bilski-and-software-patents.html

12 SOFTWARE CONTRACTS AND LICENCES

After studying this chapter, you should:

- understand the purpose of contracts in the computer industry and the different types of contractual arrangement that are commonly used;
- be familiar with the main issues that such contracts address;
- understand the different types of liability for defective software that can arise and the factors that affect these.

12.1 WHAT IS A CONTRACT?

A contract is simply an agreement between two or more persons (the parties to the contract) that can be enforced in a court of law. The parties involved may be legal persons or natural persons. There is no specific form for a contract; in particular, in England and Wales a contract need not be written down. The following are essential:

- All the parties must intend to make a contract.
- All the parties must be competent to make a contract, that is, they must be old enough and of sufficiently sound mind to understand what they are doing.
- There must be a 'consideration', that is, each party must be receiving something and providing something.

Contract law is largely based on common law. It has a long history and is well adapted to handling the disputes that arise in fulfilling commercial agreements.

The existing contract law showed itself perfectly adequate to handle contracts for the supply of computers, software and associated services. However, the coming of the internet and ecommerce has created a need for new provisions to deal with such matters as electronic signatures and which country's laws should govern transactions made over the internet when the parties to the transaction are in different countries.

In this chapter we shall not be very much concerned with the law relating to contracts. We shall be much more concerned with what should go into contracts for providing software and services in different circumstances and with issues of liability when software fails.

12.2 LICENCE AGREEMENTS

It is very unusual for customer to 'buy' software in the strict sense of the word 'buy'. As was said in the last chapter, what is usually bought is a copy of the software together with a licence to use it in certain ways. There are two main types of licence, although there are innumerable variants of each:

- **Retail** software is software aimed at a mass market and selling for a one-off fee of a few tens or hundreds of pounds per copy. Large organisations can usually negotiate bulk licences for multiple copies at a considerable discount and in some cases site licences may be offered covering all computers on a given site. The licence is usually granted *in perpetuity* (that is, for ever).The licence offers no provision for updates or corrections to be supplied nor for any support to the user, except possibly a help line. If a new version is required, in order to interface with new versions of other software perhaps or to run on an upgraded platform, the user must buy it from scratch.

- **Corporate** software is software aimed at large organisations. It is often quite specialised and may be aimed at a market with fewer than 100 customers, although some packages, such as those for human resources management and customer relationship management, may have many thousands of customers. There is typically a substantial up-front licence fee of several tens or hundreds of thousands of pounds together with an annual charge of some 20 per cent of the initial fee, which may be described as a maintenance charge. The fees may well depend on usage: the annual fee for a payroll package, for example, will usually depend on the number of employees while that for a computer-aided design package will depend on the maximum number of simultaneous users. In return for these not inconsiderable charges, the customer gets help with the initial installation and configuration, regular upgrades (including those necessary to comply with legislative changes) and an efficient and responsive help line. There may well be a user group. Training and consultancy are available but the fees are high; suppliers of this sort of software rely on such incidental income to maintain their profitability.

Software licences are usually long and complicated. Many of their provisions are intended to protect the supplier in situations that are fairly unlikely to occur. Some of them may be unenforceable in the UK because of provisions in the Unfair Contract Terms Act 1977, which is discussed in the section below on contracts for bespoke software.

Open-source licences for software allow anyone to use the source code and other design material, either in its original form or after modification, subject to certain conditions. Software covered by an open-source licence is usually, but not invariably, available free of charge. Typical conditions to be found in open-source licences include requirements to keep the names of the authors and a statement of copyright in the code and only to re-distribute the software under identical licence conditions; the latter requirement prevents code that was acquired free from being redistributed for profit. The Open Source Initiative, which was launched in 1998, exists to promote software licensed in this way. Closely related to open-source software is 'free software', a concept promoted by the Free Software Foundation, established by Richard Stallman in 1985 to support the GNU project. The OSI and the Free Software Foundation have been successful in getting free or open-source software accepted and widely used. The underlying ideological principles that motivate, and separate, the two movements have not, however, achieved the same degree of acceptance.

A completely different type of licence is a marketing licence. Companies that produce software packages frequently do not have the resources or expertise to market the software outside their own countries and they therefore license agents to sell it for them in other countries. Computer games are usually produced by fairly small companies that have no capacity to market their games. Marketing licences are normally granted for a fixed period; they may be restricted to a specified geographical area or to specific types of platform. Thus a UK company that produces an HR (human resources) package may grant a licence to an Australian company to market the package in Australia and New Zealand for a period of two years. The marketing company agrees to pay the supplier a fixed percentage of the income it receives from each sale of the package. At the end of the two-year period, the supplier may choose to renew the licence, if sales have been satisfactory, or it may look for a new agent in the hope of increasing sales. Marketing licences may be exclusive, that is, they stipulate that no other company will be allowed to market the software in the prescribed geographical area. Exclusive licences generally encourage the marketing company to market the product more energetically than they would do if other companies were competing to sell the same product in the same area.

12.3 OUTSOURCING

IT outsourcing contracts are inherently complex and depend very much on individual circumstances. It is not appropriate to go into detail here about such contracts but the following is a list of just some of the points that need to be addressed:

- How is performance to be monitored and managed?

- What happens if performance is unsatisfactory:

- Which assets are being transferred? It is often the case that the customer outsourcing its IT operations already has equipment and software and that it wishes the supplier to take this over. It is important to agree on precisely what is to be transferred.

- Very often IT staff will be transferred to the supplier. How this is to be done is covered by the TUPE regulations, discussed in Chapter 9 in the section on takeovers and outsourcing.

- Audit rights. The customer needs to ensure that both its external auditors and its internal auditors have adequate access rights to be able to fulfil their duties.

- Contingency planning and disaster recovery.

- Ownership of the intellectual property rights in software developed during the contract.

- Duration of the agreement and termination provisions.

The first two items above are key element in IT outsourcing and are often treated as a separate agreement known as a **service level agreement**.

Related to outsourcing is the provision of application services over the internet using a client-server system with a remote server. This is an instance of what is commonly known as 'cloud computing'. It is not a new idea. Payroll services have been provided in this way since the late 1960s. Because of the provisions of the Data Protection Act 1998, it is important to ensure that all the servers potentially involved meet the EU data protection requirements described in Chapter 13, in particular the eighth data protection principle.

12.4 CONTRACTS FOR BESPOKE SOFTWARE

Although private individuals normally buy software by purchasing a licence for a standard package and then, possibly, configuring it to meet their needs, commercial organisations quite commonly want to purchase a system configured specifically to meet its needs. Such systems are known as **tailor-made** or **bespoke** systems. A bespoke system may consist of a single PC equipped with a word processor, a spreadsheet, and a set of macros adapted to the customer's needs or it may consist of several thousand PCs spread across 50 offices in different parts of the world, connected by a wide-area network, with large database servers and a million lines of specially written software.

Contracts for bespoke software are often long and complicated. We shall describe here only the main points of such a contract, as they affect the information systems staff likely to be involved, whether on the client side or the supplier side.

12.4.1 What is to be produced

It is clearly necessary that the contract states what is to be produced. Information systems engineers will be familiar with the problems of producing requirements specifications. A specification sets out the detailed requirements of the client. Ideally, the specification should be complete, consistent and accurate and set out all that the client wants to be done in the performance of the contract. Unfortunately, we know that it is very difficult to achieve this ideal standard and, even if we succeed, the requirements of the client may evolve as the contract proceeds, and sometimes the changes may be substantial. How are these changes to be accommodated by a contract which, in a sense, freezes the requirements of the parties to those at one particular time by incorporating the original specification into the contract? The answer is that the contract should provide a procedure for making variations to the specification or job description, then follow this through by providing a method of calculating payment for work done to facilitate the changes, and also perhaps provide for a variation of the level of anticipated performance, and maybe also vary the method of acceptance testing. In other words, the contract should anticipate events and provide an agreed formula for modification.

Producing software for a client is not, usually, a matter of simply handing over the text of a program which does what is required. It is important, therefore, that the contract states what precisely is to be provided. The following is a non-exhaustive list of possibilities:

- source code;
- command files for building the executable code from the source and for installing it;

- documentation of the design and of the code;
- reference manuals, training manuals and operations manuals;
- software tools to help maintain the code;
- user training;
- training for the client's maintenance staff;
- test data and test results.

Alongside the issues of what is to be produced, there is the question of the standards to be used. The supplier is likely to have company standards, methods of working, quality assurance procedures, etc. and will normally prefer to use these. More sophisticated clients will have their own procedures and may require that these be adhered to. In some cases, the supplier may be required to allow the client to apply quality control procedures to the project. The contract must specify which is to apply.

12.4.2 Intellectual property rights

When an organisation commissions bespoke (that is, tailor-made) software from another company, it is important that both sides think carefully about the licensing and ownership of the copyright in the software produced. There was a time when the customer would expect to take ownership of the copyright in all the software supplied. This is no longer realistic. Parts of the software supplied are likely to be proprietary products that the supplier has developed to enable him to construct such systems quickly and efficiently; they are part of his fixed assets and it would be absurd to transfer ownership of them to a customer. Other parts of the software may be products acquired from other sources (possibly open source software) and the supplier will not have the right to assign copyright in them. The customer's needs can almost certainly be satisfied by a suitable licence. However, the customer must take into account the long-term need for maintenance and ensure that he has the right, for example, to give another contractor access to the source code and documentation for maintenance purposes.

It is important that the contract should also state just what legal rights are being passed by the software house to the client under the contract. Ownership in physical items such as books, documents or discs will usually pass from the software house to the client, but intellectual property rights, discussed in the previous chapter, present more problems. It is important for the contract to state precisely who is to own these rights.

A related topic is confidentiality. It is almost inevitable that, when a major bespoke software system is being developed, the two parties will acquire confidential information about each other. The commissioning client may well have to pass confidential information about its business operations to the software house. On the other side of the coin, the software house may not want the client to divulge to others details of the program content or other information gleaned about its operations by the client. It is usual in these circumstances for each party to promise to maintain the confidentiality of the other's secrets, and for express terms to that effect to be included in the contract.

12.4.3 Management of the contract

It is important that each party should understand the framework for making decisions relating to the contract and the mechanism by which these decisions will be agreed and recorded. Failure in this respect is ultimately responsible for most of the contractual wrangles that affect software contracts. Each party needs to know who, of the other party's staff, has day to day responsibility for the work and what the limits of that person's authority are. Each party should therefore be required party to nominate, in writing, a Project Manager. The Project Managers must have at least the authority necessary to fulfil the obligations which the contract places on them. It is particularly important that the limits of their financial authority are explicitly stated, i.e. the extent to which they can authorise changes to the cost of the contract.

Regular progress meetings are essential to the successful completion of a fixed price contract and the contract should require that they are held. The minutes of progress meetings, duly approved and signed, should have contractual significance in that they constitute evidence that milestones have been reached (so that stage payments become due) and that delay payments have been agreed.

In almost all cases where work is being carried out for a specific client, the client will have to fulfil certain obligations if the contract is to be completed successfully. The following is a (non-exhaustive) list of possibilities:

- provide documentation on aspects of the client's activities or the environment in which the system will run;
- provide access to appropriate members of staff;
- provide machine facilities for development and testing;
- provide accommodation, telephone and secretarial facilities for the company's staff when working on the client's premises;
- provide data communications facilities to the site.

A particular difficulty may arise if the client does not provide critical information on time, since this can lead to delays that cost the contractor money. The contract should provide a clear mechanism for calculating payments due for such delays. A similar mechanism will be required for calculating extra payments due when the client requests changes at a late stage – a very common occurrence.

Delay payments and payments for variations to the original requirements are, perhaps, the commonest cause of contractual disputes, not only in software engineering but in most other contracting industries - the construction industry is a notorious example. One reason for this is that competitive bidding for fixed price contracts often means that the profit margin on the original contract is very low so that companies seek to make their profit on these additional payments.

12.4.4 Acceptance procedure

Acceptance procedures are a critical part of any fixed price contract for they provide the criteria by which successful completion of the contract is judged. The essence of the acceptance procedure is that the client should provide a fixed set of acceptance tests and expected results and that successful performance of these tests shall constitute acceptance of the system. The tests must be provided at or before the start of the acceptance procedure; within reason, there may be as many tests as the client wishes but extra tests cannot be added once the test set has been handed over. The purpose of this restriction is to ensure that the acceptance procedure can be completed in reasonable time.

Other points to be addressed under this heading include who shall be present when the tests are carried out and what happens if the tests are not completed successfully.

12.4.5 Termination of the contract

There are many reasons why it may become necessary to terminate a contract before it has been completed. It is not uncommon, for example, for the client to be taken over by another company which already has a system of the type being developed, or for a change in policy on the part of the client to mean that the system is no longer relevant to its needs. It is essential, therefore, that the contract make provision for terminating the work in an amicable manner. This usually means that the supplier is to be paid for all the work carried out up to the point where the contract is terminated, together with some compensation for the time needed to redeploy staff on other revenue earning work. The question of ownership of the work so far carried out must also be addressed.

12.5 CONTRACTS FOR CONSULTANCY AND CONTRACT HIRE

Contract hire is an arrangement in which the supplier agrees to supply the customer with the services of a certain number of staff at agreed daily or hourly charge rates. The customer takes responsibility for managing the staff concerned. Either party can terminate the arrangement at fairly short notice, typically one week, either in respect of a particular person or as a whole. The supplier's responsibility is limited to providing suitably competent people and replacing them if they become unavailable or are adjudged unsuitable by the client.

Because the supplier's involvement and responsibility are so much less than in a fixed price contract, the contract for such an arrangement is usually fairly simple. Payment is on the basis of a fixed rate for each man day worked; the rate depends on the experience and qualifications of the staff. Issues such as delay payments, acceptance tests and many others simply do not arise; however, as mentioned earlier, ownership of intellectual property rights generated in the course of the work must be addressed.

Contract hire is sometimes referred to disparagingly as 'body shopping'. Closely related are the freelance agreements under which individuals sell their own services to clients on a basis similar to contract hire.

Consultancy is essentially an up-market version of contract hire. Consultants are experts who are called in by an organisation to assess some aspect of its operations or its strategy and to make proposals for improvements. This means that the end product of a consultancy project is usually a report or other document.

Consultancy projects are usually undertaken for a fixed price but the form of contract is very much simpler than the fixed price contracts so far described. There are two reasons for this. First, the sums of money are comparatively small and neither side stands to lose a great deal. Second, although it is possible to demonstrate beyond doubt that a piece of software does not work correctly and thus that the supplier has failed to fulfil the contract, it is not usually possible to demonstrate unequivocally that a report fails to fulfil a contract. The client has to rely on the desire of the supplier to maintain a professional reputation and in practice this usually proves sufficient to ensure that the work is of an acceptable standard.

There are four important aspects of a consultancy contract:

- Confidentiality. Consultants are often in a position to learn a lot about the companies for which they carry out assignments and may well be in a position to misuse this information for their own profit.

- Terms of reference. It is important that the contract refers explicitly to the terms of reference of the consultancy team and, in practice, these are perhaps the most common source of disagreements in consultancy projects. As a result of their initial investigations, the consultants may discover that they need to consider matters which were outside their original terms of reference but the client may be unwilling to let this happen, for any one of a number of possible reasons.

- Liability. Most consultants will wish to limit their liability for any loss that the customer suffers as a result of following their advice. Customers may not be happy to accept this and, in some cases, may insist on verifying that the consultant has adequate professional liability insurance, that is, insurance to cover damages that might be imposed by a court for any professional failure.

- Who has control over the final version of the report. It is common practice for the contract to require that a draft version of the final report be presented to the client. The client is given a fixed period to review the report and ask for changes. The revised version that is then submitted by the consultant should be the final version.

A time and materials contract (often referred to as a 'cost plus' contract) is somewhere between a contract hire agreement and a fixed price contract. The supplier agrees to undertake the development of the software in much the same way as in a fixed price contract but payment is made on the basis of the costs incurred, with labour charged in the same way as for contract hire. The supplier is not committed to completing the work for a fixed price, although a maximum payment may be fixed beyond which the project may be reviewed. Many of the complications of fixed price contracts still occur with time and materials contracts – ownership of rights, facilities to be provided by the client, progress monitoring arrangements, for instance – but others, such as delay payments and acceptance testing do not; this is not to say that no acceptance testing is done, only that it has no contractual significance since nothing contractual depends on its outcome.

It may be wondered why any client should prefer a time and materials contract to a fixed price contract – surely it is better to have a contract which guarantees performance for a fixed price rather than one in which the price is indeterminate and there is no guarantee of completion? In the first place, it often happens that the work to be carried out is not sufficiently well specified for any supplier to be prepared to offer a fixed price; part of the supplier's task will be to discover what is required and to specify it in detail. Secondly, a supplier always loads a fixed price contract with a contingency allowance, to allow for the risk that unexpected factors will cause the project to require more resources than originally estimated. If all goes well, the supplier makes an extra profit; this is the reward for risk taken. By accepting a time and materials contract, this risk and the possibility of extra profit (in the form of a lower cost) are effectively transferred to the client, who also avoids the dangers of having to pay excessive sums to have minor changes incorporated into the specification. All this having been said, it remains the case that there has been a strong movement away from time and materials towards fixed price, noticeably in the defence field.

12.6 LIABILITY FOR DEFECTIVE SOFTWARE

Suppliers of software and hardware are very reluctant to give a contractual commitment that it is fit for any purpose whatsoever. Standard terms and conditions will invariably contain a clause that tries to limit the supplier's liability if it turns out that the software or hardware is defective. The law, however, limits how far such clauses can be effective.

Most contracts will limit the extent of any liability either to the purchase price of the product or to some fixed maximum figure. This means that, if the product completely fails to work, the supplier agrees to refund the purchase price or possibly a bit more if some other maximum is specified.

The Unfair Contract Terms Act 1977 restricts the extent to which clauses in standard terms and conditions limiting liability can be effective. In particular, it is not possible to limit the damages payable if a defect in the product causes death or personal injury. This applies as much to software as it does to motor vehicles, say. Thus if a company supplies software to control a light railway link and a defect in the software leads to an accident in which people are killed or injured, then any clause in the contract for the supply of that software that claims to restrict liability will not be enforceable in respect of the claims for damages for the deaths and injuries.

This restriction is an important one for companies that produce safety critical software and it also led at least one hardware supplier to refuse to sell its products to the nuclear industry. However, although this is very relevant when buying, say, a motor car, it is not very relevant to most individuals or companies when dealing with software, because the software that they use or develop is very unlikely to cause death or personal industry. They are much more likely to be concerned about software that doesn't do what it was claimed to do or that has too many bugs to be usable.

At this point we need to distinguish between consumer sales and non-consumer sales. For a sale to be treated as a consumer sale, the buyer must be a private person; the buyer must buy from a seller who is acting in the course of a business; and the goods must be of a type ordinarily supplied for private use or consumption. In a consumer sale, the requirements of the Sale of Goods Act 1979 and the Supply of Goods and Services Act 1982 cannot be excluded. The most important requirement of the Sale of Goods Act in the context of software is that goods sold must be fit for the purpose for which such goods are commonly supplied. This means, for example, that if you buy a printer for use on your computer at home, it must be capable of printing reliably and clearly, at a usable speed.

There is, unfortunately, a problem about software. Because software is intangible, it has never been satisfactorily decided whether or not it comes under the definition of 'goods' and hence it is not clear whether the Sale of Goods Act 1979 applies to the sale of software. It was generally thought that it applied to the sale of retail software or software sold under 'shrink-wrapped' licences, that is, licences that are deemed to come into operation when the package containing the disk on which the software is supplied is opened. However, with the coming of the internet, software is typically downloaded and users are asked to tick a box saying that they accept the licence conditions. It is not at all clear that the Sale of Goods Act applies in such cases. Instead, they would come under the Supply of Goods and Services Act 1982. This only requires that 'reasonable skill and care' has been used. This is a very difficult test to apply and, in practice, provides little protection.

The Unfair Contract Terms Act 1977 again comes to the rescue. Whether or not the sale is a consumer sale, it allows liability to be limited or excluded only to the extent that it is reasonable to do so.

A COURT CASE

The view that a court will take depends very much on the circumstances of a particular case but a particularly illuminating example is the 1996 case of *St Albans City and District Council v International Computers Ltd (ICL)*. The facts were that the council had ordered a computer system from ICL to enable it to compute the Community Charge (a system of local taxation that is no longer in use) for the forthcoming year. ICL insisted on using its standard terms and conditions which stated that its liability 'will not exceed the price or charge payable for the item of Equipment, Program or Service in respect of which liability arises or £100,000 (whichever is the lesser). . .'. Errors in the software and incorrect advice from ICL's project manager meant that the population of the area was overestimated, so the residents were undercharged and the council lost £1.3 million.

The judge at the initial hearing found that the software was not fit for the purpose for which it was provided and that ICL's project manager had been negligent. ICL was therefore in breach of contract. The clause limiting liability had to be measured against the requirement of reasonableness. The judge noted that ICL was a substantial organisation with world-wide product liability insurance of £50 million; that all potential suppliers of the system dealt on similar standard terms; that the council was under pressure to install the system before the Community Charge was introduced; that although the council was a business and not a consumer, that it did not usually operate in the same commercial field as a normal business and that it would be impractical for it to insure against commercial risks. On balance, the judge found that the clause limiting liability to £100,000 was not reasonable and was therefore ineffective. ICL appealed, but the Court of Appeal confirmed the judgement. However, the value of this case as a precedent will be limited, for each case turns on its facts.

12.7 HEALTH AND SAFETY

The Health and Safety at Work Act (1974) completely changed the approach to safety in Britain. European thinking was also affected by the Act and there has been fruitful exchange of ideas.

It is not appropriate to go into detail about the provisions of the Act here but it is important to understand the implications that the Act has for information systems engineers. The Act states 'It shall be the duty of every employer to ensure, so far as is reasonably practicable, the health, safety and welfare at work of all his employees'. It breaks this duty up into a number of more specific duties; the ones that are of particular concern to software engineers are as follows:

- provision and maintenance of safe plant;
- provision and maintenance of safe systems of work;
- provision of such information, instruction, training, and supervision as necessary;
- ensuring the workplace is maintained in a safe condition; and
- provision and maintenance of a safe working environment and adequate welfare arrangements.

The Act also requires employers to ensure that their activities do not expose the general public to risks to their health and safety. Manufacturers of equipment to be used at work also have a responsibility to ensure that it is safe.

Failure to comply with the Health and Safety at Work Act is a criminal offence and, in serious cases, can lead to criminal proceedings being taken against individuals.

Trains, ships and aeroplanes are all places where people work and where the general public are present. The safety obligations listed above therefore apply to them. Furthermore, they all involve equipment that is controlled by software and accidents may occur as a result of defects in that software.

Modern manufacturing plant is usually software-controlled and can be dangerous; robots in particular can be dangerous for people working with them. Modern chemical plants, oil refineries and power stations, especially nuclear ones, are all software-controlled and software failures can result in accidents that affect not only the workforce but also the general public.

This book is not the appropriate place to discuss how software is or should be written in order to meet the high levels of reliability required for safety-related applications. You should understand clearly, however, that there is an extensive literature on the subject and that there are national and international standards relating to it. An organisation that undertakes to develop safety-related software without employing staff who are familiar with the appropriate development techniques is likely to be in breach of the Health and Safety at Work Act. The following clauses in the BCS Code of Conduct (and similar clauses in other codes) are of particular relevance in this area:

> You shall:
>
> 1a have due regard for public health, privacy, security and wellbeing of others and the environment.
>
> 2a only undertake to do work or provide a service that is within your professional competence.
>
> 2b NOT claim any level of competence that you do not possess.
>
> 2c develop your professional knowledge, skills and competence on a continuing basis, maintaining awareness of technological developments, procedures, and standards that are relevant to your field.
>
> 2d ensure that you have the knowledge and understanding of Legislation and that you comply with such Legislation, in carrying out your professional responsibilities.

FURTHER READING

The Open Source Initiative:
    http://opensource.org

The Free Software Foundation:
    www.fsf.org

The Gnu project:
    www.gnu.org/

The following book, from the BCS/Springer Practitioner series, covers IT outsourcing in depth and is written specifically for information systems professionals. It contains a chapter dedicated to contractual matters:
    Sparrow, E. (2003) *Successful IT outsourcing*. Springer Verlag, London.

Fuller coverage of the material in this chapter, including health and safety issues, can be found in Chapters 5, 9 and 10 of the following book:
    Bott, M.F., Coleman, J.A., Eaton, J., and Rowland, D. (2000) *Professional issues in software engineering*, 3rd ed. Taylor and Francis, London.

13 DATA PROTECTION, PRIVACY AND FREEDOM OF INFORMATION

After studying this chapter, you should:

- *be able to identify situations in which legislation relating to data protection, privacy and freedom of information is likely to impose obligations on you;*

- *understand, in straightforward cases, what your obligations in respect of data protection, privacy and freedom of information are;*

- *be able to recognise more complicated situations, in which you need to ask for expert advice.*

13.1 BACKGROUND

Public concern about data protection was first aroused when it was realised that a very large amount of data about individuals was being collected and stored in computers and then used for purposes that were different from those intended when the data was collected, and unacceptable. There were also concerns that unauthorised people could access such data and that the data might be out of date, incomplete or just plain wrong. These concerns surfaced in the 1970s. They were particularly strong in the UK and the rest of Europe, and led to a Council of Europe Convention on the subject. The first UK Data Protection Act, passed in 1984, was designed to implement the provisions of the Convention. It was designed to protect individuals from:

- the use of inaccurate personal information or information that is incomplete or irrelevant;

- the use of personal information by unauthorised persons;

- the use of personal information for purposes other than that for which it was collected.

It was meant primarily to protect individuals against the misuse of personal data by large organisations, public or private. Such misuse might occur, for example, if data-matching techniques are used on credit card records to build up a picture of a person's movements over an extended period. Further, errors can often creep into data that has been collected or data may be interpreted in a misleading way, and it was difficult to persuade the holders of the data to correct these. For example, credit rating agencies might advise against giving a person a loan because someone who previously lived at the same address defaulted on a loan.

By the mid-1990s, a different danger had become apparent. As individuals began to use the internet for an ever wider range of purposes, it became possible to capture information about the way individuals use the internet and to build profiles of their habits that could be used for marketing purposes and also, perhaps, for more sinister purposes such as blackmail. What is more, this can be done by much smaller and much shadowier organisations than those that were the object of the 1984 Act. These and other concerns led in 1995 to the European Directive on Data Protection which, in turn, led to the 1998 Data Protection Act.

A related but more general concern is that of individual privacy. Most people feel that they are entitled to keep personal information, such as their bank balance, their medical history or how they vote in elections, private. This extends to other things that don't obviously fall under the heading of information – personal correspondence, phone calls, or photographs taken on private occasions, for example. UK law does not recognise any general right to privacy but the European Convention on Human Rights, which forms part of UK law, states, in section 8(1), 'Everyone has the right to respect for his private and family life, his home and his correspondence.' Concern over telephone tapping and email monitoring, by employers as much as by the security services, led to the Regulation of Investigatory Powers Act (2000).

Although most people will accept that individuals have a right to privacy, they do not feel that this should extend to governments. Governments are traditionally reluctant to release information to their citizens, even when no question of security arises. There have been many cases where governments appear to have kept information secret in order to avoid acknowledging their responsibilities or compensating individuals for government mistakes. As a result, there has been pressure for more open government and for legislation that will guarantee freedom of information. Australia, Canada, the US and a few other countries enacted such legislation in the 1970s and 1980s. In the UK it had to wait for the passing of the Freedom of Information Act 2000. Many countries still have no legislation in this area.

(You should notice that the terms **data** and **information** are used in a very confused way in UK legislation and you should not read any significance into the use of one rather than the other!)

13.2 DATA PROTECTION

As we have seen, the first UK legislation on data protection was the 1984 Data Protection Act. However, this was superseded by the 1998 Act and it is on this that we shall base our discussion.

13.2.1 Terminology

The Act defines a number of terms that are widely used in discussions of data protection issues. In some cases these are different from the terms used in the 1984 Act.

Data means information (!) that is being processed automatically or is collected with that intention or is recorded as part of a relevant filing system (see below).

Data controller means a person who determines why or how personal data is processed. This may be a legal person or a natural person.

Data processor, in this context, means anyone who processes personal data on behalf of the data controller and who is not an employee of the data controller. This might include an application service provider, such as a company that provides online hotel booking services.

Personal data means data that relates to a living person who can be identified from data, possibly taken together with other information the data controller is likely to have (but see the subsection below on the scope of the Act). It includes expressions of opinion about the person and indications of the intentions of the data controller or any other person towards the individual (for example, whether their manager is planning to promote them).

Data subject means the individual who is the subject of personal data.

Sensitive personal data means personal data relating to the racial or ethnic origin of data subjects, their political opinions, their religious beliefs, whether they are members of trade unions, their physical or mental health, their sexual life, or whether they have committed or are alleged to have committed any criminal offence. The rules regarding the processing of sensitive personal data are stricter than for other personal data.

Processing means obtaining, recording or holding the information or data or carrying out any operations on it,

including:

a.   organisation, adaptation or alteration of the information or data,
b.   retrieval, consultation or use of the information or data,
c.   disclosure of the information or data by transmission, dissemination or otherwise making available, or
d.   alignment, combination, blocking, erasure or destruction of the information or data.

This is an extremely comprehensive list and it is difficult to imagine anything that one might do to personal data that is not included within it.

13.2.2 Data protection principles

The 1998 Act lays down eight **data protection principles**, which apply to the collection and processing of personal data of any sort. Data controllers are responsible for ensuring that these principles are complied with in respect of all the personal data for which they are responsible.

First data protection principle

Personal data shall be processed fairly and lawfully and in particular shall not be processed unless (a) at least one of the conditions in Schedule 2 is met and (b) in the case of sensitive personal data, at least one of the conditions in Schedule 3 is also met.

The most significant condition in Schedule 2 of the Act is that the data subject has given his consent. If this is not the case, then the data can only be processed if the data controller is under a legal or statutory obligation for which the processing is necessary.

For processing sensitive personal information, Schedule 3 requires that the data subject has given explicit consent. The difference between 'consent' and 'explicit consent' is not spelt out in the Act. In either case, existing case law suggests that something more positive than, for example, failing to tick an opt-out box when ordering a product is required. 'Explicit consent' almost certainly requires the nature of the likely processing and any likely disclosure to be made explicit to the data subject before he or she gives consent.

The requirement for consent was first introduced in the 1998 Act; it was not required by the earlier Act. One consequence of the change is that, because cookies may be used to gather personal data, it is now necessary to inform users of a website explicitly if it uses cookies and to give them the opportunity of refusing to accept them.

This principle requires that the processing of personal data is fair. The courts have ruled that establishing a person's credit rating only on the basis of their address constitutes unfair processing.

Second data protection principle

> Personal data shall be obtained only for one or more specified and lawful purposes, and shall not be further processed in any manner incompatible with that purpose or those purposes.

Data controllers must notify the Information Commissioner of the personal data they are collecting and the purposes for which it is being collected.

Third data protection principle

> Personal data shall be adequate, relevant and not excessive in relation to the purpose or purposes for which they are processed.

Many violations of this principle are due to ignorance rather than to intent to behave in a way contrary to the Act. Local government has a bad record of compliance with this principle, for example requiring people wanting to join a public library to state their marital status. Shops that demand to know customers' addresses when goods are not being delivered are also likely to be in breach of this principle.

Fourth data protection principle

> Personal data shall be accurate and, where necessary, kept up to date.

Although this principle is admirable, it can be extremely difficult to comply with. In the UK, doctors have great difficulty in maintaining up-to-date data about their patients' addresses, particularly patients who are students, because students change their addresses frequently and rarely remember to tell their doctor. Universities have similar difficulties.

Fifth data protection principle

Personal data processed for any purpose or purposes shall not be kept for longer than is necessary for that purpose or those purposes.

This principle raises more difficulties than might be expected:

- It is necessary to establish how long each item of personal data needs to be kept. Auditors will require that financial data is kept for seven years. Action in the civil courts can be initiated up to six years after the events complained of took place so that it may be prudent to hold data for this length of time. It is appropriate to keep some personal data indefinitely (e.g. university records of graduating students). In all cases, the purpose for which the data is kept must be included in the purposes for which it was collected;
- Procedures to ensure that all data is erased at the appropriate time are needed, and this must include erasure from backup copies.

Sixth data protection principle

Personal data shall be processed in accordance with the rights of data subjects under this Act.

The rights of data subjects are discussed in the next subsection.

Seventh data protection principle

Appropriate technical and organisational measures shall be taken against unauthorised or unlawful processing of personal data and against accidental loss or destruction of, or damage to, personal data.

Of the eight principles this is the one that has the most substantial operational impact. It implies the need for access control (through passwords or other means), backup procedures, integrity checks on the data, vetting of personnel who have access to the data and so on.

Eighth data protection principle

Personal data shall not be transferred to a country or territory outside the European Economic Area unless that country or territory ensures an adequate level of protection for the rights and freedoms of data subjects in relation to the processing of personal data.

This means that companies operating in the EU are not allowed to send personal data to countries outside the European Economic Area (a group that includes slightly more countries than the EU) unless there is a guarantee that the data will receive adequate levels of protection. Such protection may be at the country level (if the country's laws offer adequate protection) or at the level of the individual organization (if a multinational organization has its own internal controls on personal data. United States legislation in general is not considered to offer adequate protection but there is a mechanism, known as the Safe Harbour Privacy Principles that allows individual American companies to register their compliance with the EU requirements.

It is important to realise that this principle means that if personal data is being processed using the 'cloud', all the computers processing it must be in countries that meet the EU data protection requirements.

This principle can be viewed in two ways. It can be seen as protecting data subjects from having their personal data transferred to countries where there are no limitations on how it might be used. It can also be seen as specifically allowing businesses to transmit personal data across national borders provided there is adequate legislation in the destination country. In practice, of course, if a website is physically located in a country that does not have adequate data protection legislation, a visitor to that website from a country that does have such legislation has no protection.

13.2.3 Rights of data subjects

The 1984 Act gave data subjects the right to know whether a data controller holds data relating to them, the right to see the data, and the right to have the data erased or corrected if it is inaccurate.

The 1998 Act extends this right of access so that data subjects have the right to receive:

- a description of the personal data being held;
- an explanation of the purpose for which it is being held and processed;
- a description of the people or organisations to which it may be disclosed;
- an intelligible statement of the specific data held about them;
- a description of the source of the data.

All these rights apply to data that is held electronically and, in some cases, to data that is held in manual filing systems. If, however, the data is processed automatically and is likely to be used as the sole basis for taking a decision relating to data subjects – for example, deciding whether to grant them a loan – they have the right to be informed by the data controller of the logic involved in taking that decision. They can also demand that a decision relating to them that has been taken on a purely automatic basis be reconsidered on some other basis.

The 1998 Act also gives data subjects the right:

- to prevent processing likely to cause damage and distress;
- to prevent processing for the purposes of direct marketing;
- to compensation in the case of damage caused by processing of personal data in violation of the principles of the Act.

13.2.4 Scope of the Act

The directive applies not only to data processed automatically but also to manual data provided it is contained in a 'relevant filing system' or 'accessible record'. A **relevant filing system** means any information relating to individuals which, although not processed automatically, is structured either by reference to individuals or by reference to criteria relating to individuals, in such a way that specific information relating to a particular individual is readily accessible. This includes, for example, a set of paper files relating to individuals and organised in any sort of systematic way. This is in contrast to the earlier, 1984, Act, which referred only to data held on a computer. Following a recent judgement by the Court of Appeal, however, very few manual filing systems are likely to fall into the category of 'relevant filing systems' (see the Further Reading section below).

The same case also clarified the question of what constitutes personal data. It ruled that, in order to constitute personal data, the information must, among other things, have the individual 'as its focus rather than some other person with whom he may have been involved or some transaction or event in which he may have figured or have had an interest'. This means, for example, that a list, in the minutes of a meeting, of the names of those attending does not constitute personal data about them.

The Act provided for the appointment of a Data Protection Commissioner and the establishment of Data Protection Tribunals. Their powers were subsequently extended to cover freedom of information and they were renamed Information Commissioner and Information Rights Tribunals respectively. (See section below on freedom of information.) Data controllers are required to notify the Information Commissioner of any processing of personal data that they carry out, including the purposes for which it is held and processed. However, the Act applies to the processing of personal data, whether or not there has been a notification.

There are two classes of personal data that are exempt from all the provisions of the Act. These are data related to national security and data used for domestic or household purposes (including recreation).

There are a number of important exceptions or limitations to the right of subject access, for example:

- Where disclosing the information may result in infringing someone else's rights.
- Where the data consists of a reference given by the data controller.
- Examination candidates do not have the right of access to their marks until after the results of the examinations have been published.
- Personal data consisting of information recorded by candidates during an academic, professional or other examination are exempt from the right of access.

In addition to these (and many other) specific cases included in the Act, the Secretary of State is given the power to make further exemptions in other areas.

Operation of the Act

The Act provides for the Information Commissioner's Office (ICO) to impose a 'monetary penalty' (in effect, a fine) on organisations that fail to comply with the Act. Some of the most serious of these cases arise in local government, the Civil Service and the National Health Service and in most instances it is the seventh data protection principle that is breached. Some typical examples are the following:

- In June 2013, the ICO imposed a monetary penalty of £150,000 on Glasgow City Council following the loss of a laptop holding the unencrypted personal data relating to 20,143 people, including the bank details of 6,069 of them. The culpability of the Council was aggravated when the ICO found that a further 74 laptops were unaccounted for, six of which were known to have been stolen, this despite the fact that the Council had been issued with an enforcement notice in 2010, requiring it to tighten up its procedures.

- In February 2013, the ICO imposed a £150,000 monetary penalty on the Nursing and Midwifery Council after it lost three DVDs related to a nurse's misconduct hearing, which contained unencrypted confidential personal information and evidence from two vulnerable children.

- In July 2013, a monetary penalty of £200,000 was imposed on NHS Surrey after more than 3,000 patient records were found on a second-hand computer bought through an online auction site; a further ten computers disposed of in the same way were found to be still holding personal data but many more computers could not be traced. NHS Surrey had disposed of the computer through a data destruction company without assuring itself that the data would be properly destroyed.

An example of a case involving a private company is the following:

- In January 2013, a monetary penalty of £250,000 was imposed on Sony after its PlayStation Network Platform was hacked, compromising the personal information of millions of customers. The ICO found that the hacking was a serious and sophisticated criminal attack but it could have been prevented had the software been up to date. The hackers in question were subsequently convicted of offences under the Computer Misuse Act (CMA), as described in Chapter 15 in the section on operation of the CMA.

The 1998 Act also makes it a criminal act for individuals to access personal data in contravention of the Act. The ICO has been active in pursuing such cases. Many of these cases involve domestic matters:

- A bank clerk was fined £500 plus costs for unlawfully accessing the bank statements of her partner's ex-wife.

- A former receptionist at a GP surgery was fined £750 plus costs for unlawfully obtaining sensitive medical information relating to her ex-husband's new wife.

- In a more commercial context, a former Community Health Promotions Manager at a council-run leisure centre was fined £3,000 plus costs for sending the sensitive medical information relating to 2,471 patient to his private email address. He had been made redundant and used the data to contact the patients in an effort to persuade them to sign up to his new, private service.

The ICO has expressed concern that the penalty for criminal access to personal data in contravention of the Act is limited to a fine and it is pressing for a prison sentence to be available in the most serious of cases.

One unfortunate and unforeseen consequence of the Data Protection Act has been that it has been used by many organisations as an excuse for not doing things that they ought to do. In some cases this may be because of a genuine lack of understanding coupled with an unwillingness to find out; in other cases, it is clearly just an excuse for not doing something that they don't want to do.

13.3 PRIVACY

The general issue of privacy and the law is far too large and complex to be considered here. We shall therefore consider only those specific issues that relate to the use of information systems and the internet. The starting point is the Regulation of Investigatory Powers Act 2000 (RIPA), which sets up a framework for controlling the lawful interception of computer, telephone and postal communications. The Act allows government security services and law enforcement authorities to intercept, monitor and investigate electronic data only in certain specified situations such as when preventing and detecting crime. Powers include being able to demand the disclosure of data encryption keys.

Under the Act and the associated regulations, organisations that provide computer and telephone services (this includes not only ISPs and other telecommunications service providers but also most employers) can monitor and record communications without the consent of the users of the service, provided this is done for one of the following purposes:

1. to establish facts, for example, on what date was a specific order placed;
2. to ensure that the organisation's regulations and procedures are being complied with;
3. to ascertain or demonstrate standards which are or ought be to be achieved;
4. to prevent or detect crime (whether computer-related or not);
5. to investigate or detect unauthorised use of telecommunication systems;
6. to ensure the effective operation of the system, e.g. by detecting viruses or denial of service attacks;
7. to find out whether a communication is a business communication or a private one (e.g. monitoring the emails of employees who are on holiday, in order to deal with any that relate to the business);
8. to monitor (but not record) calls to confidential, counselling help lines run free of charge by the business, provided that users are able to remain anonymous if they so choose.

Organisations intercepting communications in this way are under an obligation to make all reasonable efforts to inform users that such interception may take place.

The Act itself granted certain government agencies – the police, intelligence services and HM Revenue & Customs – the right to ask for interception warrants to allow them to monitor communications traffic to or from specific persons or organisations. Subsequent regulations have, however, extended the right to a ragbag of bodies (including, for example, fire authorities and local councils) that have little obvious reason for needing such information and no track record of being able to handle it. This extension has caused particular concern to civil liberties groups and also to many members of Parliament. They are concerned that the powers it confers have been used are being used for purposes that do not justify such intrusions into personal privacy, for example, by local education authorities

The Act and the regulations issued under it have also been heavily criticised by security experts and by some sectors of the telecommunications industry. They argue that there are many ways in which the Act can be rendered ineffective and that the provisions that allow for the seizure of keys undermine the security of public key systems.

The security services are eager to amend RIPA. At present, the telephone from which a call has been made or a text message sent can be identified, along with the time and location. However this cannot be done for internet-based communications such as email or Skype. The Communications Data Bill would require ISPs to hold sufficient information to be able to do this. It would cost ISPs a great deal of money to implement the necessary record keeping and the proposals have caused much political controversy. Despite repeated attempts by successive governments, the bill has not been passed. In part, at least, this is because of the unhappiness of individual MPs with the way in which RIPA has been misused.

We should emphasise that there are many other aspects of privacy that we cannot deal with here. These include, for example, the publication on the internet of photographs taken without the consent of the subject or the use of parabolic microphones to eavesdrop on private conversations at a distance.

13.4 FREEDOM OF INFORMATION

The primary purpose of the Freedom of Information Act (FoI) is to provide clear rights of access to information held by bodies in the public sector. Under the terms of the Act, any member of the public can apply for access to such information. The Act also provides an enforcement mechanism if the information is not made available.

The legislation applies to Parliament, government departments, local authorities, health trusts, doctors' surgeries, universities, schools and many other organisations.

The main features of the Act:

- A general right of access to information held by public authorities in the course of carrying out their public functions, subject to certain conditions and exemptions.

- In most cases where information is exempted from disclosure there is a duty on public authorities to disclose where, in the view of the public authority, the public interest in disclosure outweighs the public interest in maintaining the exemption in question.

- A new office of Information Commissioner and a new Information Rights Tribunal were created with wide powers to enforce the rights. This was done by extending the powers of the Data Protection Registrar and the Data Protection Tribunal.

- A duty was imposed on public authorities to adopt a scheme for the publication of information. The schemes, which must be approved by the Commissioner, specify the classes of information the authority intends to publish, the manner of publication and whether the information is available to the public free of charge or on payment of a fee.

Information in this context has a rather wider meaning than in normal usage so that it includes the text of documents such as minutes of meetings. The Act does not apply to personal information: the Data Protection Act already gives individuals access to information held about themselves and prevents a member of the public having access to personal information held about anyone else. There is, however, a possible conflict with the DPA in cases where documents include personal information, because the information that has to be released under the FoI may include personal data that must be kept confidential under the Data Protection Act. The ICO has ruled that in some cases the provisions of the FoI override those of the DPA. Thus, for example, bodies covered by the FoI are expected to reveal the salaries of their senior staff (or, at least, the salary scale on which each senior member of staff is positioned) and any expenses that they claim.

The United States also has a Freedom of Information Act. It was passed in 1967 and is thus much older than the UK Act. It is fundamentally different from the UK Act. In particular, since 1975, the US Act has applied to personal data, including that held by the law enforcement agencies and has, notoriously, been used by criminals to force those agencies to reveal the information they hold about the applicant's criminal activities. It has created a very substantial administrative burden for US government agencies; the FBI, for example, claims to have handled over 300,000 requests under the Act.

Unlike the other legislation discussed in this chapter, the Freedom of Information Act creates a requirement for new information systems and for packages that can be used to develop them. Such systems are commonly known as record management systems and document management systems.

FURTHER READING

The website of the Information Commissioner:
    www.ico.org.uk
contains much useful information relating both to data protection and to freedom of information. In particular, it contains guidance regarding what constitutes personal data and what is meant by a relevant filing system. The site contains press releases relating to all the cases mentioned in the section on operation of the Data Protection Act.

The text of the DPA can be found at:
    www.legislation.gov.uk/ukpga/1998/29/contents

that of the RIPA at:
    www.legislation.gov.uk/ukpga/2000/23/contents

and that of the FoI at:
    www.legislation.gov.uk/ukpga/2000/36/contents

The following book provides a much fuller treatment of the topics covered in this chapter:
    Room, S. (2006) *Data protection and compliance in context.* British Computer Society, Swindon.

In contrast,
    Bott, M.F., Coleman, J.A., Eaton, J., and Rowland, D. (2000) *Professional issues in software engineering.* 3rd ed. Taylor and Francis, London
describes the development of data protection legislation and the thinking behind it, starting from the Younger Committee's report of 1972.

14 INTERNET ISSUES

After studying this chapter, you should understand:

- *the reasons why misuse of the internet gives cause for concern;*
- *the scope and limitations of the legislation that governs the use of the internet at present;*
- *why it is difficult to enact legislation that will effectively regulate the use of the internet.*

14.1 THE EFFECTS OF THE INTERNET

The benefits that the internet has brought are almost universally recognised. It has made access to all sorts of information much easier. It has made it much easier for people to communicate with each other, on both an individual and a group basis. It has simplified and speeded up many types of commercial transaction. And, most importantly, these benefits have been made available to very many people, not just to a small and privileged group – although, of course, the internet is still far from being universally available, even in developed countries.

Inevitably, a development on this scale creates its own problems. In this chapter we shall be looking at three topics – pornography, defamation and spam – that are a matter of concern to everyone professionally involved in the internet, as well as to many other people. These are topics that cannot sensibly discussed in technical terms alone. There are social, cultural and legal issues that must all be considered. Different countries approach these issues in very different ways but the internet itself knows no boundaries.

Every country has laws governing what can be published or publicly displayed. Typically, such laws address defamation, that is, material that makes unwelcome allegations about people or organisations, and pornography, that is, material with sexual content. They may also cover other areas such as political and religious comment, incitement to racial hatred or the depiction of violence.

Although every country has such laws, they are very different from each other. Some countries, for example, consider that pictures of scantily clad women are indecent and have laws that prevent them from appearing in publications and advertisements. In other countries, such pictures are perfectly acceptable. In some countries, publication of material criticising the government or the established religion is effectively forbidden, while in others it is a right guaranteed by the constitution and vigorously defended by the courts.

The coming of the internet (and satellite television) has made these differences much more apparent and much more important than they used to be. Since material in digital form flows across borders so easily, it is both much likelier that material that violates publication laws will come into a country and more difficult for the country to enforce its own laws.

The roles and responsibilities of internet service providers (ISPs) are a central element in the way these issues are addressed and we therefore start by discussing the legal framework under which ISPs operate. Then we shall look at the problems of different legal systems. Only then can we address the specific issues of defamation, pornography and spam. Finally, we shall look at the more mundane issue of commerce over the internet and the protection of consumers.

14.2 INTERNET SERVICE PROVIDERS

The central issue we need to consider is how far an ISP can be held responsible for material generated by its customers.

In Europe, the position is governed by the European Directive 2000/31/EC. In the UK this directive is implemented through the Electronic Commerce (EC Directive) Regulations 2002. These regulations follow the EC Directive in distinguishing three roles that an ISP may play: mere conduit, caching and hosting.

The role of **mere conduit** is that in which the ISP does no more than transmit data; in particular, the ISP does not initiate transmissions, does not select the receivers of the transmissions and does not select or modify the data transmitted. It is compatible with the role of mere conduit for an ISP to store information temporarily, provided this is only done as part of the transmission process. Provided it is acting as a mere conduit, the regulations provide that an ISP is not liable for damages or for any criminal sanction as a result of a transmission.

The **caching** role arises when the information is the subject of automatic, intermediate and temporary storage, for the sole purpose of increasing the efficiency of the transmission of the information to other recipients of the service upon their request. An ISP acting in the caching role is not liable for damages or for any criminal sanction as a result of a transmission, provided that it:

1. does not modify the information;
2. complies with conditions on access to the information;
3. complies with any rules regarding the updating of the information, specified in a manner widely recognised and used by industry;
4. does not interfere with the lawful use of technology, widely recognised and used by industry, to obtain data on the use of the information; and

5. acts expeditiously to remove or to disable access to the information it has stored upon obtaining actual knowledge of the fact that the information at the initial source of the transmission has been removed from the network, or access to it has been disabled, or that a court or an administrative authority has ordered such removal or disablement.

These apparently complicated conditions are simply designed to ensure that an ISP that claims to be playing a caching role is behaving in accordance with industry practice.

Where an ISP stores information provided by its customers, it is acting in a **hosting** role. In this case, it is not liable for damage or criminal sanctions provided that:

1. it did not know that anything unlawful was going on;
2. where a claim for damages is made, it did not know anything that should have led it to think that something unlawful might be going on; or
3. when it found out that that something unlawful was going on, it acted expeditiously to remove the information or to prevent access to it, and
4. the customer was not acting under the authority or the control of the service provider.

In the US, ISPs enjoy much broader immunity than in Europe. In effect, even when they are hosting, they enjoy the immunity that in Europe is only granted to ISPs acting as mere conduits.

It seems very reasonable that an ISP should cease to enjoy immunity if it fails to remove unlawful material once it has been informed about it. However, this places the ISP in the position of having to judge whether or not material is unlawful. ISPs are not qualified to make such judgements and if they are forced to make them they will play safe, that is, they will usually accept that the material complained about is unlawful and will remove it. The person who posted the material has no legal redress. This means, for example, that if a website is set up to collect and display comments about a major company – be it a supermarket chain, a car manufacturer or a fast food chain – the company can, in effect, censor the comments that appear by complaining to the ISP that the material is defamatory. The ISP, aware that the complainant can deploy an army of expensive lawyers, is likely to play safe by requiring that the material be removed, regardless of whether it is true and in the public interest. There is no easy legal remedy that the owners of the website can use. This is a difficult issue and there is no obvious solution.

A further issue regarding ISPs is the question of anonymous and pseudonymous postings. It is common for contributors to bulletin boards and newsgroups to use pseudonyms for their postings. Their ISP will be aware of their true identity. Is the ISP allowed to release, and can it be compelled to release, this information to someone wishing to take legal action against the contributor? In the UK, the ISP is allowed to release the information and can be compelled to do so by a court. In the USA, ISPs cannot in general be required to release the information, although they may be required to do so in the case of serious crimes.

14.3 THE LAW ACROSS NATIONAL BOUNDARIES

How law operates across national boundaries is a difficult and intensely technical topic but one that is very important in the context of the internet. We can only give the most superficial description here.

14.3.1 Criminal law

Suppose a person X commits a criminal offence in country A and then moves to country B. Can country A ask that X be arrested in country B and sent back to A so that he can be put on trial? Or can X be prosecuted in country B for the offence committed in country A?

The answer to the first of these questions is that, provided there exists an agreement (usually called an **extradition treaty**) between the two countries, then in principle X can be extradited, that is, arrested and sent back to face trial in A. However, this can only be done under the very important proviso that the offence that X is alleged to have committed in A would also be an offence in B. What is more, extradition procedures are usually extremely complex, so that attempts at extradition often fail because of procedural weaknesses. Within the EU, the recent proposals for a European arrest warrant are intended to obviate the need for extradition procedures. The case of Gary McKinnon, discussed in the next chapter, raised issues related to extradition in an acute form.

In general, the answer to the second question is that X cannot be prosecuted in B for an offence committed in A. However, in certain cases some countries, including the UK and the USA, claim **extraterritorial jurisdiction**, that is the right to try citizens and other residents for crimes committed in other countries; in particular, this right is used to allow the prosecution of people who commit sexual offences involving children while they are abroad. However, the issue of extraterritoriality is much wider than this and attempts to claim extraterritorial jurisdiction make countries very unpopular.

What does this mean in the context of the internet? Suppose that you live in country A and on your website there you publish material that is perfectly legal and acceptable in country A but which it is a criminal offence to publish in country B. Then you can't be prosecuted in country A and it is very unlikely that you would be extradited to country B. You might, however, be unwise to visit country B voluntarily.

14.3.2 The international convention on cybercrime

In 2001, the Council of Europe approved a draft convention on 'cybercrime'. It deals with child pornography on the internet, criminal copyright infringement, computer-related fraud and hacking. There is an additional protocol relating to incitement to religious or racial hatred, to which signatories to the protocol may also sign up.

International conventions inevitably are slow to take effect. Governments sign the treaty showing that they approve of it. However, in many cases they will have to persuade their legislature to approve it and the laws necessary to implement it. This process, known as **ratification**, can take a long time and is often not at the top of a government's priorities. Governments may be replaced and the incoming government may not feel committed to ratification.

The Council of Europe, which is quite separate from the EU, has 47 members; four countries outside Europe (the USA, Canada, Japan and South Africa) are associated with it. As of May 2013, 39 of these 51 countries have signed and ratified the treaty while 12 have signed it but not yet ratified it. The USA has explicitly indicated that it will not sign up to the protocol relating to hate material because this would be contrary to the First Amendment (see subsection below on the regulation of pornography in other countries)

14.3.3 Civil law

There are some parts of the civil law where the position is reasonably clear cut. Any contract that involves parties from more than one country should, and usually will, state explicitly under which jurisdiction (that is, which country's laws) it is to be interpreted. Where intellectual property law is concerned, there are international agreements to which most countries are signatories so that there is a common framework, even if it can be very difficult to enforce the rights in certain countries.

In many cases, the plaintiff will have some choice about where to take action. Very often the decision will be taken on practical grounds – there is little point in taking action in a country in which defendant has no legal presence or few assets and it is probably unwise to take action in a country where the legal process is well known to be lengthy and expensive.

Consider the case of an ISP based in the USA, with a European office in London. One of its customers is an Italian, resident in Italy, who posts on his website, which is hosted by the ISP, an accusation about a French politician. The French politician complains but the ISP does nothing to remove the allegation. If the French politician wishes to take action, he can, in theory, take action in any of the four countries involved – England, France, Italy or the USA. His best hope of winning a court action may well be in France but there is little point in bringing an action in France unless the ISP has some sort of legal presence there. The same applies to Italy, a country where, in any case, the law is not renowned for bringing cases to a rapid conclusion. The politician will probably opt for action in England, on the grounds that, in such cases, English law is much more sympathetic to the person claiming to be wronged than is American law. It may still be necessary to persuade the English court that this is a matter that it can properly consider.

One concrete example is that a court in New Zealand recently ruled that an organisation based in New Zealand could take action in a New Zealand court against an Australian newspaper that, it was claimed, had published defamatory statements about it on its website in Australia.

14.4 DEFAMATION

Consider the following scenario. A university provides internet services for its students and allows them to mount personal web pages. One student, who is a passionate fan of Llanbadarn United football club, believes the referee in their last game made a bad decision that caused them to lose the match. He believes that the decision was so obviously wrong that the referee must have been bribed. He puts a statement on his web page saying that the referee is corrupt. Someone draws the referee's attention to this allegation. The referee believes that his reputation has been badly damaged by this and he wants compensation.

This situation is covered by the law of defamation. Defamation means making statements that will damage someone's reputation, bring them into contempt, make them disliked, and so on. In England and Wales, a distinction is made between **slander**, which is spoken, and **libel**, which is written or recorded in some other way (including email).

There can be little doubt that, on the face of it, the statement in question constitutes libel. The first issue to consider, however, is who should the referee take action against. He could sue the student, but the student probably doesn't have enough money to pay any damages that might be awarded. Can he also sue the university, which presumably could pay damages?

The Defamation Act 1996 states that a person has a defence if he can prove that:

    a.   he was not the author, editor or publisher of the statement complained of,

    b.   he took reasonable care in relation to its publication, and

    c.   he did not know, and had no reason to believe, that what he did caused or contributed to the publication of a defamatory statement.

(Presumably, this is intended to read $a \lor (b \land c)$.)

The author, the editor and the publisher of the libel can all be held responsible. If the allegation had been published in a traditional student newspaper, printed on paper and sold to students and others through newsagents or the students' union, the referee would have been able to sue the publisher of the newspaper – probably the students' union if it had a separate legal existence, if not, the university – and the editor. This is reasonable because everything published in the newspaper is directly under the control of the editor, who is the agent of the publisher.

When the libel is published on a web page, on the university site, the university can reasonably argue that it cannot possibly vet everything that every one of its 10,000 students puts on their personal web page. It is not, in fact, publishing the pages, it is only providing an infrastructure that allows students to publish their own web pages. In the terminology used in the 2002 Regulations it is acting in a hosting role. Provided therefore that it removed the offending material, as soon as it had reason to suspect its presence and that the student was not acting under its authority or control, the university cannot be subject to an action for damages.

ISPs receive a significant number of complaints, many apparently from companies. As we have already stated, given the cost and management time involved in defending a libel action, it is not surprising that in these circumstances ISPs make no attempt to assess whether a complaint is justified. Instead, they immediately remove or block access to the offending material, with the result that they can avail themselves of the defence that the 2002 Regulations provide. This may not always be in the public interest. There may well be occasions when allegations of corruption, for example, are justified and that it is in the public interest for this to be publicised. In such circumstances, in suppressing the allegations, the ISP is carrying out a function that more properly belongs to the courts.

Despite the provisions of the 2002 Regulations, there are many areas of uncertainty regarding the position of ISPs and also many practical problems with complying with the law. We have given a very simplified picture here. The reader who wishes to pursue the matter further is referred to the Law Commission report referenced in the Further Reading section at the end of this chapter.

Because so much material on the internet originates in the US, it is appropriate here to say a little about the position there. US law relating to defamation is much more favourable towards authors and publishers than is the law in the UK. The First Amendment to the United States Constitution guarantees a right to free speech that the US courts have always been eager to defend. The result is that many statements that might be considered defamatory in the UK would be protected as an exercise of the right of free speech in the USA. This is particularly the case where the defamatory statement refers to a public figure. In this case, to succeed in a libel action, the public figure needs to show not only that the statement was factually incorrect but also that it was made maliciously or recklessly.

Suppose that an internet site in the USA, hosted by an American ISP, contains a statement about someone living in the UK that would be considered defamatory in the UK but not in the USA (a statement accusing a British politician of corruption, for example). The person who is the subject of the statement can reasonably say, 'I am British. I live in the UK. This statement can be read by anyone in the UK. Surely, I am entitled to the protection offered by British law'. The author of the statement and the ISP can both say, 'We live in the United States and we are governed by its laws. We understand those laws and we comply with them. We cannot be expected to know the law as it exists in all the other countries of the world and we cannot be expected to comply with those laws'. The complainant may be able to take action in the UK against the ISP, provided the ISP has a legal presence in the UK, but only in respect of the circulation of the defamatory statement in the UK. A court in the United States will not enforce British law over such matters.

This is a case in which the global nature of the internet magnifies an issue. American newspapers and magazines do not contain much material about British politics nor do they have a very wide circulation in the UK. If the statement had appeared in an American newspaper or magazine, it would not have achieved a wide circulation in the UK. But it is nowadays more likely that such a statement will be made on the internet and it is more likely that it will then be read in the UK.

All these considerations apply to defamatory information published on other social media, as two recent cases involving tweets on Twitter show.

Lalit Modi, the former Chairman of the Indian Premier League (a cricket league) tweeted an allegation that New Zealand cricket star Chris Cairns had a history of match fixing. Although the tweet initially went to only 65 people, it was picked up by the cricket website cricinfo, where it was read by a further 1,000 or so readers. Cairns sued both Modi and cricinfo for damages to his reputation. cricinfo quickly acknowledged the libel and settled out of court, paying £7,000 in damages and around £8,000 in costs. Modi however refused to withdraw the libel and was ordered to pay Cairns £90,000 in damages. This was confirmed on appeal in October 2012. Note that the legal action took place in London rather than in India or New Zealand.

In November 2012 the BBC Newsnight programme made allegations that a high-profile Tory politician had been involved in the sexual abuse of young boys at a children's home in North Wales. The programme did not specifically name the politician in question but there had been tweets on Twitter before the programme was broadcast alleging that Lord McAlpine was the politician involved. After the broadcast, Sally Bercow, the wife of the Speaker of the House of Commons, tweeted 'Why is Lord McAlpine trending? *innocent face*'. It proved that there was no substance in the allegations and the BBC agreed to pay substantial damages. Mrs Bercow, however, who had some 56,000 followers on Twitter claimed that her tweet was just a neutral enquiry. The judge in the High Court held that the innuendo was clear and that the damage to Lord McAlpine's reputation was potentially severe. Mrs Bercow was forced to pay substantial damages and costs.

14.5 PORNOGRAPHY

More or less every country has laws concerned with pornography. Beyond this simple statement it is almost impossible to generalise. What is considered pornographic varies widely from country to country. What is accepted as normal by everyone in one country may be considered pornographic in another country. In some countries the possession of pornography may be a criminal offence, in others possession is not an offence but distribution and/or publication are. We are not concerned here with what should or should not be considered pornographic or what should or should not be prohibited. We are concerned simply with a country's ability to enforce the laws that it has chosen to enact.

Until the early 1980s, a country could expect to enforce its laws regarding pornography reasonably effectively. It was a comparatively simple matter for the police to stop the sale of material that was regarded as pornographic. It was easy to prevent cinemas showing films considered pornographic; again this could be done by the police. And, apart from a few areas near its borders, the only television broadcasts that could be received in the country would be ones that were broadcast from within the country and could therefore be controlled.

Three developments changed this. It became possible to broadcast television programmes via satellite, which meant that programmes could be broadcast from one country to be received in another. Secondly, the advent of the internet meant that individuals could receive pornographic material, in the form of images or text, in a way that was extremely difficult for the authorities to detect. In other words, pornography became available in an intangible form. And finally, the advent of the digital camera allowed photographs to be produced without the need for externally provided development services.

There is a second aspect to the problem of pornography. This is the problem of unsolicited pornography sent to people who find it offensive. This, however, is part of the wider problem of spam, which we deal with in the next section. In this section, we are concerned with the problems that a country faces in enforcing its laws against pornography, in the face of internet users who are willing receivers of it.

There is one important difference between laws regarding defamation and laws regarding pornography. In most instances of defamation, any legal action will be under the civil law and will be initiated by the person or organisation who is the target of the defamation. In most cases concerning the publication of pornography, action will be under the criminal law and will be initiated by state prosecution services on the basis of information provided by the police.

14.5.1 The law in the UK

In England and Wales, the law relating to pornography is based on the Obscene Publications Acts of 1959 and 1964. The 1959 Act repealed both existing legislation and the common law offences relating to obscene material. It created a criminal offence of publishing an obscene article, whether for profit or not, and the 1964 Act extended that offence to include possessing an obscene article with a view to for publication for gain. It is not an offence simply to possess an obscene article. In the context of these Acts, 'article' is to be taken to mean any type of article 'containing or embodying matter to be read or looked at or both, any sound record, and any film or other record of a picture or pictures'. The definition of publishing was amended in 1994 so that it explicitly includes the transmission of electronically-stored data.

The 1959 Act states that 'an article shall be deemed to be obscene if its effect or the effect of any one of its items is, if taken as a whole, such as to tend to deprave and corrupt persons who are likely, having regard to all relevant circumstances, to read, see or hear the matter contained or embodied in it'. Although the Act has been modified by subsequent legislation, some intended to bring it provisions into line with the world of computers and the internet, the definition of obscenity has not been changed. However, its interpretation has changed considerably; much material that would almost certainly have been found by a court to be obscene at the time that the Act was passed would now be regarded as quite acceptable.

Two important features of this definition are that the effect is to be 'taken as a whole' and that it is the effect on 'persons who are likely... to read, see or hear' the material that matters. The 'taken as a whole' provision means that a prosecution under the act cannot be based simply on a short excerpt, possibly taken out of context. Thus a 400-page novel, five pages of which contain graphic and explicit descriptions of sexual activity, must be judged as a whole. The Act also states explicitly that a defendant should not be found guilty of an offence if it is proved that publication is 'for the public good on the ground that it is in the interests of science, literature, art or learning, or of other objects of general concern'. Furthermore, it is explicitly states that 'the opinion of experts as to the literary artistic, scientific or other merits' of the article can be taken into account. The effect of these provisions has been that, starting with the famous case of *Lady*

Chatterley's Lover, attempts to prosecute works that have any literary or artistic merit at all have proved unsuccessful and have now been abandoned by the authorities.

The phrase 'tend to deprave and corrupt persons who are likely, having regard to all relevant circumstances, to read, see or hear the matter contained or embodied in it' is potentially of importance in relation to the internet. In the 1980s, pornographic material was usually purchased in printed form from newsagents, where it was kept in a less accessible position and not sold to under-18s. Thus, those who were likely to read or see the material were likely to be adults who were deliberately looking for it. It could be argued that when the same material is posted on the internet, younger people are much more likely to gain access to it, possibly unintentionally. This could mean that material that a court would not judge to be obscene when it is printed and sold in a newsagent becomes obscene when it is posted on the internet, because it is likely to be seen or read by a larger group of people.

The position regarding child pornography is very different. The Protection of Children Act 1978 and subsequent legislation make the simple possession of indecent, that is, sexually explicit, material involving children a serious criminal offence. It is much easier to prove in court that material is sexually explicit than that it tends to deprave or corrupt. And mere possession is an objective fact in a way that possession with a view to publication is not. For these reasons, prosecutions under the Protection of Children Act are much more straightforward than prosecutions under the Obscene Publications Act. Sections 63 to 67 of the Criminal Justice and Immigration Act 2008 introduce provisions making mere possession of certain other types of obscene material – so-called 'extreme pornography' – an offence, thus simplifying prosecutions related to such material.

14.5.2 The regulation of pornography in other countries

The First Amendment to the US Constitution famously states that:

> Congress shall make no law respecting an establishment of religion, or prohibiting the free exercise thereof; or abridging the freedom of speech, or of the press; or the right of the people peaceably to assemble, and to petition the government for a redress of grievances.

The clauses about freedom of speech and of the press have been enthusiastically defended by the courts since the 1950s. In particular, attempts by individual states to enact provisions against pornography have been struck down as unconstitutional by the Supreme Courts of the states themselves and an act of Congress that would have made the internet subject to much stricter control than other media was struck down by the Federal Supreme Court. As a result, despite the fact that much of American society is very conservative in its attitude to sexual matters, there is little legal control over pornography.

Within Europe, the level of legal control over pornography covers a wide spectrum, with some countries, such as Denmark and Sweden, having very few controls whilst others are as restrictive or, in some cases, more restrictive than the UK. Quite often, controls are limited to material that depicts violent, non-consensual sexual acts. Worldwide, the range is still broader, ranging from countries in which the depiction of a woman in a modest one-piece bathing costume would be unlawful to countries in which there are apparently no restrictions whatsoever.

Notwithstanding this wide variation in the control of pornography in general, there is wide (though not universal) international agreement that child pornography should be banned. Some ambiguity can arise because of differences in the age of consent from country to country – pictures involving 14-year olds might be regarded as child pornography in one country but not in another. And, indeed, a painting of Romeo and Juliet could be considered to be child pornography, since Shakespeare's play explicitly states that Romeo is 14 and Juliet is 13. But despite this ambiguity 'at the boundary', there is generally a clear understanding of what constitutes child pornography.

14.5.3 The Internet Watch Foundation

In the UK, the Internet Watch Foundation (IWF) was set up in 1996 to monitor and, where desirable and possible, take action against illegal and offensive content on the UK internet. It has the support of the UK government, the police and the internet service providers. It can act against material on the web that contain:

- images of child sexual abuse, originating anywhere in the world;
- adult material that potentially breaches the Obscene Publications Act in the UK;
- non-photographic child sexual abuse images (e.g. cartoon material) hosted in the UK.

When originally founded, the IWF's remit included material inciting racial hatred, but this has now become a police responsibility, for which there is a dedicated website. Obscene adult material was added to the IWF remit at the same time as responsibility for material inciting racial hatred was transferred to the police. The restrictions to the UK for adult obscene material and non-photographic material reflect the fact that there is no international agreement that such material should be banned.

The IWF operates a 'hotline' through which members of the public can report any internet content that they believe may be illegal. The IWF will locate and assess the material. If the material is considered illegal and falls within the IWF remit, the IWF will pass the information to the police and inform the ISP that is hosting it in the case that the material is hosted in the UK. If it is hosted abroad, the IWF will inform all its ISP members so that access from the UK can be blocked. If images of children originating in other countries are involved, it will also inform Interpol and the police in the countries concerned.

The IWF receives around 20,000 complaints per year, of which about a third relate to material that is assessed as being potentially illegal. In the first full year of IWF operation, 18 per cent of the illegal material was traced to sources within the UK. By 2003, this had been reduced to one per cent and it has remained at this low level; furthermore, it is typically removed within 60 minutes of being reported.

In the UK, the provisions of the Electronic Commerce (EC Directive) Regulations 2002, discussed in the section on the effects of the internet, apply to pornography as well as to defamatory material. This means that ISPs will not be subject to criminal action in respect of pornographic material on sites that they host provided that:

- they did not know of its presence;
- they removed it when they became aware of its presence; and
- those responsible for publishing it were not under the ISP's authority or control.

If ISPs were left to deal directly with complaints from the public, they would inevitably feel they have to remove all the material complained about, regardless of whether it is potentially illegal, in order to keep their immunity from prosecution. This, however, would lead to legitimate public complaints that private companies were acting as internet censors. Having the complaints routed through the IWF, means that an ISP only receives those that the specialised staff at the IWF believe relate to potentially illegal material. Complaints about material that is offensive to the complainant but not potentially illegal never reach the ISP. Although this is not a perfect solution, it is a reasonable one and has proved to work well in practice.

THE ICRA

The Internet Content Rating Association (ICRA) was an international, independent organisation whose mission, it claimed, was 'to help parents to protect their children from potentially harmful material on the internet, whilst respecting the content providers' freedom of expression'. Its board included representatives from the major players in the internet and communications markets, including AOL, BT, Cable and Wireless, IBM, Microsoft and Novell. Despite its claim to be international, it was largely US-based.

The ICRA provided a framework that enabled content providers to label their sites or individual pages systematically with labels that described the nature of the content under such categories as nudity and sexual content, bad language, violence, use of drugs and alcohol, and so on. The ICRA also provided filter software, which could be used to control which sites and pages could be accessed. A user could download and install this software and then configure it to allow access only to webpages and sites that satisfy particular labelling criteria. This allowed parents discretion about how they controlled their children's use of the internet. Some parents might be quite unconcerned about their children viewing material involving nudity but might feel that they want to protect them from violent images, a common view in Sweden, for example. Others might take the opposite approach.

ICRA failed. It failed because it could not persuade enough sites to label their contents using its system and because it could not persuade browser developers to make their products read and act on the ICRA labels. For a much fuller analysis of the causes of the ICRA failure, see the paper referred to in the Further Reading section.

There are many other internet filtering products, some at least of which are useful in appropriate situations. They may be used by parents to control the amount of time their children spend playing online games or using social media; they may be used by employers to prevent employees using work time to surf the net; and they can be used to block what may potentially be dangerous software, such as viruses. However, many filtering products aimed at blocking access to offensive material are linguistically naïve and result in harmless material being blocked. Typically this arises because an innocent word – often a place name or a personal name – contains a string of letters that are in other contexts an obscenity. Examples include Scunthorpe (a town in Lincolnshire) and Cockburn (a common Scottish surname). The local history website RomansInSussex.co.uk, which was specifically aimed at school children, was blocked by the filtering software used in many schools because the URL contains the substring 'sex'.

14.5.4 Future developments

As we have seen, the IWF has been very effective in blocking child pornography, even if the press and politicians have failed to appreciate what has been achieved. The effectiveness of the IWF's work is the result of several factors:

- There is general international agreement that this sort of material should be suppressed.

- Sites that supply the material are not attractive to advertisers. Thus, in order for such a site to be profitable, it must charge its customers. Since the payments will be necessarily electronic the customers can be traced.

- Prosecution is comparatively straightforward.

These conditions, in particular the first, do not apply in relation to other types of pornographic material and there is little likelihood of effective action being taken against them in the same way. In some countries, for example, representation of the naked body is regarded as pornographic and is forbidden by law; in other countries, paintings and sculptures by great artists, depicting the naked body, are considered to be among the countries' greatest artistic treasures. Novels that are enjoyed as great literature in some countries are banned as pornographic in others. In some countries, homosexuality is illegal and so is the depiction in text or images of homosexual relationships; in other countries, the rights of homosexuals are guaranteed by law and any discrimination is illegal. Furthermore, constitutional provisions guaranteeing freedom of speech and expression will often lead to a country tolerating pornographic material that most of its population would find extremely offensive, and more general considerations of individual freedom make it unlikely that many countries would want to make simple possession of pornography illegal.

There is, however, increasing concern about pornography on the internet, whipped up by the populist press and politicians looking for bandwagons to climb on. In response to this, in a speech delivered on 22 July 2013, the UK prime minister announced that the government had signed an agreement with the country's four largest ISPs (BT, TalkTalk, Virgin and Sky) under which all broadband connections will be automatically fitted with a 'family friendly' filter unless customers specifically request that the filter not be activated. The prime minister stated explicitly that the purpose of the agreement was to protect children from viewing inappropriate material. He was unable or unwilling to be specific about the type of material that would be blocked.

It has been suggested that search engines should block searches that include terms from a forbidden list. If implemented, this will certainly run into the 'Scunthorpe problem' mentioned above. What is more, it would effectively ban searches looking for legitimate websites covering medical information about aspects of sexual health. In practice, anyway, it is not necessary to use obscene terms in a search in order to find pornographic material on the web.

The prime minister also said that it was wrong that material that would not be allowed in a newsagent's shop was available on the internet. Although we may sympathise with this sentiment, we must recognise the advent of the internet has made it almost impossible to stop this happening – it could only be achieved by censorship of cross-border internet traffic on a scale so massive as to be completely unacceptable to society as a whole as well as so demanding of resources as to be unaffordable.

14.6 SPAM

Spam is best defined as 'unsolicited email sent without the consent of the addressee and without any attempt at targeting recipients who are likely to be interested in its contents'. Any regular user of email will be familiar with spam. We find our mailboxes filled with emails offering Viagra, penis enlargement treatments, incitements to visit pornographic sites, advertisements for dubious financial investments and so on. It is estimated that around half of the traffic on the internet is spam. Internet users find it irritating and often offensive. If they respond to any of these invitations, they may also find themselves defrauded and their bank accounts raided. It is easy to miss important emails in the welter of spam. Some spam carries viruses. The effectiveness of the internet is much reduced by the load of spam that it carries. Not surprisingly, there is considerable pressure on governments to legislate to eliminate or at least alleviate the problem and a number of organisations have been set up specifically to fight spam.

There are some technical means of fighting spam, for example:

- closing loopholes that enable spammers to use other people's computers to relay bulk messages;
- the use of machine learning and other techniques to identify suspicious features of message headers;
- the use of virus detection software to reject emails carrying viruses;
- keeping 'stop lists' of sites that are known to send spam.

Most of these methods require constant vigilance, however, and are more suitable for use by organisations than by an individual. Furthermore, they carry a real risk that genuine email will be mistaken for spam and rejected.

The problem of spam is perceived as being of the utmost importance by the industry and substantial efforts are being made to develop technical solutions but these need to be backed up by effective legislation.

14.6.1 European legislation

The European Community Directive on Privacy and Electronic Communications (2002/58/EC) was issued in 2002 and required member nations to introduce regulations to implement it by December 2003. In the UK, the directive was implemented by the Privacy and Electronic Communications (EC Directive) Regulations 2003.

The directive addresses many issues that are not relevant here but includes essential features relating to unsolicited email:

- Unsolicited email can only be sent to individuals (as opposed to companies) if they have previously given their consent;
- Sending an unsolicited email that conceals the address of the sender or does not provide a valid address to which the recipient can send a request for such mailings to cease is unlawful;
- If an email address has been obtained in the course of the sale of goods or services, the seller may use the address for direct mailings, provided that the recipient is given the opportunity, easily and free of charge, with every message, to request that such mailings cease.

In the UK, the enforcement of the regulations is in the hands of the Information Commissioner. The maximum penalty is a fine of £5,000 in a magistrate's court but the matter can be taken to a higher court, where an unlimited fine can be imposed.

The directive is widely seen as a step in the right direction. Its main weakness, however, is that it can only be effective in relation to spam sent from within the EU; it is estimated that some 90 per cent of the spam received in the UK originates in the USA. It has also been criticised because it does not prohibit the sending of spam to companies and because the penalties are felt to be too light.

A second weakness in the UK legislation is the difficulty of enforcing it effectively. Since it is not an offence to send unsolicited email to companies, it falls to individuals to take action against UK spammers. Few individuals are prepared to make the effort that this involves, particularly as any damages awarded will inevitably be comparatively small. Furthermore, if the spammer is a company it may frighten the individual off by threatening to fight the matter to the highest court. In one case, after judgement had been given in favour of the complainant, the company repeatedly delayed payment of the damages and costs until it suddenly disappeared. (See the Further Reading section.)

14.6.2 Legislation in the United States

A superficially similar act came into force in the USA at the start of 2004. This is the Controlling the Assault of Non-Solicited Pornography and Marketing Act 2003, otherwise known as the CAN SPAM Act. Unfortunately, the Act has fundamental weaknesses; the main one is that it is legal to send spam provided that:

- the person sending the spam has not been informed by the receiver that they do not wish to receive spam from that source; and

- the spam contains an address that the receiver can use to ask that no more spam be sent.

These provisions means that email users will have to respond to every piece of spam they receive, asking for no more to be sent. Dishonest spammers will be able to use these messages to confirm the validity of the email addresses. In Europe, it is the responsibility of the spammer to get the recipient's permission before sending the spam; in the USA it is the responsibility of the recipient to inform the spammer that they don't want to receive the spam.

The law actually has some very good provisions, mostly the technical ones that require valid return addresses and make it illegal to forge other routing information that accompanies each message. Coupled with some changes in the architecture of internet mail handling and increased anti-spam vigilance by ISPs and network operators, these could, over time, have real impact on spam volumes.

The CAN SPAM Act allows ISPs to sue for damages in certain cases and several ISPs have initiated successful court action against spammers. In 2005, Microsoft won a $7.8 million civil judgement against Robert Soloway for sending spam through MSN and Hotmail services and Robert Braver, a small ISP in Oklahoma, was awarded over $10 million in a judgement against Soloway. It is not clear whether either claimant actually received the money awarded. In 2008, Soloway was sentenced to 47 months imprisonment and ordered to pay $700,000 on email fraud and related charges. Other large-scale spammers have also been successfully prosecuted, many of the cases involving both spamming and other criminal activities. Despite these cases, there is little sign of a decrease in the overall amount of spam originating in the USA, which accounts for nearly 20 per cent of all spam worldwide.

14.6.3 Registration

Both the USA and the UK operate successful schemes that allow individuals to register their telephone numbers as ones to which unsolicited direct marketing calls must not be made. On the face of it this should act as a model for preventing spam; indeed, the CAN SPAM Act specifically requires the Federal Trade Commission to produce plans for such a register within six months. Unfortunately, the technical differences between the internet and the telephone network mean that this model is unlikely to work with spam. In order to enforce the law, it is necessary to be able to identify reliably the source of the communication. Telephone operators keep records of calls showing the originator and the destination of the call; such records are needed for billing purposes. It is therefore easy, in most cases, to identify the source of any direct marketing call about which a consumer complains and then take the action necessary to enforce the law, although this is not effective when the direct marketing call originates from overseas.

In most cases, use of the internet is not charged on the basis of individual communications but on the basis of connect time, so there is no recording of individual emails and it costs no more to send an email from Australia to the UK than it does to send an email to one's colleague in the office. Furthermore, 'spoofing' (forging the sender's address on an email) and relaying (using other people's mail servers to send your spam) are easily achieved. This means there are no reliable records that can be used to identify where the spam really came from and the use of relaying may mean that it is impossible even to determine in which country it originated. In these circumstances, there is little possibility that a prohibition on sending unsolicited email to addresses on a register could be enforced effectively.

14.7 ECOMMERCE REGULATIONS

The basic law regarding selling over the internet is contained in the European Directive 97/7/EC, which was incorporated into UK law by the Consumer Protection (Distance Selling) Regulations 2000. They apply to both goods and services ordered over the telephone or over the internet. Two important aims of the Directive were to ensure 'that consumers should be able to have access to the goods and services of another Member State on the same terms as the population of that State' and to provide 'a new impetus for consumer protection policy'.

The regulations require suppliers to provide the following information before any contract is agreed:

- the name of the supplier and an address;
- a description of the what is being offered;
- the cost, including tax;
- the delivery charge, if any, and the method of delivery;
- the method of payment;
- the customer's right of cancellation;
- any communication costs for concluding the contract (the cost of a premium rate telephone call, for example;)
- how long the offer is valid for;
- the duration of the contract, if it is not a one-off.

The information must be clear and understandable and it must be provided, along with all terms and conditions, either in physical form or in a digital form that the consumer can store. The supplier must fulfil the contract within 30 days of its being made.

The consumer has an automatic right to cancel the contract for up to seven days after the goods are delivered or, in the case of contracts for the supply of services, up to seven days after the contract has been agreed. If the supplier has failed to provide all the information listed above, however, the customer has an automatic right to cancel the contract up to three months and seven days after delivery of the goods or, in the case of services, from the date of the contract. The supplier must reimburse the customer within 30 days of the customer cancelling. (The right to cancel does not apply in certain cases, such as customised products or newspapers and magazines.)

The regulations also stipulate that, if a customer's credit card is charged fraudulently, the card holder must be reimbursed by the card issuer.

In the case of transactions over the internet, the above provisions are strengthened by the EU Electronic Commerce Directive 2000/31/EC, incorporated into UK law by the Electronic Commerce (EC Directive) Regulations 2002. The main additional provision is that the supplier must acknowledge the order by electronic means without undue delay and provide information explaining how to amend any input errors made.

FURTHER READING

The issues discussed in this chapter change rapidly. The best sources of information are therefore usually to be found on the internet but it is important to make sure that you know the date of any article you look at. An article on spamming dated 1997, for example, cannot reflect the current situation. You should also realise that many websites are maintained by small groups of people who have very strong views. You should not assume that what you read is necessarily balanced or even factually correct.

In December 2002, the Law Commission (an official UK body responsible for reviewing UK law) produced a report entitled *Defamation and the internet*. The report is clearly written and (comparatively) easy for a non-lawyer to understand. If you want to know more about this topic it is strongly recommended. It can be found on the internet at:
>   http://www.lawcom.gov.uk/files/defamation2.pdf

Although it dates from 1997, the following reference is a valuable and comprehensive source of information:
>   Akdeniz, Y. (1997) 'Governance of pornography and child pornography on the global internet: a multi-layered approach'. In Edwards, L. and Waelde, C. (eds), *Law and the internet: regulating cyberspace*. Hart Publishing, Oxford.

It is also available on the internet:
>   www.cyber-rights.org/reports/governan.htm

The Internet Watch Foundation:
>   www.iwf.org.uk

The failure of the ICRA initiative is well documented and analysed by Phil Archer, in a paper to be found on his website:
>   http://philarcher.org/icra/ICRAfail.pdf

A summary of the UK spam case referred to in the subsection on European spam legislation:
>   www.scotchspam.org.uk/transcom.html

The Robert Soloway case mentioned in the subsection on spam legislation in the United States is described in more detail online:
>   www.pcworld.com/article/148780/spam.html

15 COMPUTER MISUSE

After stuyding this short chapter, you should:

- understand the legal position regarding the misuse of computers and how common offences are handled under the law;
- appreciate why the law has had only a limited effect on the extent of computer misuse.

15.1 THE PROBLEM

In recent years, the public (or, at least, the media) has been much more concerned about the misuse of the internet than about the more general misuse of computers. Nevertheless, crimes committed using computers form a significant proportion of so-called white collar crime and it has been necessary to introduce legislation specifically aimed at such activities. Until 1990, when the Computer Misuse Act was passed, hacking, that is, gaining unauthorised access or attempting to gain unauthorised access to a computer was not in itself an offence. Attempts were made to convict hackers of stealing electricity but the quantity of electricity involved was minute and impossible to measure. Courts were reluctant to convict and, even if a conviction was obtained, the penalty was trivial.

As a result of the Court of Appeal decision in 1988 to uphold the appeal of two people who had hacked into private mailboxes, legislation to tackle computer crime was brought forward remarkably quickly, resulting in the Computer Misuse Act 1990 (CMA). The internet, although becoming widely used for email, was little known to the general public in 1990 and the CMA did not attempt to address issues arising from its misuse. The arrival of the internet and the enormous growth in its importance during the 1990s made it necessary to address some issues, such as denial of service attacks, that were not covered by the CMA, and this was done in the Police and Justice Act 2006, which made several important amendments to the CMA.

It is a good general principle that legislation should not be introduced to deal with special situations that already fall within the purview of more general laws. For this reason, the Computer Misuse Act does not address some topics, in particular computer fraud, which are better dealt with by more general legislation.

15.2 THE COMPUTER MISUSE ACT 1990

The Computer Misuse Act creates three new offences that can briefly be described as unauthorised access to a computer, unauthorised access to a computer with intention to commit a serious crime, and unauthorised modification of the contents of a computer. We shall look at each of these in more detail below. It is important to note that the offences are committed if either the computer in question or the offender (or both) are in the UK at the time of the offence. This means that someone who hacks into a computer in the UK or infects it with a virus from anywhere in the world is guilty of a criminal offence and can, in principle, be prosecuted in the UK.

Section 1 of the Computer Misuse Act 1990 states that

a person is guilty of an offence if

1. he causes a computer to perform any function with intent to secure access to any program or data held in any computer;
2. the access he intends to secure is unauthorised; *and*
3. he knows at the time when he causes the computer to perform the function that that is the case.

This is called the **unauthorised access** offence. It is punishable by a fine of up to £5,000 or up to six months' imprisonment.

There are several points that need to be emphasised. First, a person can only be guilty of the offence if they intend to gain unauthorised access and know, or should know, that the access is unauthorised. In other words, you cannot be guilty of the offence by accident.

Secondly, the wording of the Act makes it clear that a person who is authorised to access some programs or data on a computer is guilty of the offence if they attempt to gain access to other programs or data to which they are not authorised to have access.

Finally, it is no defence to claim that no harm was done. The attempt to gain unauthorised access itself constitutes the offence.

Section 2 of the Act is concerned with gaining unauthorised access to a computer with the intention of committing a more serious offence. A blackmailer might attempt to gain unauthorised access to medical records, for example, in order to identify people in prominent positions who had been treated for sexually transmitted diseases, with a view to blackmailing them. A terrorist might try to get access to a computer system for air traffic control with a view to issuing false instructions to pilots in order to cause accidents to happen.

The need for this offence arises because, if a criminal is apprehended as a result of unauthorised access before committing the more serious offence, they cannot be prosecuted for the serious offence, even though there may be ample evidence to show what they intended to do. This offence carries a penalty of up to five years imprisonment or an unlimited fine.

Section 3 of the Act states that

a person is guilty of an offence if

1. he does any act which causes an unauthorised modification of the contents of any computer; and

2. at the time when he does the act he has the requisite intent and the requisite knowledge.

The Act then goes on to explain that

the requisite intent is an intent to cause a modification of the contents of any computer and by so doing

1. to impair the operation of any computer;

2. to prevent or hinder access to any program or data held in any computer; or

3. to impair the operation of any such program or the reliability of any such data.

Furthermore, the Act goes on to make clear that it is not necessary to have any particular computer or any particular program or data in mind. Like the offence under Section 2, this offence carries a maximum penalty of five years imprisonment or an unlimited fine.

It is the offence created by Section 3 that gives the Act its power. For example, it makes each of the following a criminal offence:

- intentionally spreading a virus, worm, or other pest;

- encrypting a company's data files and demanding a ransom for revealing the key required to decrypt it;

- concealed redirection of browser home pages;

- implanting premium rate diallers (that is, programs that replace the normal dial-up code for the computer with the code for a premium rate service).

15.3 AMENDMENTS TO THE ACT

In 2004, the All-Party Parliamentary Internet Group (now part of the All-Party Parliamentary Communications Group), a group of British members of Parliament and members of the House of Lords, carried out a review of the workings of the Computer Misuse Act. It took evidence from a large number of individuals and organisations, including BCS and the IEE (now the IET), many of whom urged the need to extend the Act to include many more specific offences.

The Group concluded that the Act needed comparatively little modification. It recommended an additional offence of 'impairing access to data', which could be used to prosecute the perpetrators of denial of service attacks, which cannot always be prosecuted under Section 3 of the Act. (A denial of service attack is an attack on a website in which it is flooded with so many requests for service that either the links to the site or the site itself are no longer able to respond to legitimate requests. Such attacks have become extremely common.) It also recommended an increase from six months to two years in the maximum prison sentence for the unauthorised access offence. The recommendations of the Group were largely accepted by the Government and implemented in the Police and Justice Act 2006 (PJA), which made a number of important amendments to the CMA.

First, the penalties for the basic offence of unauthorised access were increased. The maximum penalty on summary conviction (i.e. conviction in a Magistrates' Court) was increased to imprisonment for up to twelve months (six months in Scotland) and/or a fine of up to £5,000. Under the CMA, the basic offence could only be dealt with in a Magistrates' Court. The PJA allows for trial in a Crown Court (i.e. before a judge and jury), with a maximum prison sentence of two years. The main purpose of the change was to make it apparent that Parliament regarded the offence as a serious one. It also had the side-effect of making the offence an extraditable one, that is, for which a person in Britain charged with committing the offence in another country could be sent by a British court to stand trial in that country.

Second the PJA amends the offence defined in section 3 of the CMA so that it covers unauthorised acts with intent to impair, or with recklessness as to impairing (i.e. not caring that they might impair), the operation of any computer, etc. The point of this change is that it removes the requirement that the hacker has modified something. Thus it covers denial of service attacks where the operation of the computer targeted is impaired not by modifying its contents but by flooding it with messages or other requests. The maximum penalty for the new offence on summary conviction is the same as for unauthorised access but on indictment (i.e. in a Crown Court) it is raised to ten years imprisonment and/or an unlimited fine. The maximum penalty is intended to recognise the fact that such attacks may be intended to compromise a nation's security or to damage a large company permanently.

Third, the PJA introduces a new offence of 'making, supplying or obtaining articles for use in computer misuse offences'. This offence is designed to attack the growing market in hackers' tool kits, sets of software tools that facilitate the unauthorised penetration of computer systems. The penalties are the same as for unauthorised access.

15.4 OPERATION OF THE ACT

EXAMPLES OF PROSECUTIONS

The CMA has been used to prosecute a significant number of high-profile cases successfully, as shown in some recent examples:

- On 16 May 2013, at Southwark Crown Court, Ryan Cleary and three other men were sentenced for offences under the Act. During a three-month period in 2011, the group had hacked into the websites of Sony, News International, PBS and Fox, amongst others, and carried out denial of service attacks on the various sites, including those of the UK Serious Organised Crimes Agency and the CIA. It was this group that was responsible for the breach of security at Sony Entertainments, mentioned in Chapter 13 in the subsection on operation of the Data Protection Act. Cleary was sentenced to 32 months, and two other men to 30 months and 24 months respectively. The fourth, who at the age of 18 was the youngest member of the group, was sentenced to 20 months in a young offenders' institution. Cleary is also awaiting sentence after being found guilty on a separate charge of possessing 172 indecent images of children, which were found on his computer when he was arrested. At the time of writing a fifth member of the group is awaiting sentence in New York.

- James Jeffery hacked into the website of the British Pregnancy Advisory Service and acquired the records of some 10,000 women who had had pregnancies terminated. In April 2012, he was sentenced to 32 months in prison. He had been threatening to publish the information on the web.

- Active Investigation Services was set up by two moonlighting police officers, Scott Gelsthorpe and Jeremy Young, in 1999. It indulged in a wide range of illegal activities, including many that were offences under the CMA. In one instance, they were hired by a waste disposal company to spy on the activities of Environmental Agency staff who were monitoring its activities. Following a tip-off from BT, the firm's offices were raided in September 2004 and 27 people were arrested. Young and Gelsthorpe were given prison sentences of 27 months and 24 months respectively; many other members of staff and others associated with the company received shorter sentences.

Notwithstanding a few such high profile cases, there is a general feeling that given the extent of hacking and the number of viruses and other malware in circulation, these figures are extraordinarily low. In the first 16 years that the Act was in force, only 214 defendants were proceeded against in magistrates' courts in England and Wales under the Act, of whom 161 were convicted. The number of prosecutions brought in Crown Courts would be much lower.

A number of reasons for this low number of prosecutions have been suggested:

- A company that has suffered an attack that constitutes an offence under the CMA will often prefer to avoid the adverse publicity that could result from a trial, particularly since the rules of the court might prevent them rebutting it. A bank, for example, might be reluctant to see an apparent security weakness publicised because this might cause it to lose customers as well as possibly exposing it to the risk of further attacks. In other words, by prosecuting it risks further losses and there is little likelihood of any significant gain.

- Since the police do not have the resources or the expertise to investigate more than a tiny fraction of the cases, the decision to prosecute would almost certainly mean devoting much management time to the case and calling in external experts, whose fees may be high.

- Too many prosecutions under the Act have failed because of legal technicalities.

- Where convictions have been obtained, the sentences imposed have been at the lower end of those that the Act provides for and have not reflected the seriousness of the offences. Despite the theoretical maximum of a ten year jail sentence, no one has been sentenced to more than 32 months imprisonment for an offence under the Act.

- Far more publicity has been given to cases in which the defendant was acquitted or received a very light penalty than to those in which the defendant was convicted and sentenced appropriately. Thus, for example, in 1993 at Southwark Crown Court, Paul Bedworth, then 18, who had hacked into and made changes to the *Financial Times* database that cost the newspaper £25,000 and had also hacked into systems at the European Organisation for the Research and Treatment of Cancer that resulted in it receiving £10,000 telephone bill, was acquitted on the grounds that he was addicted to hacking. This verdict received a great deal of publicity but much less publicity was given to the fact that two men arrested with Bedworth were each sentenced to six months imprisonment. (The acquittal of Bedworth was widely held to be perverse – the jury seems to have ignored the judge's instructions.)

The well-publicised case of Gary McKinnon served further to muddy the waters. McKinnon admitted gaining unauthorised access to US defence computers from the UK and causing them to become temporarily inoperable, although he denied malicious intent. He claimed that his motivation was to reveal information about free energy and UFOs, which was being deliberately suppressed by the USA. Following indictment in 2002, the US sought his extradition. He fought against this, asking to be tried in the UK, and claiming that, because he was suffering from Asperger's syndrome, it would be a violation of his rights under the European Convention on Human Rights to extradite him to the USA. Every court hearing ruled against him but a massive popular campaign, founded on anti-American feeling and opposition to the 2003 extradition treaty between the UK and the USA, led the Home Secretary to withdraw the extradition order in 2012, and it was subsequently announced that he would not be prosecuted in the UK. Thus a confessed law-breaker, who had committed serious damage to computer systems in a friendly foreign country, was allowed to avoid trial.

15.5 COMPUTER FRAUD

Computer fraud involves manipulating a computer dishonestly in order to obtain money, property, or services, or to cause loss. Most of the techniques that are used are much older than computers. Such tricks as placing fictitious employees on the payroll or setting up false supplier accounts and creating spurious invoices are still the commonest type of fraud, as they were before computers appeared. The introduction of computers has made it possible to carry out more spectacular frauds and, because of the reluctance that many people have to question computer output, has perhaps made it less likely that these will be uncovered. Nevertheless, the offences are the same as before.

The law relating to fraud in England, Wales and Northern Ireland is largely contained in the Fraud Act 2006, which substantially clarified what had been a complicated and confused area of the law. It also removed several technical problems related to cases of fraud where a computer was involved. There is thus nothing special about fraud cases in which a computer has been involved. That having been said, it is important to realise that the collection and preservation of evidence generated by, or arising from, computer systems requires specialised expertise.

In Scotland, there is and always has been, a single common law offence of fraud and it has not been felt necessary to introduce a statutory offence.

FURTHER READING

The Computer Misuse Act:
    www.legislation.gov.uk/ukpga/1990/18/contents

The first three sections are fairly easy to read but the succeeding sections, although necessary, are highly technical (in the legal sense) and relate to questions of jurisdiction and mechanisms for enforcing the Act.

The following articles give a fuller description of the operation of the Act than has been possible in this chapter:

Akdeniz, Y. (1996). 'Section 3 of the Computer Misuse Act 1990: an antidote for computer viruses!'. *Web Journal of Current Legal Issues*. Can be accessed at: http://webjcli.ncl.ac.uk/1996/issue3/akdeniz3.html.

MacEwan, N. (2008) 'The Computer Misuse Act 1990: lessons from its past and predictions for its future.' *Criminal Law Review* 955. Can be accessed at: http://usir.salford.ac.uk/15815/7/MacEwan_Crim_LR.pdf

Cases brought under the CMA rarely involve legal subtleties and are therefore usually only reported in newspapers rather than in law journals. The resulting reports are usually rather superficial. Newspaper reports about the cases mentioned in the section on operation of the Act can readily be found by typing the name of the accused into a search engine. In the case of Gary McKinnon, however, there is a huge amount of material on the internet, most of it biased in one direction or another. Two court judgements that are readily available and which give some idea of the issues can be found at:
    www.bailii.org/ew/cases/EWHC/Admin/2009/2021. html
    and
    www.publications.parliament.uk/pa/ld200708/ldjudgmt/jd080730/mckinn-1.htm

APPENDIX
SAMPLE CONTRACT OF EMPLOYMENT

CAMBRIAN CONSULTANTS LIMITED

Contract of Employment for Permanent Professional Employees below the Rank of Director

This contract of employment is made between *<employee name>* ('the employee') and Cambrian Consultants Limited ('the company').

1. This contract shall become effective on *<start date of the employment>* and shall subsist until either it is terminated by either side in accordance with section 8 or until the employee reaches the retiring age as specified in section 9.

2. This contract supersedes all other contracts or agreements between the parties, whether oral or written.
   [As usual, the contract needs to make sure that things that may have been said during negotiations have no legal weight.]

3. The employee shall be employed as a *<job title>* (grade *<A to F>*) at an initial salary of *<starting salary>* pounds per annum, which shall be paid monthly in arrears, no later than the last day of the month. This grade and salary will be reviewed after the first six months of employment and annually thereafter.

4. The employee's normal place of work shall be the company's premises located *<full address of place of work>*. The employee may be required from time to time to work elsewhere; in such cases travel and subsistence expenses shall be payable in accordance with the company's usual rates and procedures.

5. Normal office hours shall be from 9.00 am to 5.30 pm, Mondays to Fridays, with an hour's break for lunch. The employee shall normally work these hours, or such other hours as may be agreed with the company, and may from time to time be required to work longer hours.

6. The employee shall be entitled to 24 days annual holiday per calendar year, in addition to statutory holidays. Holiday entitlement can only be carried over from one calendar year to the next with the written permission of a director or authorised manager. For employees starting or terminating their employment during the year, holiday entitlement is accrued at the rate of two days per complete calendar month; employees who have holiday entitlement outstanding when their employment terminates shall be entitled

to a payment in lieu of one 1/240th of their annual salary for each complete day of holiday outstanding.

7. The duties of the employee shall be such as are from time to time assigned to him or her by the Board of Directors or by authorised management.

8. After the employee's first month of completed service, the contract of employment may be terminated by either party giving one week's notice in writing to the other for each year of the employee's completed years of service, subject to a minimum of four weeks and a maximum of twelve weeks. *[There are lots of other ways that notice conditions may be specified. It is quite common for all employees above a certain grade or with more than one year's service to be on three months notice.]*

9. An employee shall retire at the age of 65 or on the date at which he or she becomes eligible to receive the state retirement pension, whichever is earlier, unless otherwise agreed in writing by the company. The company does not operate any pension scheme and a contracting out certificate issued by the Occupational Pensions Board is not in force for this employment. After the employee has completed one year of service with the company, the company will contribute to an approved private pension scheme held by the employee; the amount of this contribution shall be the same as that contributed by the employee, up to a maximum of 6 per cent of the employee's salary.

10. In the event of the employee being unable to work due to sickness or injury, the company will pay the employee's full basic salary for a period of eight weeks. Thereafter the employee will be entitled to statutory sick pay up to the expiry of 28 weeks from the first notification of the incapacity. *[Sick pay can be an expensive business.]*

11. All intellectual property developed by the employee as part of his or her employment shall be the property of the company and the employee shall, at the request of the company and at its expense, undertake any actions necessary to confirm such ownership, including but not limited to the filing of patent applications.

12. Unless otherwise agreed by the company, the employee shall treat as confidential all information he or she acquires as a result of the employment, unless and until that information enters the public domain. In particular, the employee shall obtain the permission of the company before publishing any material arising from the employment, such permission not to be unreasonably withheld. The obligation of confidentiality shall continue for a period of five years following the termination of the employment.

13. The employee shall at all times act in good faith and in such a way as to promote the best interests of the company.

14. The employee shall abide by all the rules and procedures promulgated within the company.

15. The employee shall not make any financial commitment on behalf of the company except as duly authorised.

16. The employee shall not, for a period of twelve months following the termination of the employment, solicit business from, or otherwise approach, any client of the company, except with the prior agreement in writing of the company.

17. The employee shall not, for a period of twelve months following the termination of the employment, entice or seek to entice any employee of the company to leave its employment, except with the prior agreement in writing of the company.

18. The employee shall abide by any additional conditions that may from time to time be imposed as a result of the company's contracts with its clients.

19. At the request of the company, the employee shall apply for, and maintain, professional registration and corporate membership of an appropriate professional body.

20. The employee shall ensure that his or her dress and personal appearance are appropriate to the environment in which he or she is working.

21. The employee accepts that he or she has a responsibility for the health and safety of all employees and shall abide by all health and safety regulations promulgated by the company and its clients.

22. An employee who believes that he or she has a grievance against the company shall, in the first instance, raise the matter in writing with the Managing Director, who will endeavour to settle the matter to the employee's and the company's satisfaction. If the matter cannot be satisfactorily resolved in this way, the employee and the Managing Director shall each submit to the Chairman of the Board of Directors a written statement of the grievance and the efforts made to resolve it. The decision of the Chairman shall be final.

Signed . . . .(Director)
for and on behalf of Cambrian Consultants
Limited
Date . . . .
Signed . . . .(the employee)
Date . . . .

INDEX